Transmedia Change

This book examines and illustrates the use of design principles, design thinking, and other empathy research techniques in university and public settings, to plan and ethically target socially-concerned transmedia stories and evaluate their success through user experience testing methods.

All media industries continue to adjust to a dispersed, diverse, and dilettante mediascape where reaching a large global audience may be easy but communicating with a decisive and engaged public is more difficult. This challenge is arguably toughest for communicators who work to engage a public with reality rather than escape. The chapters in this volume outline the pedagogy and practice of design, empathy research methods for story development, transmedia logics for socially-concerned stories, development of community engagement and the embrace of collective narrative, art and science research collaboration, the role of mixed and virtual reality in prosocial communication, ethical audience targeting, and user experience testing for storytelling campaigns. Each broad topic includes case examples and full case studies of each stage in production.

Offering a detailed exploration of a fast-emerging area, this book will be of great relevance to researchers and university teachers of socially-concerned transmedia storytelling in fields such as journalism, documentary filmmaking, education, and activism.

Kevin Moloney is Assistant Professor in the Center for Emerging Media Design and Development at Ball State University, USA. He researches transmedia storytelling in journalism, documentary, activism, and other socially-concerned genres. For 20 years, he was a regular contributor to the *New York Times* covering the Rocky Mountain region of the United States and Latin America. He visually reported more than 960 stories for the *Times*, 50 of which appeared on page 1. His work has also appeared in news magazines worldwide, including *National Geographic*, *Time*, *Stern*, and *Paris Match*.

Routledge Advances in Transmedia Studies
Series Editor: Matthew Freeman

This series publishes monographs and edited collections that sit at the cutting-edge of today's interdisciplinary cross-platform media landscape. Topics should consider emerging transmedia applications in and across industries, cultures, arts, practices, or research methodologies. The series is especially interested in research exploring the future possibilities of an interconnected media landscape that looks beyond the field of media studies, notably broadening to include socio-political contexts, education, experience design, mixed-reality, journalism, the proliferation of screens, as well as art- and writing-based dimensions to do with the role of digital platforms like VR, apps and iDocs to tell new stories and express new ideas across multiple platforms in ways that join up with the social world.

Transmediality in Independent Journalism
The Turkish Case
Dilek Gürsoy

Theory, Development, and Strategy in Transmedia Storytelling
Edited by Renira Rampazzo Gambarato, Geane Carvalho Alzamora, Lorena Tárcia

Place and Immersion in Contemporary Transmedia Storytelling
Donna Hancox

Telenovelas and Transformation
Saving Brazil's Television Industry
Rosane Svartman

Transmedia Practices in the Long Nineteenth Century
Edited by Christina Meyer and Monika Pietrzak-Franger

Transmedia Change
Pedagogy and Practice for Socially-Concerned Transmedia Stories
Edited by Kevin Moloney

Transmedia Change
Pedagogy and Practice for
Socially-Concerned Transmedia Stories

Edited by Kevin Moloney

LONDON AND NEW YORK

First published 2022
by Routledge
4 Park Square, Milton Park, Abingdon, Oxon OX14 4RN

and by Routledge
605 Third Avenue, New York, NY 10158

Routledge is an imprint of the Taylor & Francis Group, an informa business

© 2022 selection and editorial matter, Kevin Moloney; individual chapters, the contributors

The right of Kevin Moloney to be identified as the author of the editorial material, and of the authors for their individual chapters, has been asserted in accordance with sections 77 and 78 of the Copyright, Designs and Patents Act 1988.

All rights reserved. No part of this book may be reprinted or reproduced or utilised in any form or by any electronic, mechanical, or other means, now known or hereafter invented, including photocopying and recording, or in any information storage or retrieval system, without permission in writing from the publishers.

Trademark notice: Product or corporate names may be trademarks or registered trademarks, and are used only for identification and explanation without intent to infringe.

British Library Cataloguing-in-Publication Data
A catalogue record for this book is available from the British Library

Library of Congress Cataloging-in-Publication Data
A catalog record has been requested for this book

ISBN: 978-0-367-71432-1 (hbk)
ISBN: 978-0-367-71437-6 (pbk)
ISBN: 978-1-003-15086-2 (ebk)

DOI: 10.4324/9781003150862

Typeset in Sabon
by Apex CoVantage, LLC

To our students, who take theories and ideas and put them into practice in order to better the world.

Contents

List of Figures ix
List of Contributors x
Acknowledgments xiii

1 Introduction 1
KEVIN MOLONEY

2 Native, Emergent, and Feral Transmedia Storyworlds 8
KEVIN MOLONEY

3 Design Thinking and the Storytelling Goal 23
SARAH JANSSEN

4 Deploying Design Thinking for Story Design: Case Studies 37
SARAH JANSSEN

5 Contextualizing the American Opioid Crisis: A Case Study in Transmedia Harm Reduction 47
MATT SLABY

6 Storylines and Conceptual Lineage: Tomas van Houtryve and the Contextualization of History 63
MATT SLABY

7 Challenging Hegemonic Narratives: Power of Story-Based Design Strategies in Activating Sustainable Social Change 76
FRANCESCA PIREDDA AND MARIANA CIANCIA

8 Teaching Transmedia Practice in a Design School: The Plug Social TV Experience — 91
MARIANA CIANCIA AND FRANCESCA PIREDDA

9 Transmedia Action Research: Progressive Pedagogy and Community Engagement — 107
LESLIE L. DODSON

10 Water From Fog: Transmedia Storytelling and Humanitarian Engineering — 125
JAMILA BARGACH AND LESLIE L. DODSON

11 Encounters: Art, Science, Clouds, and Water — 140
ANA REWAKOWICZ

12 Addressing Social Issues Through Immersive Media — 161
KUO-TING HUANG

13 Immersive Storytelling Case Studies: Eva: A-7063, Lesson Learned From That Dragon Cancer and Coming Home Virtually — 169
KUO-TING HUANG

14 Design Thinking as a Tool for Ethical Audience Targeting — 178
KEVIN MOLONEY

15 *The Revolutionist: Eugene V. Debs*: A Transmedia Experience for Public Media Audiences — 193
KYLE TRAVERS

16 User Experience Design and Testing for Socially-Concerned Storytelling — 210
JENNIFER PALILONIS

17 User Experience Case Study: Professor Garfield's 21st-Century Literacy Project — 225
JENNIFER PALILONIS

18 Conclusion: Defining a Flexible Framework for Analysis or Design of Socially-Concerned Transmedia Stories — 237
KEVIN MOLONEY

Index — 245

Figures

2.1	A spectrum of native, emergent, and feral transmedia stories	12
5.1	Two overdose diptychs	55
5.2	Michigan opioid harm reduction billboard	59
6.1	Anna Maria Gallegos de Houser and the Bonneville Salt Flats diptych	64
6.2	Nathan Alexander Steiner and Green River diptych	66
10.1	Ballad of the Fiancé of Fog	130
10.2	"Brui-Art: Le son du paysage" (*Fog-Art: Landscape Sound*)	132
11.1	*Inside Out* and *Traveling With My Inflatable Room*	142
11.2	*Through the Looking Mist . . .*	150
11.3	*Misty Way*	152
11.4	*Nephelograph (Mist Impressions)*	157
14.1	The Indiana Donut	184
15.1	Elements of The Revolutionist booth at Wine Fest	200
15.2	The Medical History Museum in Indianapolis	201
15.3	Website banner showing Terri Jett promoting "Simple Civics" episodes related to Eugene Debs	202
15.4	Prototype social media post	204
17.1	Digital literacy exercise sample	230
17.2	Loop 11 structure	233

Contributors

Jamila Bargach is co-founder and Executive Director of NGO Dar Si Hmad which built the largest fog collection initiative in the world and manages other environmental educational initiatives in southwestern Morocco. She has worked extensively promoting civil society and has taught at the National School of Architecture, Rabat, Morocco.

Mariana Ciancia is a researcher in the Department of Design at Politecnico di Milano, Italy. She is a member of Imagis Lab and Deputy Director of the master's degree in brand communication. She researches new media and participatory culture to understand how multichannel phenomena (crossmedia and transmedia) are changing narrative environments' production, distribution, and consumption.

Leslie L. Dodson is Co-Director of The Global Lab at Worcester Polytechnic Institute in Massachusetts, USA, which supports international project-based learning and global activism. The Lab engages in transmedia storytelling, ethical media-making, humanitarian engineering, and the arts to bring socio-political awareness to engineering projects developed through faculty research and student capstone project work. As a journalist, she reported throughout the world for Reuters, NBC and CNN, NHK, and others. She worked extensively in South America, Europe, and Asia covering politics, economics, and international finance. She won numerous awards for her environmental reporting.

Kuo-Ting (Tim) Huang is Research Assistant Professor in the Department of Information Culture and Data Stewardship at the University of Pittsburgh, USA. His research focuses on the psychological, cognitive, and affective processes and outcomes of interactive media usage, with an emphasis on digital games and virtual/augmented reality (VR/AR). Specifically, he is interested in how these psychological mechanisms can be harnessed to create experiences that address digital divides and inequalities and promote educational and health outcomes.

Sarah Janssen is a strategist and storyteller currently working in product management for software products. She started her career as a newspaper education journalist before earning a master's degree in Emerging Media Design & Development (EMDD). She was a member of the Blue Roots Project team and researched, designed, and performed the "We're Still Here: Stories of the Flint Water Crisis" project. She is a software products manager.

Kevin Moloney is Assistant Professor in the Center for Emerging Media Design and Development at Ball State University, USA. He researches transmedia storytelling in journalism, documentary, activism, and other socially-concerned genres. For 20 years, he was a regular contributor to the *New York Times* covering the Rocky Mountain region of the United States and Latin America. He visually reported more than 960 stories for the *Times*, 50 of which appeared on page 1. His work has also appeared in news magazines worldwide, including *National Geographic*, *Time*, *Stern*, and *Paris Match*.

Jennifer Palilonis is the George and Frances Ball Distinguished Professor of Multimedia Journalism and a full professor in the Department of Journalism at Ball State University and is the Director of the Center for Emerging Media Design and Development (EMDD). She has been recognized for her leadership of immersive learning efforts that partner undergraduate and graduate students with real-world project partners, including USA Volleyball, the Vatican, the Professor Garfield Foundation, and David Letterman. Her research focuses on digital literacy, multimedia in education, transmedia storytelling, and user experience design. She is the author of two books *A Practical Guide to Graphics Reporting* and *The Multimedia Journalist*. In 2020, Palilonis received the Mid-American Conference (MAC) Outstanding Faculty Award for Student Success.

Francesca Piredda is Associate Professor in the Department of Design at Politecnico di Milano, Italy. She is a member of Imagis Lab and collaborates with DESIS International Network. She is scientific director of the master's degrees in brand communication, art direction and copywriting, and digital design strategy. She researches audiovisual language, participatory video, digital media, and narrative. She leads research and educational activities for community TV and social media, content strategy, worldbuilding, and storytelling techniques for social inclusion and brand communication. She develops participatory video and narrative-driven processes and tools for co-design. In 2017, she received the XXV ADI Compasso D'Oro award. Since 2015 she is a member of Fondazione Adolfo Pini board in Milan.

Ana Rewakowicz is a Polish-born interdisciplinary artist, living and working in Montreal and Paris. She is finishing her Ph.D. in art and science at École Polytechnique, Paris. Known for stimulating, interactive, inflatable works that question our relationship with the environment, she is concerned with issues of sustainability and the need for inter-/

trans-disciplinary collaborations to face growing environmental challenges. Currently, her art effectuates greater water awareness through the creation of imaginative and sensorial encounters with water. Her works are in the permanent collections of MACRO (Rome, Italy), MAC (Montreal), MNBAQ (Québec City), and Musée de Joliette, and she has exhibited in Europe, Asia, and the Americas.

Matt Slaby is a journalist and photographer whose work has been featured in publications and venues ranging from *National Geographic* to the United Nations. He began his career as a public interest lawyer before co-founding Luceo as a vehicle for story-based advocacy. In 2004, he was named as a prestigious Chancellor Scholar for his work on public interest issues during his studies at the University of Denver Sturm College of Law. Under his leadership, Luceo has focused on addressing niche public health, drug policy, and criminal justice issues.

Kyle Travers is Director of video content at WFYI Public Media in Indianapolis, for which she oversees production of video for television and emerging media platforms. She has won regional Emmy awards for "The Revolutionist: Eugene V. Debs," "The Work Around: Wrestling with American Healthcare," and "Lois Main Templeton." She also contributed her production skills to several WFYI digital shorts series, including "Simple Civics" and "Headstrong."

Acknowledgments

The editor wishes to thank the diligent contributors, many of whom worked on this book not as part of the academic system, but alongside demanding professional careers. He also humbly thanks his assiduous peer reviewers for accepting requests to help hone this volume. Thanks go to series editor Matthew Freeman for creating the opportunity to produce this work and the staff at Routledge for their encouraging support. Thanks to the partners, spouses, bosses, children, pets, and houseplants of contributors for their patience and endurance.

1 Introduction

Kevin Moloney

Readers of this book will likely have lived, studied, worked, or researched through the digital revolution and the disruption it brought to legacy media institutions. Although old business and publication models continue their slow and inexorable collapse, we now see beyond the uncertainty and into what a future of *à la carte* media holds: The once-captive audience can now select with which media they engage and can support their beliefs with confirming—rather than challenging—information. New media enterprises battle for audience attention in a mediascape that brings all the media of the globe onto one's phone. Meanwhile, what remains of legacy media institutions scramble to find routes back to public attention and business models that better fit the marketplace. In the United States, one polar outcome of this disruption can be seen in progressive social movements like #MeToo and Black Lives Matter that—fueled by the fall of gatekeepers and an extraordinary ability to build public awareness and community—are battling toxic, age-old discrimination. The once quietly simmering other pole now boils up here in the rise of white supremacy and conspiracy theories like QAnon through the use of the very same fuel. Similar contrasts around the globe demonstrate the need for a more effective socially-concerned communication paradigm. Although reaching critical publics with important, actionable, and problem-solving information has never been easy or assured, that lack of assurance is now both more evident and more problematic. In response, new approaches emerge in both the profession and the academy that strive to answer the 21st-century mediascape. Three of those approaches are described and deployed in this volume: human-centered design, transmedia storytelling, and usability and user experience evaluation.

Definitions

Although each chapter that follows is written to stand alone and will define the terms used in it, you will repeatedly encounter four key ideas. In the context of this volume, *socially-concerned communication and storytelling* include genres that seek to inform, educate, or advocate. These include journalism, documentary production, education, history, community organizing, and fact-driven social change movements. Socially-concerned communication and storytelling does not seek to market, advertise, fictionalize, nor propagandize, although the approaches that follow appear in those genres too. *Human-centered design*, and approaches and toolkits for it, such as *empathy research* and *design thinking*, work to find solutions to problems from the bottom up, involving the end user in their design and development. In the case of socially-concerned communication, this approach is useful for debunking assumptions about what information the public needs and where they should find it. It lets the public help determine the best way to accomplish the goal. *Transmedia storytelling* is designing a story to unfold across multiple media—analog, digital, and even brick-and-mortar—in an expansive rather than repetitive way. Two great advantages come from designing communication like this: We can tell richer stories that are present in the lives of their publics longer, and we can strategically aim instances of those complex stories toward the specific publics that can use them most. The most conscientious design and deployment must be verified, though. To achieve goals of audience engagement, entertainment, interest, participation, and others, we must test whether the transmedia stories we have designed are actually resonating with their intended publics. For this *usability and user experience design and testing* helps socially-concerned transmedia story designers to check, iterate, adjust, and perfect the stories we develop. This user-centered approach not only helps us better understand our public's interests, needs, preferences, and motivations but also helps monitor user interaction with the digital platforms and physical experiences that comprise a transmedia story.

Disruptions

Once aware of these techniques and patterns, their native existence in the world reveals itself in surprising places. As a photojournalist, I once spent most of the 1990s documenting the socio-political impact of the rise of Pentecostalism in Latin America (Moloney, 2012). Once the stronghold of the Roman Catholic Church, Latin America is turning Protestant. There people have been flocking for decades to upstart Protestant churches, particularly Pentecostal ones. There are many and complicated reasons for this, but among them is that these little upstarts work to directly address the needs of their communities. First, they put churches in accessible locations like old movie theaters and storefronts in low-income neighborhoods. Then, they provide daycare and job training to their congregations which are made up in significant numbers by single mothers. And by letting those congregations in on the service's conversation, they inspire a deep engagement with that community and its leaders. Services there are interactive and passionate by any observer's measure.

By contrast, the old-line Catholic churches there tend to be centered around big, elaborate, and baroque structures in the center of the cities where they are three bus transfers from the homes of the people they most hope to serve. On their altars are priests—mostly foreigners—who deliver pretty much the same information as the insurgent churches but with a time-worn and emotionless demeanor. The pews are nearly empty, and those sitting in them are mostly the elderly. Like many Catholic priests around the world, they remind the newcomers who only show up on Christmas or Easter that they will go to hell if they don't attend every Sunday.

Both kinds of church offer the same basic story, and both believe that this information is critical for the wellbeing of their congregations. It's just the style of delivery that's different, but the results have culture-changing impact on a continent where the Catholic tradition and local culture are deeply intertwined. "They are destroying Brazilian culture," anthropologist Rubem César Fernandes told me (Personal communication, 1994). "You're not supposed to samba if you're a member of one of these churches."

When the disruption of legacy media institutions began (in the same years during which I covered this religious revolution), commercial and nonprofit media industries looked a lot like the Catholic priests standing at the altar of a 300-year-old Latin American cathedral, preaching to an elderly congregation of five. A church that had become too comfortable with a captive audience and the ability to pontificate suddenly found itself flanked and outnumbered by fast-iterating newcomers. As soon as choice was available, their audience fled.

However, the future of the Latin American Catholic church appeared in Padre Marcelo Rossi, a former aerobics instructor turned priest who brought not only a youthful and effusive passion to his work, but he learned quickly—like his Pentecostal counterparts—to use any medium available to spread his message, particularly those that land straight in the path of his young target public. At the time I covered him, Padre Marcelo was producing radio shows and TV broadcasts, and releasing CDs and videos. He has acted in movies, and his multiple Twitter feeds then had more than 100,000 followers. He attracted as many as 10,000 people to weekday morning masses, many of whom were school kids who had cut class to go to church. His new sanctuary could hold 100,000. Intuitively using approaches much like the three described in this volume, Rossi and his Pentecostal counterparts listened to their publics and sought to directly answer their needs. They communicated through any media form or channel that made sense to reach those publics, and they checked their work. They made the story of Christianity engaging, in ways that broke a stodgy old paradigm. "Priests aren't showmen," Archbishop Odilo Scherer of São Paulo reportedly said in reference to Padre Marcelo. "The Mass is not to be transformed into a show" (Rohter & Fisher, 2007, para. 15). As a photojournalist, I reported not only on their successes but also the scandals and shortcomings of this sociological change. We see parallels to those problems in the wider 21st-century mediascape and its effects on culture just as I did in the religious identity change happening in Latin America.

4 Kevin Moloney

The disruption of religion in Latin America at the end of the 20th century was as inevitable as that brought by the diverse, dispersed, and dilettante mediascape at the beginning of the 21st century. The answer, however, is not to lament a past age like an aging Brazilian bishop but to respond effectively to the present one like Padre Marcelo. The stories distributed across media by Rossi and the Pentecostal insurgents build community, and through community comes more enduring social change. This volume examines the three aforementioned approaches of value to scholars studying the contemporary mediascape as well as teachers and producers of socially-concerned transmedia communication: human-centered design, transmedia storytelling, and usability and user experience testing. In the following chapters, scholars add to existing theory by defining new frames for understanding how both factual and fictional transmedia stories interact with the real world and adapt design and testing techniques from the product development industries to storytelling. Academic practitioners present case studies here of socially-concerned transmedia stories they deployed. And active, professional transmedia producers describe both their practice and the context and ethos of the stories they tell.

Labs

Six of the contributors to this volume are associated with three academic organizations that focus on socially-concerned transmedia storytelling: The Center for Emerging Media Design & Development at Ball State University, Imagis Lab at Politecnico di Milano, and the Global Lab at the Worcester Polytechnic Institute.

The Center for Emerging Media Design & Development at Ball State University is a graduate studies program in design thinking, transmedia storytelling, and usability and user experience research methods. The center pairs a traditional master's curriculum with hands-on lab experiences in which students work with public and private partners to solve community problems. External partners include local, state, and national organizations in entertainment, the arts, nonprofit journalism, sports, education, and community activism.

Imagis Lab is a collaborative and interdisciplinary design research and teaching group at Politecnico di Milano that is focused on building brands, stories, and experiences. Research and education are strongly integrated into hands-on and in-field activities that build creative content, communication strategy, gaming experience, and transmedia storytelling for branding and social innovation. Their process merges design tools and skills in audio-visual language, participatory communication design strategies, branding as identity development, and transmedia practice.

The Global Lab at the Worcester Polytechnic Institute is a collective of professors, researchers, media-makers, and students, the goal of which is to support international and global activism, on campus and off. The lab engages transmedia storytelling, technology, the humanities, and ethics to bring socio-political awareness to engineering projects developed through faculty and student capstone project work.

Chapter Outlines

In Chapter 2, Kevin Moloney, of the Center for Emerging Media Design & Development, briefly examines what storyworlds are and how we interact with them in fiction and nonfiction. He then identifies a spectrum of transmedia storyworld types, starting with *native* transmedia stories in which the transmedia story is designed as such from the very start. Moloney continues through *emergent* transmedia stories in which a single-medium story is subsequently transformed into a complex transmedia story and then extends the spectrum to *feral* transmedia stories that expand across multiple media forms and channels independently of any designer. Understanding the intentional or unintentional transmedia qualities of successful stories is critical for the design or analysis of communication strategies.

In Chapters 3 and 4, author Sarah Janssen examines the use of design thinking as a tool for developing empathetic stories and describes its history and processes. She then explores two cases of its use for global water crises: one resulting in a one-person, three-act stage play that explores lead pollution in the Flint, Michigan water supply, and another that crowdsourced media on complex global water security issues for nonprofit journalism organization Circle of Blue.

In Chapters 5 and 6, scholars Mariana Ciancia and Francesca Piredda of the Imagis Lab present strategies of *transmedia design*, a collaborative, social process that gives voice to the experiences of those at the margins. Through this collaborative narrative worldbuilding practice, audiences immerse themselves into narrative spaces and participate in creating stories that challenge hegemonic narratives. They then discuss the *Plug Social TV* experience as an example of design methodology for conceiving transmedia communication strategies. They present the concept of *transmedia design* as a fusion of the evolving practices of transmedia story production and the design approach as taught in design schools worldwide.

Chapters 7 and 8 provide a shift from the academic to the professional, as Matt Slaby contextualizes the American opioid crisis and the motivations and human story content that drive the publicly funded transmedia storytelling his partnership Luceo produces. In Chapter 7, Slaby interviews Paris-based transmedia documentary colleague Tomas van Houtryve about his motivations to reset through transmedia storytelling the historical record of U.S. expansion into the American Southwest in the 19th century.

In Chapter 9, scholar Leslie L. Dodson, of the Global Lab, posits *transmedia action research* as a new methodological construct fusing transmedia storytelling with action research theory and practice. Transmedia action research can provide a coherent engagement strategy in which stakeholders and researchers share in the translation, composition, production, and distribution of storyworlds that bolster social change.

In Chapter 10, Dodson and Jamila Bargach examine the ongoing production of the transmedia storyworld of the world's largest fog water harvesting system, located in southwest Morocco near the Sahara Desert. The Dar Si Hmad for Development, Education and Culture nongovernmental organization uses transmedia communication to build engagement with local participants, to explore research questions at the intersection of engineering and community development, and for global awareness and advocacy around culture and climate change.

In Chapter 11, artist and scholar Ana Rewakowicz, of the École Polytechnique in Paris, recounts encounters between art, science, clouds, and water through imaginative, poetic, and nonlinear narration, with the aim to bring more acute awareness to water scarcity. Her inquiry started with the question of efficiency in the science and method of collecting water from fog, and evolved into the production of artworks as a response. Driven by a desire to contribute to problem-solving methodologies, the research and storytelling project she describes emphasizes the necessity for active participation and responsibility toward what she terms "*ever-more* inclusion" when facing contemporary environmental challenges.

For Chapters 12 and 13, prosocial gaming scholar Kuo-Ting (Tim) Huang, of the University of Pittsburgh, presents a theoretical framework for analyzing and designing immersive stories that address social issues and connects the theoretical concepts of presence, social cognitive theory, and the Proteus effect to immersive storytelling. He presents recommendations for applying immersive storytelling to social issues. In the case studies that follow, Huang examines three cases of immersive storytelling that address social issues through empathy, compassion, and feeling of presence—*Eva: A-7063*, *Lesson Learned From That Dragon Cancer*, and *Coming Home Virtually*—and relates them to the theoretical frameworks offered in the prior chapter.

In Chapter 14, Moloney explores the theory and practice of transparent and ethical audience targeting through design thinking, which can provide a scalable method to ethically and transparently understand where and how to reach critical audiences with the low budget and short timeframe required by most social communication campaigns. A case study of developing and using these techniques for the Water Quality Indiana documentary project illustrates this process.

In Chapter 15, transmedia documentary producer Kyle Travers, of WFYI Public Media in Indianapolis, presents a case study of the transmedia storytelling she produced about early-20th-century labor organizer and socialist presidential candidate Eugene V. Debs, Travers describes her use of design thinking techniques to identify and co-create transmedia content to support the television documentary.

In Chapters 16 and 17, Jennifer Palilonis, of the Center for Emerging Media Design & Development, explores usability and user experience principles for transmedia storytelling that include how to collect user requirements and develop user personas for new media content systems, core usability, and user experience principles. Palilonis explores user experience for stories that cross physical and digital spaces, testing processes and data analysis, iterative design and development processes, and techniques for testing and evaluating audience engagement. She then provides a case study that chronicles a user-centered design and development process and user experience testing for a transmedia digital literacy curriculum for kindergarten through fifth-grade teachers and students.

In the concluding chapter, Moloney summarizes the volume's content and from it distills a flexible framework for analysis or design of socially-concerned transmedia stories. Built on the approaches and cases outlined here, the framework recommends examination or planning of 1) contexts, 2) empathy research, 3) storyworld, 4) targeting, 5) aesthetics, 6) story network, 7) user contribution, and 8) results testing for transmedia stories in production or under analysis.

Together these contributions present a handful of tools for the design, production, and analysis of socially-concerned transmedia stories. They offer scholars, students, and producers a look into the theories of practice and the processes of design, execution, and testing of diverse stories that aspire to positively influence communities. Neither Padre Marcelo Rossi nor his paradigm-disrupting Pentecostal counterparts would claim they had all the answers to engaging their publics, and neither do these authors. As with design thinking, we must adapt to an always-evolving mediascape with iterative processes. Like we do with transmedia storytelling, we must consider how our perceptions of a problem reflect and reform the complex and constantly evolving solutions in the wider world. Finally, as we do with usability and user experience research, we must stay attuned to how our publics engage with what we produce, and whether it is successful. The following chapters provide a start.

References

Moloney, K. (2012, July 2). Down at the Cathedral of the Immaculate Information. *Transmedia Journalism*. http://transmediajournalism.org/2012/07/02/at-the-cathedral-of-the-immaculate-information/

Rohter, L., & Fisher, I. (2007, May 9). Brazil greets Pope but questions his perspective. *The New York Times*. www.nytimes.com/2007/05/09/world/americas/09pope.html

2 Native, Emergent, and Feral Transmedia Storyworlds

Kevin Moloney

Though the study of transmedia storytelling is almost 30 years old at this writing, initial understanding of it is still beset by misconceptions. Thanks to Henry Jenkins' (2006) extensive analysis of *The Matrix* and other similarly huge blockbuster fictional entertainment storyworlds like the Star Wars galaxy or the Marvel Cinematic Universe of superheroes, we most easily see and identify transmedia stories as phenomena of entertainment, as predominantly digital, as something fairly new in the mediascape, and as complex, meticulously designed enterprises. There is certainly much to be learned by producers and analysts of socially-concerned transmedia stories from those massive cultural entities and how they build engagement. However, transmedia stories arguably unfold in every discipline, industry, or genre of storytelling. For the advertising and public relations industries, the "discovery" of this idea by Marsha Kinder (1991) is something akin to Native Americans' reaction to Columbus discovering a world they knew was there all along. Although this discovery aligns with the beginning of the digital age, thinking of transmedia stories as inherently digital is unnecessarily limiting. Media consumption on digital channels unquestionably continues to increase (Pew Research Center, 2019), but I argue that adding analog elements to a transmedia project can create longer-lasting, more personal, or more memorable engagement by contrast alone. Digital media is important, but our interaction with most instances of it is fast and shallow. Physical media will reach fewer people, but engagement with it is more likely to endure. Although most scholarly or professional analysis describes *native* transmedia stories that were designed as such from the very start, this chapter will also look at how *emergent* transmedia stories grow from the seed of a successful single story and at what we can learn from observing how *feral* transmedia stories—that have no single designer or creator behind them—develop deep and meaningful engagement from the public.

Storyworlds and Reference Worlds

At the core of transmedia storytelling is the concept of a *storyworld*, or the collection of characters in the story and the complex world in which they

DOI: 10.4324/9781003150862-2

live, love, and clash. The enormous "galaxy far, far away" of *Star Wars* is one example, as are J.K. Rowling's wizarding world of Harry Potter, the pseudo-Medieval lands in J.R.R. Tolkien's Middle Earth, and the magical world of Frank L. Baum's Oz. To best conceptualize the differences between *native, emergent,* and *feral* transmedia stories, I will first pull back the curtain on what a storyworld is and how it animates and manipulates the great and powerful wizard of both the imagined and the literal.

Narratologist Marie-Laure Ryan (2014, pp. 33–43) describes a fictional storyworld as the world a set of characters and objects inhabit, with its own physical laws, social rules, and physical and mental events that drive the plots of the stories that happen within it. Klastrup and Tosca (2014, p. 297) describe these imaginary worlds as informed by three dimensions: *mythos,* an origin story; *topos,* a setting; and *ethos,* a moral codex that drives the characters. "It is a dynamic model of evolving situations," Ryan (2014) wrote, "and its representation in the recipient's mind is a simulation of the changes that are caused by the events of the plot" (p. 33).

Mark J.P. Wolf (2014) describes imaginary storyworlds—alternate visions of the one we inhabit or that exist in a far-off galaxy—as "secondary worlds." Those worlds are created by authors and imagined by readers seated in the real, "primary world" we inhabit. They are connected, he argues:

> Secondary worlds are, to some degree, versions or variations of our own world. Likewise, the main character in stories set in secondary worlds is often a very ordinary sort of person with whom an audience can easily relate, seeing as they are experiencing the new world vicariously through the main character.
>
> (p. 63)

We see how these worlds connect when the fictional characters themselves enter alternate worlds. These worlds within a world, as in the Matrix, the Hogwarts School of Witchcraft and Wizardry, Wonderland, and Narnia, are analogous to how we mentally construct alternate experiences in the secondary storyworld. In the film *The Wizard of Oz* (Fleming et al., 1939), Dorothy Gale is a reflection of ourselves; we identify with her whether she is in Kansas or the Land of Oz. However, at the beginning and end of the film, we see Dorothy's own primary and secondary worlds collide. As Dorothy's house flies from Kansas to Oz on the winds of a tornado, the rotten, dog-snatching Miss Gulch morphs into the Wicked Witch of the West right outside the window. In the end, Dorothy wakes up in her Kansas bed, looks at Professor Marvel and farmhands Hunk, Zeke, and Hickory, and insists, "And you . . . and you . . . and you . . . and you were there. You couldn't have been, could you?" We and Dorothy recognize the four as the Wizard, the Scarecrow, the Cowardly Lion, and the Tin Man from Oz with the same basic character across both of Dorothy's primary and secondary worlds. Many fictional stories do this slip in some self-awareness. In *The Matrix*

(Wachowski & Wachowski, 1999), the hero Neo is offered a choice to take a red pill and leave the illusory world for the dystopian real one, or a blue pill to forget the question and stay where he is. Shortly after he chooses the red pill, Cypher quips to him, "Buckle your seatbelt Dorothy, 'cause Kansas is going bye-bye."

A nonfiction storyworld, however, is not an imaginary second realm of the somewhat familiar; it is a part of the world we inhabit already. We are separated by time, distance, culture, familiarity, or experience from the subset world presented in a nonfiction story, and like we do with a fictional world, we must still imagine ourselves into it through the characters and events in the narrative. Factual or fictional, a storyworld is a mental construct. The stories we tell each other or ourselves about the world we inhabit can be as flawed and human as the characters in them. Ryan (2014) writes:

> Nonfictional stories are told as true of the real world, but they do not necessarily live up to this ideal. The storyteller can be lying, misinformed, or playing loosely with the facts. It is therefore necessary to distinguish the world as it is presented and shaped by a story from the world as it exists autonomously. The former is a storyworld, the latter is a reference world. Assessing the truth of a story means assessing to what extent the storyworld corresponds to the reference world.
>
> (p. 33)

Although nonfiction storytelling is an effort to tell stories that reflect the empirical facts and data of the reference world, it is still a very human act. We filter facts through our own internal mythos, topos and, in particular, ethos. In the *narrative paradigm*, Walter Fisher (1987) described how readers accept the truthfulness of a story based on how well its characters and their actions agree with our own understanding of the world. "Determining a character's motives is prerequisite to trust, and trust is the foundation of belief," he argued (p. 47). Real-world storyworlds are as constructed as the fictional ones, whether that construction is conscious or unconscious.

When we read a nonfiction story, we are transported to a subset of the real world. Though that transportation is not necessarily an escape as it is with fiction, we temporarily find ourselves in a different place or time, we still imagine engagement with its characters, and we evaluate its ethos. For example, when the cathedral of Notre Dame caught fire in April 2019, news coverage might have transported us halfway around the world to Paris to vicariously experience the grief and anguish of the Parisians. When we read history or visit a museum or historical site, we are transported to another time. When we remotely watch social change movements unfold, we briefly inhabit the world of civil, immigrant, or environmental rights activists and perhaps even mentally argue back to those characters or their opponents. Like fictional storyworlds, these subsets of the real world can also be hypothetical. When we engage with coverage of climate change, we might be transported to a probable future of greater famine, drought, and more extreme weather events. This ability to enter a storyworld, whether it is in another galaxy or another part of town, is as active in the creation of a transmedia storyworld as the design efforts of a Lucas, Wachowski, or Tolkien.

Transmedia Origin Stories

Many scholars have described the internal structures of transmedia stories, made frameworks for them, and analyzed the economic forces and advantages of the form. After first putting flesh on Marsha Kinder's (1991) identification of the form, Jenkins broke the idea apart into Seven Principles of Transmedia Storytelling, adding granularity to the understanding of what goes on within a transmedia story (Jenkins, 2009a, 2009b): *Spreadability vs. Drillability, Continuity vs. Multiplicity, Immersion, Extractability, Worldbuilding, Seriality, Subjectivity*, and *Performance*. Since their posting on his blog, these principles have been continually refined by scholars and practitioners of the form and have been used as a frequent framework of analysis.

In 2016, he described differing contemporary logics, goals, and economic models, and tied them to global locations (Jenkins, 2016). He argued that culture and economics influence how a transmedia story is structured, from the media mix of Japan, to Hollywood's mothership franchises, New York's game-like experiences, Canada's ethos of public service, The European Union's efforts at cultural enrichment, to Brazil's burgeoning hybrid of all of the above.

Producers such as Robert Pratten (2011) and Andrea Phillips (2012) have described how to create the network of stories that build transmedia worlds. Scholars continue to design analysis frameworks to study the internal structures of transmedia stories (Aarseth, 2006; Ciancia, 2015; Gambarato, 2018; Javanshir et al., 2020; Jung et al., 2017; Moloney, 2018, 2019; Ruppel, 2012; Scolari, 2013). However, none of them have yet examined how and from where a transmedia story originates. The focus of analysis are stories designed from the start as transmedia entities, the stories Jenkins (2016) described as "born transmedia" (p. 235).

It is limiting, however, to only analyze or design transmedia stories that originate as such. If intentional design were a requirement, then transmedia stories could not have existed before the term was coined by Kinder (1991). Oz and Middle Earth are common examples of transmedia storyworlds that predate her identification of this structure. Jenkins (2006, p. 119) wrote of how the Christian story was told in the middle ages across books, architecture, sculpture, and ritual. If transmedia storytelling is at least a thousand years old, then where did those early storyworlds come from? Who, if anyone, designed them?

Native, Emergent, and Feral Transmedia Stories

I argue that the origins of transmedia stories should be plotted somewhere on a spectrum of possibilities. This spectrum could either begin or end with *native* transmedia stories that are conceptualized as such from the start by their producers—Jenkins' "born transmedia." But not all transmedia stories debut that way. Some of our favorites, as I'll describe shortly, begin as simple, single, monomedia stories that soon gain so much traction with the public that their or other producers design transmedia experiences around them. These are *emergent* transmedia stories. Further down this spectrum of continuity are the stories that are experienced by their fans, their believers, or their embracers as transmedia stories. These *feral* transmedia stories have no Wachowski, Lucas, or Disney guiding the transmedia nature of the experience. Instead, they are created by multitudes of amateurs, professionals, and fans all spreading pieces of the story independently.

These three definitions cannot be separated by distinct lines; no truly effective transmedia story, despite how intentionally it might be designed, is free of external or preexisting contexts. Inevitably, a well-designed storyworld will have elements of all three of these ideas. The poles of the spectrum are easy to reverse if one is so inclined, so long as on one end is *native* and the other *feral*. I start the spectrum here with the most familiar idea—the *native* or intentionally designed transmedia stories—only because it is the most familiar.

Native Transmedia Stories

Native transmedia stories are conceptualized as transmedia projects from the start, embracing in their design the logic of telling richer, additive stories through many media forms, and reaching diverse or specifically targeted publics through carefully chosen media channels. Though new media and story extensions may be added to a native transmedia project later, these

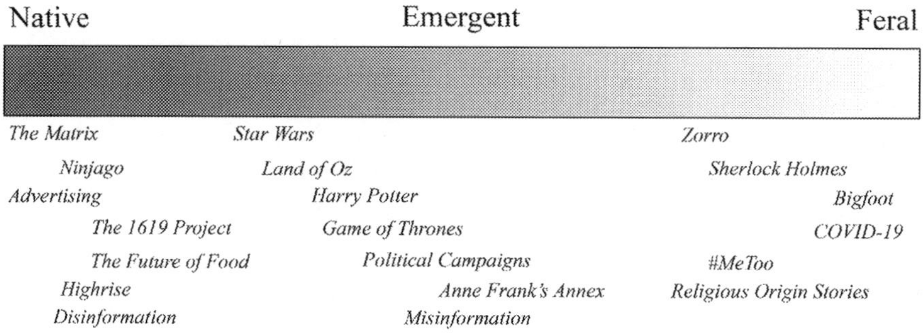

Native	Emergent	Feral
The Matrix	Star Wars	Zorro
Ninjago	Land of Oz	Sherlock Holmes
Advertising	Harry Potter	Bigfoot
The 1619 Project	Game of Thrones	COVID-19
The Future of Food	Political Campaigns	#MeToo
Highrise	Anne Frank's Annex	Religious Origin Stories
Disinformation	Misinformation	

Figure 2.1 A spectrum of native, emergent, and feral transmedia stories

differ from emergent and feral transmedia projects by their original intention and planning. An emergent transmedia story arises from the success of what was originally a discrete story. A feral transmedia project has no designer behind it at all.

In biological taxonomy, a type specimen is the individual exemplar of a species. It is the reference point for how a category like that species is defined. If there is a type specimen of transmedia storytelling, it is *The Matrix* franchise. Jenkins (2006) illustrated his definition of transmedia storytelling through a detailed case study of the popular films and their preplanned transmedia extensions. Not only does its preplanned story unfold across four movies but the storyworld was also intentionally built further through a series of short animated films, games, comic books, and action figures. Matrix producer Joel Silver told Jenkins:

> I remember on the plane ride back, [Lana] sat down with a yellow pad and kinda mapped out this scheme we would do—where we would have this movie, and these video games and these animated stories, and they would all interact together.
>
> (p. 101)

Like any effective transmedia production, the storyworld diffuses down the origin spectrum through fan fiction, fan art, cosplay, and remix and parody. With the core stories being the highly profitable theater films, The Matrix models Jenkins' Hollywood "mothership" logic perfectly.

The transmedia studies' subdiscipline has spent a lot of time analyzing and critiquing entertainment productions like *The Matrix*—ones that are native transmedia stories. Other examples include Lego's *Ninjago* storyworld, which is populated by movies, games, and books in addition to the toy bricks themselves; the anime-, manga-, and game-fueled Pokémon; and the early-social-media-centered storyworld of LonelyGirl15. The expansive, targeted, media-agnostic contemporary advertising campaign has long exemplified native transmedia publication, and so has their nefarious evil twin, the disinformation campaign (del Mar Ramirez-Alvarado, 2020).

Socially-concerned native transmedia storyworlds appear in documentary, journalism, activism, and public information campaign projects. The National Film Board of Canada's transmedia documentary *Highrise* (Cizek, 2009) centered on five online multimedia experiences from 2010 to 2015. The citizen media projects explore life in public-subsidized high-rise apartment towers around the world through the eyes of residents. They unfold as nonlinear explorations through homes and lives as if the viewers have slipped in unnoticed. One of the five, "A Short History of the Highrise" (Cizek, 2013), was produced in collaboration with the *New York Times*, introducing the project to a vast new public. The project also engaged the interested through "mixed media, interactive documentaries, mobile productions, live presentations, installations and films" (Cizek, n.d.).

Though native transmedia stories remain relatively rare in journalism, the National Geographic Society's Future of Food project (Foley et al., 2014) explored how the world would feed nine billion people by 2050. The project deployed through more than 800 stories and 450 social media posts on 41 different media channels. Though initially planned for eight months of publication, the project extended for more than a year. The channels used in the project ranged from monthly issues of the famed yellow-bordered magazine to mobile apps, cable television miniseries, a blog series, social media, museum exhibitions, tours, food tastings, and a hackathon. The Future of Food project was an experiment in interdepartmental collaboration designed to coordinate the many media channels at the disposal of the National Geographic Society on behalf of a single subject of planetary importance. The project was not well scoped, however, resulting in a massive, sprawling project that might intimidate even those most interested in the subject (Moloney, 2015).

Five years later, however, the New York Times Company managed to produce a rich, well-scoped, and defined storyworld with the Pulitzer-Prize-winning 1619 Project (Hannah-Jones, 2019). Named for the date 400 years earlier that the first slaves were sold into what is now the United States, the 1619 Project explored the lingering aftermath of slavery through an expansive multi-year project. The 1619 Project included a special interactive website section, three issues of the printed magazine, a special print section of the *New York Times* newspaper, articles in the Sports section and the print-only *New York Times for Kids*, a five-episode podcast, live symposia at the Smithsonian Institution and The Times Center, online presentations, and a primary education curriculum matched to Common Core Standards. A book series still in development at this writing will include an expanded version of the existing project content, a graphic nonfiction book, and four other books for young readers. The television production *The Weekly* and podcast *The Daily* aired connected stories about ongoing race issues, and the weekly email newsletter *Race/Related* contributes to the project scope with both directly and indirectly related stories and commentary. The 1619 Project was advertised by the New York Times Company on the 2020 Academy Awards broadcast (Moloney, 2020). Although the project is most easily accessed online, the analog components they deployed provided exclusive, singular experiences through the symposia, and physically durable ones through printed materials. Reprints of original 1619 magazine and newspaper sections were available through the *New York Times* online store through 2020, and original copies are selling on eBay at this writing for two hundred dollars. For some readers, these print materials could one day be heirlooms. Although the aforementioned list of interconnected stories is large, the preplanning by journalist Nicole Hannah-Jones and *New York Times Magazine* editor Jake Silverstein created a concise and approachable storyworld centered on a handful of illustrative subjects. Unlike the sprawling and fuzzy-bordered *National Geographic* project mentioned earlier, the 1619 Project is approachable in scope.

Massive scale is not a prerequisite for a transmedia story, however. This volume features extensive description and analysis of five native, socially-concerned transmedia projects produced effectively by a handful of people each, on a modest array of media: The Blue Roots Project (Chapter 4), LUCEO's harm reduction campaign in response to the U.S. opioid crisis (Chapter 5), Tomas van Houtryve's Lines and Lineage project on the former United States –Mexico border (Chapter 6), the Plug Social TV project in Milan (Chapter 8), Dar-Si Hmad's water from fog project (Chapter 10), and Ana Rewakowicz's Mist Collector Project (Chapter 11). These projects spread modestly across the left end of the spectrum (Figure 2.1), positioned roughly by how much of the project content depends on preexisting stories drawn into their scope. However, through their intentional design, the creators of these stories are able to seize all of the advantages of transmedia storytelling, from nonlinear structures, to serialization, to the targeting of particular publics through the use of specific media channels. Whether used for entertainment, for social good, or for evil, the design gives producers the ability to better achieve their project goals.

Emergent Transmedia Stories

Not all successful, familiar, or beloved transmedia storyworlds began with intentional design, however. The now at this writing 44-year-old *Star Wars* galaxy started life as a one-off movie in 1977. Lucas struggled to get his single movie made. According to Frank Rose (2011):

> the only studio that would take a chance on the space opera Lucas wanted to make was Fox—and so low were its expectations that Lucas was able to keep the sequel rights and the merchandizing rights as well.
> (p. 68)

Thanks to those key intellectual property rights and enormous public traction, that film soon became three, then six, then a seemingly unending stream, combined with novels, comic books, games, TV, and committed fandom across generations. That rapid and massive expansion did not start with the careful planning of a native transmedia story, however. According to Rose:

> *Star Wars* was accompanied by a cascade of spin-offs, but few of them had any direct connection with the movie. Del Rey Books published a novel, purportedly written by Lucas himself but in fact ghosted by a science fiction writer whose only guide was an early draft of the script. Marvel brought out a series of comics that began veering off in weird

directions as early as episode 8, when Han Solo (played in the movie by Harrison Ford) and his Wookiee sidekick Chewbacca encounter Jaxxon, a giant rabbit that Marvel's writers dreamed up as an homage to Bugs Bunny. Only the toy line—hurriedly released by Kenner, a second-tier manufacturer, after bigger companies passed—maintained any faithfulness to the universe Lucas had conjured up in his head. Nobody—not Fox, not the fans, not Lucas himself-seemed to think this was odd. It was just the way things worked.

(p. 68)

Ultimately, Lucasfilm seized control of the storyline and designed rigid guidelines for the mythos, topos, and ethos of the *Star Wars* galaxy. Lucasfilm's private *Holocron* database, and the fan-created, online *Wookieepedia* both define the canonicity of information about the storyworld, and continue to do so through further expansion by Disney.

Stories like this—that start as monomedia but soon gain enough traction that producers then expand the storyworld—cover the broad middle of this spectrum. Like *Star Wars* you could plot storyworlds such as Frank L. Baum's Oz, The Wizarding World of Harry Potter, or George R.R. Martin's Westeros from the *Game of Thrones* franchise on the spectrum of emergent transmedia stories. Here again, the originating authors launched complex, well-defined, and controlled storyworlds upon the success of a seed novel. They all expanded into multiple novels from their storyworlds, and into film or television, theater, comics, games, toys, and more. After intermittent success on the big and small screens, Marvel's expansion of old comic-book storyworlds quickly evolved into a complex and interconnected multiverse under their and Disney's careful direction. Contemporary political campaigns, which though they are deeply designed, start from the candidate's preexisting story and constantly react to the feral mediascape (Kreiss, 2009; Tenderich, 2013). This is also reflected in the spread of the fuzzy semi-design of fear- and bias-driven misinformation (Alzamora & Andrade, 2019). Again, these projects usually begin with a compelling story in a single media form and channel, and, after they gain public traction, the owners of the intellectual property expand them into transmedia experiences. They emerge from a single story, but their variation plots them across wider bands of the spectrum.

The Diary of a Young Girl, by Anne Frank (1996), is a venerable example of socially-concerned, emergent transmedia storytelling, the trajectory of which is similar to the aforementioned examples. Frank's well-crafted diary of life within the tiny storyworld of The Annex was published in Dutch in 1947, two years after Frank's murder at the Bergen-Belsen concentration camp in Nazi Germany. It quickly came to embody parts of the Jewish experience of the Holocaust in Europe and by 1952 had been published in multiple languages worldwide. On the traction of this story the Anne Frank Fonds, a Swiss foundation that holds the copyright to the diary, licensed adaptations of the story on stage, film, opera, radio, and anime. Adaptation alone does not define a transmedia story, however. The transmedia storyworld of Frank's wartime experience expands through museums such as the Anne Frank House in Amsterdam where visitors walk in Frank's footsteps and gaze through the same windows as she. Others, such as the United States Holocaust Memorial Museum, and the Children's Museum of Indianapolis move the story into physical space through evocative scenes and settings for visitors. And generations of school children have read and explored Frank's world as they learn about the history of the Holocaust.

One case presented in this volume (Chapter 16) exemplifies how emergent transmedia storytelling works in documentary film: *The Revolutionist: Eugene V. Debs*, a documentary by WFYI public television in Indianapolis, evolved from an hour-long broadcast documentary film into an eleven-part transmedia campaign to open new doors to the storyworld around the regional mediascape, create experiences and new modes of engagement for the public, and to lengthen and broaden engagement with the storyworld. The tightly targeted and concise storyworld emerged after preproduction for the documentary film—originally planned only as a broadcast film—had started.

As discussed previously, all nonfiction transmedia storyworlds are subsets of the real world. Anne Frank's storyworld from within the annex is a subset of the storyworld of the Holocaust, which is a subset storyworld of the Second World War. By reading her diary, watching a film or anime, students her same age around the world enter the storyworld of the annex. Inevitably that storyworld is contextualized by the larger terror of the Holocaust and the cataclysm of the global war. These subsets of the real-world nest within each other, or overlap like Venn diagrams, or interconnect as a network in our minds. We contextualize these stories through prior knowledge, revisit them after new experiences, use them for analogy and metaphor, or make other novel mental connections first between stories within the storyworld, then between connected storyworlds, and then to our own lives. All transmedia stories interlink this way, whether they connect the imaginary to the real, or one part of our physical or mental world to another. Emergent transmedia storyworlds arguably connect to other storyworlds more than the native stories do. However, *feral* transmedia storyworlds exist entirely in the connections the public makes, either collectively or individually.

Feral Transmedia Stories

At the right end of the spectrum fall feral transmedia stories. These are stories that gain so much public traction that the storyworlds expand across media and assemble in the minds of believers, fans, or concerned citizens. Feral transmedia stories have no single designer behind their structure; storyworlds are built through the independent contributions of many producers and many more fans. These stories demonstrate all of the principles, logics, locations, and dynamics of intentionally designed projects. Bigfoot, the Yeti, el Chupacabra, and other mythical terrors have stalked us for centuries through distributed, uncoordinated, grassroots storytelling in any media available. In fiction and entertainment, we see these qualities in the 100-year-old story of el Zorro, the swashbuckling hero of Spanish California introduced in 1919 as serialized pulp fiction by Johnston McCulley. Though first McCulley then Zorro Productions Inc. have held the copyright to the character, neither has done anything other than license that character. Zorro has appeared in a multiplicity of forms, in additive or alternative storylines through a multitude of books, films, television series, stage plays and musicals, comics, toys, and games. Zorro entered midcentury modernism as Batman, and dozens of other international characters borrow his qualities. He even echoes in the mascot of Texas Tech University. Similarly, feral transmedia storytelling might be observed in the Sherlock Holmes storyworld. Though Sir Arthur Conan Doyle wrote four novels and 56 short stories about the character, the detective continues to outlive his creator through countless other novels, films, plays, television series, and unnumerable popular culture references.

As Jenkins (2006, p. 119) observed in the Christian story as told in the middle ages, most of the world's religious stories embody transmedia storytelling through their use of any storytelling form or channel available to spread the message. Judeo-Christian religions, Hinduism, Buddhism, and others relate their stories through books, architecture, art, iconography, reenactment, ritual, and personal testament to build a complex storyworld with which their faithful engage as fact, fiction, or both. Though throughout history sects and specific organizations have sought to control those stories, no one organization is in charge of the storytelling in the same way that a Wachowski or Lucas is.

Aside from familiar entertainment storyworlds, these transmedia experiences are easily seen in how we engage with breaking news stories. Throughout the ongoing COVID-19 pandemic, each of us independently assembles the storyworld of the pandemic expansively, through multiple media. We read newspapers, watch TV reports, and listen to radio broadcasts, engage with social media, converse at home or online, jeer or applaud political actors, bake bread, sew masks, or simply walk around the community where permitted, among myriad other ways of gathering information we individually trust. Like COVID-19, we can see these mediated experiences in the #MeToo movement which shows a mix of emergent and feral qualities. Though the #MeToo movement sprang from a 2006 Myspace post by activist Tarana Burke and subsequent launch of a focused organization, the movement exploded into a public consciousness and expanded into a feral transmedia story with accusations against Hollywood producer Harvey Weinstein in 2017 (Renkl, 2017). Though a committed organization exists to promote the message of #MeToo, the hashtag and ethos extend far beyond its reach.

There are varying degrees of wildness in these feral stories. They spread toward the emergent in their varying degrees of domestication. This spectrum is valuable to the study of all transmedia stories, whether they come from the entertainment and advertising industries or from socially-concerned communication. It is a helpful framework to understand the role of design in the expansion of a storyworld.

Embracing Wildness in Transmedia Storytelling

Whether for entertainment, education, or social change, the best transmedia stories allow room for the wildness of feral transmedia storytelling in their mix. Whether conscious or not, Katarina Cizek's *Highrise* storyworld depends on the viewer's experience and prior understanding with subjects of architecture, development, public housing, and culture to be fully understood. Jenkins (2006) wrote:

> When the Greeks heard stories about Odysseus, they didn't need to be told who he was, where he came from, or what his mission was. Homer was able to create an oral epic by building on "bits and pieces of information" from preexisting myths, counting on a knowledgeable audience to ride over any potential points of confusion. This is why high school students today struggle with *The Odyssey*, because they don't have the same frame of reference as the original audience. Where a native listener might hear a description of a character's helmet and recognize him as the hero of a particular city-state and, from there, know something of his character and importance, the contemporary high school student runs into a brick wall, with some of the information that once made these characters seem so real buried in some arcane tome.
>
> (pp. 119–120)

For designers of any native or emergent transmedia story—socially-concerned stories in particular—an understanding of how the designed or delineated storyworld connects to, reflects, or depends upon other real or fictional storyworlds for context is crucial to an effective design. Socially-concerned transmedia stories in particular are less likely to have abundant resources to develop an effective information campaign; few are made for-profit and funding either comes from donors, grants, or the personal funds of the producer. By explicitly connecting a modest socially-concerned project to the wider, feral storyworld's history and context, a producer can provide their publics with rich depth and complexity. This effort can be made as mysterious and complex as the clues hidden within *The Matrix* films (1987) or as explicit as the hotlinks to off-site contextual information provided for the Future of Food or 1619 Projects.

Beyond context, designers can also open new doors to their storyworld, expand reach, and build scale beyond their budget and personnel by exploring what other storyworlds connect to or overlap with their own. During the research and planning phases for any transmedia story, producers will likely encounter other subset storyworlds about their broader subject that would provide new and related information to their publics. For example, the 1619 Project explicitly linked to external reporting by the *Miami Herald, HuffPost* and the Organisation for Economic Co-operation and Development. Implicit connections to Alex Haley's *Roots*, and films *Selma* and *12 Years a Slave* expand reader understanding of the complexities of slavery's impact on the history and culture of the United States (Moloney, 2020, pp. 4691–4692). By linking to real or fictional stories as a fundamental element of design, the depth, reach, and complexity of a storyworld can grow, and with it the long-term and valuable engagement of the story's public.

One might imagine Dorothy Gale, still resting on her bed post-adventure, gobsmacked by hallucination or dream, connecting her experience, knowledge, and recognition across two worlds. Through its connection to real life, her secondary dream world in Oz becomes richer and more meaningful. As analysts and designers of transmedia stories, we benefit from the same understanding of how our primary world connects with, informs, and influences the secondary worlds we study and create.

References

Aarseth, E. J. (2006). The culture and business of cross-media productions. *Popular Communications*, 4(3), 202–211.

Alzamora, G. C., & Andrade, L. (2019). The transmedia dynamics of fake news by the pragmatic conception of truth. *Matrizes*, 13(1), 109–131. https://doi.org/10.11606/issn.1982-8160.v13i1p109-131

Ciancia, M. (2015). Transmedia design framework: Design-oriented approach to transmedia research. *International Journal of Transmedia Literacy*, 1(1), 131–146.

Cizek, K. (2009). *Highrise*. National Film Board of Canada. http://highrise.nfb.ca

Cizek, K. (2013, October 28). A short history of the Highrise. *The New York Times*. www.nytimes.com/interactive/2013/08/28/opinion/highrise-trailer.html

Cizek, K. (n.d.). *About*. Highrise. http://highrise.nfb.ca/about/

del Mar Ramirez-Alvarado, M. (2020). Post-truths and fake news in disinformation contexts: The case of Venezuela. In *Handbook of research on transmedia storytelling, audience engagement, and business strategies* (pp. 306–320). IGI Global. www.igi-global.com/chapter/post-truths-and-fake-news-in-disinformation-contexts/253400

Fisher, W. R. (1987). *Human communication as narration: Toward a philosophy of reason, value and action*. University of South Carolina Press.

Fleming, V., Cukor, G., LeRoy, M., Taurog, N., Thorpe, R., & Vidor, K. (1939, August 15). *The Wizard of Oz*. Metro-Goldwyn-Mayer (MGM).

Foley, J., Steinmetz, G., & Richardson, J. (2014, March 15). The future of food. *National Geographic Magazine*. www.nationalgeographic.com/foodfeatures/feeding-9-billion/

Frank, A. (1996). *The diary of a young girl: The definitive edition*. Anchor Books/Doubleday.

Gambarato, R. R. (2018). A design approach to transmedia projects. In M. Freeman & R. R. Gambarato (Eds.), *The Routledge companion to transmedia studies*. Routledge.

Hannah-Jones, N. (2019, August 14). The 1619 project. *The New York Times*. www.nytimes.com/interactive/2019/08/14/magazine/1619-america-slavery.html

Javanshir, R., Carroll, B., & Millard, D. (2020). Structural patterns for transmedia storytelling. *PLoS One*, 15(1), 1–45. https://doi.org/10.1371/journal.pone.0225910

Jenkins, H. (2006). Searching for the origami unicorn. In *Convergence culture: Where old and new media collide* (pp. 93–130). New York University Press.

Jenkins, H. (2009a, December 12). The revenge of the origami unicorn: Seven principles of transmedia storytelling (Well, two actually: Five more on Friday). *Confessions of an Aca-Fan*. http://henryjenkins.org/2009/12/the_revenge_of_the_origami_uni.html

Jenkins, H. (2009b, December 12). The revenge of the origami unicorn: The remaining four principles of transmedia storytelling [Weblog]. *Confessions of an Aca-Fan*. http://henryjenkins.org/2009/12/revenge_of_the_origami_unicorn.html

Jenkins, H. (2016). Transmedia logics and locations. In B. W. L. D. Kurtz & M. Bourdaa (Eds.), *The rise of transtexts: Challenges and opportunities* (pp. 220–240). Routledge.

Jung, J. E., Lee, O.-J., You, E.-S., & Nam, M.-H. (2017). A computational model of transmedia ecosystem for story-based contents. *Multimedia Tools and Applications*, 76(8), 10371–10388. https://doi.org/10.1007/s11042-016-3626-5

Kinder, M. (1991). *Playing with power in movies, television, and video games: From Muppet babies to teenage Mutant Ninja turtles*. University of California Press.

Klastrup, L., & Tosca, S. (2014). Game of Thrones: Transmedial worlds, fandom, and social gaming. In M.-L. Ryan & J.-N. Thon (Eds.), *Storyworlds across media: Toward a media-conscious narratology*. University of Nebraska Press.

Kreiss, D. (2009). Developing the "good citizen": Digital artifacts, peer networks, and formal organization during the 2003–2004 Howard Dean Campaign. *Journal of Information Technology & Politics*, 6(3–4), 281–297. https://doi.org/10.1080/19331680903035441

Moloney, K. (2015). *Future of story: Transmedia journalism and National Geographic's future of food project* [Doctoral dissertation, University of Colorado]. https://scholar.colorado.edu/downloads/2227mp94w

Moloney, K. (2018). Designing transmedia journalism projects. In R. R. Gambarato & G. C. Alzamora (Eds.), *Exploring transmedia journalism in the digital age* (pp. 83–103). IGI Global. www.igi-global.com/chapter/designing-transmedia-journalism-projects/198024

Moloney, K. (2019). Proposing a practical media taxonomy for complex media production. *International Journal of Communication*, 13(2019), 3545–3568.

Moloney, K. (2020). All the news that's fit to push: The New York Times Company and Transmedia Daily News. *International Journal of Communication*, 14(2020), 4683–4702.

Pew Research Center. (2019, July 23). *Digital news fact sheet*. State of the News Media. www.journalism.org/fact-sheet/digital-news/

Phillips, A. (2012). *A creator's guide to transmedia storytelling: How to captivate and engage audiences across multiple platforms*. McGraw Hill Professional.

Pratten, R. (2011). *Getting started with transmedia storytelling*. CreateSpace Independent Publishing Platform. https://www.google.com/books/edition/Getting_Started_with_Transmedia_Storytel/BHANswEACAAJ?hl=en

Renkl, M. (2017, October 20). Opinion | The raw power of #MeToo (Published 2017). *The New York Times*. www.nytimes.com/2017/10/19/opinion/the-raw-power-of-metoo.html

Rose, F. (2011). *The art of immersion: How the digital generation is remaking Hollywood, Madison Avenue, and the way we tell stories*. W. W. Norton & Company.

Ruppel, M. (2012). *Visualizing transmedia networks: Links, paths and peripheries*. University of Maryland. http://drum.lib.umd.edu/handle/1903/13589

Ryan, M.-L. (2014). Story/worlds/media: Tuning the instruments of a media-conscious narratology. In *Storyworlds across media: Toward a media-conscious narratology* (pp. 25–49). University of Nebraska Press.

Scolari, C. A. (2013). *Narrativas transmedia: Cuando todos los medios cuentan*. Deusto.

Tenderich, B. (2013). *Design elements of transmedia branding*. USC Annenberg Innovation Lab. www.edee.gr/content/files/white_papers_cases_articles/design%20elements%20of%20transmedia%20branding.pdf

Wachowski, L., & Wachowski, L. (1999, March 31). *The Matrix* [Action, Sci-Fi]. Warner Bros.

Wolf, M. J. P. (2014). *Building imaginary worlds: The theory and history of subcreation*. Routledge. https://doi.org/10.4324/9780203096994

3 Design Thinking and the Storytelling Goal

Sarah Janssen

The process of design thinking (Brown, 2009; Buchanan, 1992; Cross, 1982; Norman, 2013)—an iterative five-phase method of design popularized by design firm IDEO and Stanford University's d.school—can be a valuable tool in the transmedia creator's toolkit. Consumers have thousands of options for content consumption right in their living rooms or from the smartphones in their pockets, and traditional ways of reaching consumers and potential audiences are inadequate for businesses or creators who want to cut through the noise of all that content. When, for example, was the last time you acted on information from a billboard? While creators still succeed with traditional media, many are exploring more creative and innovative options, including transmedia stories that place audiences in a more active role within the storyworld. Similarly, the product and experience design world has undergone a shift toward greater awareness and consideration of the user, paving the way for better products and services. This change was the result of experts questioning design as a "self-contained creative act" (Chesluk & Youngblood, 2020, pp. 16–17) and instead advocating that design make a difference in the lives of the people for whom the design is intended (Norman, 2013). Designers refer to those people as "users," for which the equivalent in storytelling is the audience, reader, or anyone who experiences the story. The design thinking process and its strategies of research through empathy for the users of a product, service, or story provide transmedia creators methods that can be adapted to different stories and generate innovative ideas. Creators of socially-concerned transmedia experiences in particular can benefit from the use of design thinking to define what is technologically feasible within a project's unique constraints, what is engaging to an audience, and what is economically viable. In an ever-changing world, creators need processes and methods that are both flexible and reliable to apply to the world's most complex social problems.

Being a human- or user-centered process, design thinking relies heavily on stories to understand the current state of people's lives and how it relates to the problem or challenge at hand. Designers then work to reframe the story in a new way to create a solution. "Thus, stories that inform—about contradictions, workarounds, normative, and success or failure—are the

DOI: 10.4324/9781003150862-3

input to the design process. Stories that inspire are its output" (Beckman & Barry, 2009, p. 158). Design thinking is human-centered, and so too is storytelling—a tool humans have been using for millennia to communicate, educate, influence, and entertain. Design thinking provides strategies that can enhance transmedia storytelling, offering creators methods for developing clear goals, refining and iterating ideas, and innovating on how the story unfolds. Design thinking—also variously described as *empathy research* or *human-centered design*—relies on a foundation of empathy with end users, which can provide important insights for storytellers and result in stories that inspire. Design thinking is already being applied to social problems as a way to identify and build solutions (Design Kit, 2020), and transmedia storytellers can benefit from how design thinkers engage with end users and stakeholders to enhance creativity and innovation. Socially-concerned stories should inspire audiences to act.

Origins of Design Thinking Process

Design thinking requires at minimum a problem, possibility of a solution, and users who care about the former and whose lives would be improved by the latter. In *The Design of Everyday Things*, Norman (2013) argues that designers, even if given a problem, will always be looking to solve the "right" problem, or the root problem of which other problems are merely symptoms. It was Stanford University professor David Kelley who is credited with adding the word "thinking" to design to describe the way that designers approach problems (Camacho, 2016). In his work at Stanford, Kelley combined ideas of the psychology of design with understanding of its creative processes, and deployed them using interdisciplinary teams of professors and students to tackle product design problems (Camacho, 2016). These courses he created evolved into Stanford's d.school design program, founded in 2005 (d.school, 2021). In 1991, Kelley took these methods to consulting firm IDEO where design thinking is employed using interdisciplinary creative teams to help businesses develop innovative, human-centered solutions (Camacho, 2016). Initially, IDEO focused primarily on product design, but after a decade, companies began bringing them other types of problems. If design thinking is about tackling the right (or root) problems, it's unlikely that the solution to every problem would be a new, well-designed consumer product. Advocates believe the spread of design thinking beyond traditional industrial or graphic design and the expanded expertise that these design thinkers could bring to old problems would allow society to more effectively tackle bigger problems (Buchanan, 1992).

Experts describe the activities of design thinking differently based upon to which industry it is being applied. What they share is more about what design thinking is not—a list of prescriptive steps performed in a particular order. Instead, those who use design thinking move among activities or phases as they iterate and refine their ideas. In the application of design thinking as popularized by IDEO, design thinkers navigate their way through the process, exploring what's possible to determine what solution strikes a balance among what is desirable, feasible, and viable within client or contextual constraints (Brown, 2009).

The approach to design thinking practiced at Stanford's d.school encourages design teams to move iteratively through empathize, define, ideate, prototype, and test phases as required by the project. The *empathize* phase serves as the foundation for the human-centered design process, requiring design thinkers to stand in the shoes of their users. The *define* phase is often a reframing of the problem into an actionable statement, called a problem statement, created using insights from the empathy conducted with actual users. This is fundamental to the next phase, *ideate*, in which design thinkers generate many ideas for a solution to address their problem statement. They are able to then *prototype* those ideas and *test* them (d.school, 2018). The process is not intended to be sequential; teams may find that after prototyping, more empathy research is needed to further define the problem statement. Or teams might conduct several rounds of prototyping and testing before landing on an idea they will take to market. The process and methods are intended to help guide design teams toward an idea that fulfills the needs of the users, meets the constraints of the brief, and is something that can be accomplished within the project timelines and budget. The d.school's application of design thinking, which is careful and specific about the goals of the activities, serves as a way to create masters of the process (Camacho, 2016). Its abundant available online resources could be helpful to those who wish to implement design thinking with little or no formal training.

Application of Design Thinking to Social Problems

In the past decade, design thinking has become more widely known and more broadly applied and adopted, primarily by businesses looking to become more efficient and stay ahead of their competition. During this time, both Stanford's d.school and IDEO have become more involved in tackling social problems like poverty and sustainability. IDEO heard specifically from clients that if they were a nonprofit organization they could work more extensively on issues of social or environmental concern. In response, IDEO created the nonprofit ideo.org, now OpenIDEO (Camacho, 2016). Beyond the business value of using design thinking for social problems, the process can infuse creativity and innovative thinking into organizations not widely known for technological advancement or innovation.

Foundations and nonprofit organizations emerged from the Great Recession in 2008–2009 having lost money in investments and facing fewer funding prospects. They needed to do more with even less (Pastorek, 2013). Working with OpenIDEO and using the design thinking process offered a way to explore the right problems and identify the ideas most likely to succeed and provide value to end users. Though social enterprises, foundations, or nongovernmental organizations might use user-engaged aspects of design thinking, they often fall short in designing innovative solutions by using traditional top-down problem-solving techniques. Design thinking strategies ultimately lead to better outcomes for the organizations and the people they serve (Brown & Wyatt, 2010). OpenIDEO co-founder Jocelyn Wyatt said of her time working on projects for the U.S. government:

> We were going to Uganda or Bolivia and kind of telling people, like, "Okay, this is the way we think you should do it." It seemed like those projects had really high budgets, little impact, and almost no sustainability in terms of what happened at the end of the project. It just seemed to me that there must be a better way to do things.
> (Pastorek, 2013, para. 4)

These issues can be some of society's most complex, at least on the surface. Design thinking is well suited for taking complex problems and breaking them down into simpler, more actionable problem statements.

Empathy in Design Thinking and Socially-Concerned Stories

Pine and Gilmore (2020) wrote about a looming shift to an experience economy of active participation from one that was primarily service-based with passive consumption. It's no longer enough for businesses to sell a well-designed product with pleasing packaging. In the experience economy, consumers expect the purchase and use of said product to be an experience, and one in which they are an active participant. In *Change by Design*, Brown (2009) explains that consumers expect that experiences "be as finely crafted and precision-engineered as any other product" (111). Industries that rely on storytelling, such as entertainment, publishing, and journalism, are not immune or exempt from this shift, though some have been slower to react than others. Transmedia storytelling is an integral part of these larger experiences. An early example is The Walt Disney Company, founded in the 1920s as a cartoon studio but soon emerged as an entertainment and media empire. The company brings its stories and characters to life beyond books and movies through theme parks, resorts, and cruises, in addition to merchandise like books, video games, and apparel. More specifically, what Disney offers are transmedia storytelling experiences that resonate with children and adults alike. Disney makes fans a part of the story and they sometimes are affected or even changed by it. Families vacationing at a Disney resort don't just leave with mouse ears or T-shirts; they leave with lasting memories of the experience and how it made them feel. In the following chapter, I will provide more detail about socially-concerned story experiences and how design thinking helped in their design and distribution.

Today, the lines between product, service, and experience are continuously blurred, but each requires design to reach end users and consumers, who make decisions and selections based on how something makes them feel. Emotions are what move people to trade money or time for an experience, and it's the job of designers to understand and harness those emotions to motivate people to action (Lupton, 2017). "Designers tap into people's emotions to trigger feelings of delight, desire, surprise, and trust. Designers train their emotion intelligence defined as the ability to read people's feelings and respond in ways that build understanding and cooperation by exploring empathy" (p. 59). Designers who develop empathy for the people they're designing for to understand their values, culture, and aspirations create better experiences by using design thinking.

Creators of socially-concerned stories face a similar task—enticing users to choose to spend their time or money on their story experience and harnessing the users' or audience's emotions through storytelling to create staying power—enough to encourage a change in thinking or action. Design thinking strategies leverage innate human abilities like intuition, pattern recognition, self-expression, and communication, to move designers and creators closer to the people for whom they create as opposed to traditional top-down solution processes. The human-centered process produces results that are also human-centered (Brown & Wyatt, 2010). With design thinking, designers and creators can use their empathy and understanding of people to encourage active engagement and participation in the experiences, products, and services they design (Brown, 2009).

In the same way, storytellers can leverage empathy research with their audience and stakeholders to capture the right emotions for the story. Conducting empathy research can help storytellers strike the right tone for an experience that, for example, critiques the actions of the society in contributing to climate change. The design thinking process can help creators present information and next steps that encourage the audience to act, instead of retreating to feelings of overwhelm and despair. As consumers' expectations have shifted toward active participation in experiences, so to have audiences' expectations changed in how they wish to engage with stories. Andrea Phillips (2012) wrote that "the realm of deep experiences and completely immersive stories" of transmedia experiences evoke emotions from an audience that are unmatched by a movie or single book (p. 5). Audiences expect to be able to engage with a story and its characters across multiple media. Design thinking can assist storytellers, especially those without the budgets of Hollywood or Madison Avenue, to develop and refine the story they're telling, the ways in which it will target audiences, and how those audiences will engage. Creators can incorporate publicly available design thinking tools into their story design process and hopefully contribute to the greater social good.

Methods for Empathy Research

Empathy is all about stepping into the shoes of users through observations, conversations, simulations, and other activities. Much of what follows is based on strategies from Stanford University's d.school and IDEO, but there are a number of organizations and resources that promote these methods, even if they are not called design thinking or are associated with Stanford or IDEO. Storytellers can adjust these methods or combine aspects of multiple methods to fit the needs of their project or brief.

An important habit to adopt when conducting empathy research, or even throughout the design thinking or story-building process, is to assume a beginner's mindset. A beginner's mindset is open to opportunities and possibilities; it is one of curiosity and wonder. Each member brings knowledge, experience, and expertise to form an interdisciplinary team. However, this point of view can also include beliefs, biases, and assumptions that could contribute to misconceptions or stereotypes that can be harmful, at worst, and at best, prevent building empathy and understanding for others. Journalists, particularly those who cover a specific topic area or beat, adopt a beginner's mindset every day. They keep in mind their audience and their level of understanding to balance the insider expertise they carry from being highly involved in topics like education, local government, or politics. Assuming a beginner's mindset means setting aside biases—even ones of which we might not be immediately aware—and approaching a problem or challenge with fresh eyes to increase creativity, innovation, and diverse thought.

Tips for assuming a beginner's mindset:

- Learn to recognize the emotional, mental, and physiological cues that you're in an expert mindset: feeling proud or defensive; thinking that an activity is a waste of time or won't be beneficial; crossing your arms; or slouching.
- Pause, take a few breaths, and adjust your modes to the opposite of your own warning signs: feeling open and curious; showing interest and being present; and leaning in and looking around to take in the environment.
- Intentionally adopt a beginner's mindset or if needed, assume the persona of a child or someone from another place or time to reset and bring an open mind to the task.

(Chan & Norris, 2021)

Imposing Constraints

Constraints are part of most design or storytelling projects by default. They can be deadlines, timelines, or budgets. They may be viewed negatively, but in reality, can force a creator or project team to develop very clear goals. In *The Paradox of Choice*, Schwartz (2004) warns that the freedom to choose bogs us down in endless possibilities, each requiring evaluation and attention. Instead of fearing constraints, they should be embraced, freeing individuals and teams to focus more on choices that matter to them or choosing to make the choices most critical for the project. Though it sounds counterintuitive, constraints are also important to unleashing and sustaining creativity. Especially for teams, constraints lead to increased encouragement by team members and helping behaviors that enable the team to be more creative (Saleh, 2015).

Though constraints have proven to be beneficial, teams should be cautious about imposing unnecessary constraints on the process. With experience, designers and storytellers will be to determine when and what constraints may be necessary and when team members' or stakeholders' bias, personal opinions and preferences, or other filters are being forced upon the project.

Tips for imposing constraints:

- Use another design thinking method such as brainstorming to enlist the help of stakeholders to add constraints to the project; employing others' opinions and ideas helps them feel like they're a part of the process.
- Time constraints are a simple way to start using constraints. Timelines can be imposed on a project overall (the team has four weeks to prepare to pitch an experience) or on smaller aspects of the project (each team member has 20 minutes to sketch five prototypes).
- Retrospectives or debriefs on projects and their constraints can be helpful to acknowledge the benefits of constraints and recognize when they're hindering instead of helpful.

Empathy Interviewing

Design thinkers conduct interviews to build empathy and better understand people's behaviors, choices, attitudes, preferences, and needs. Storytellers can use empathy interviews to glean insights from audiences, story subjects, or even other creators, to help inform the characters, storyline, or implementation of their transmedia experience. In-person interviews are often the most effective in building trust, engagement, and rapport with the interview subject. Interviews should feel comfortable for both the interviewer and interviewee. This is why care should be taken to prepare and plan for the interview. Questions should be crafted to elicit stories, not just simple yes or no answers, and promote a conversation with follow-up or clarifying questions added as needed. The interview setting should also be an appropriate and neutral place where all parties can be comfortable, not somewhere noisy where either party could struggle to hear the other.

Preparation is also critical to avoid squandering an interviewee's valuable time. Design thinking teams should be very clear about the goals of empathy interviews, what they hope to learn, and how it can be applied to best prepare for these interviews. Brainstorming questions based on the defined goal, identifying themes, and whittling down to the most necessary questions can be helpful in maximizing time with users. To capture insights and data, it's best to record the interviews, as any good journalist would, or bring a partner to capture the information.

Tips for Empathy Interviews

- Ask why, even if the answer might be obvious. Be careful not to lead the interviewee to an answer unintentionally through the phrasing of the question.
- Encourage stories to reveal how users think about the world. Pay attention to what might be inconsistent between what a user says and what they do.
- Don't be afraid of silence. Allowing silence provides participants the opportunity to process and reflect on the question and may give space for deeper, more thoughtful answers to questions.

(d.school, 2018, p. 4)

Analogous Empathy

Analogies can be helpful to gain understanding or clarity through comparison. In empathy research, analogies can help uncover insights that may not be obvious through a more direct approach. Teams struggling to innovate often benefit from exploration beyond their organization. Analogies encourage teams to consider different industries or offerings and provide a new perspective (d.school, 2018, p. 36). It can also provide a reset for those with experience to more easily assume a beginner's mindset by researching something that may seem less familiar. Analogous research and observation can also serve as a useful workaround when direct observation is difficult or impossible (d.school, 2010, p. 12). Socially-concerned storytellers can explore how people become involved with a different social cause or care about another social problem in order to inform how they might build involvement in their own.

Tips for analogous empathy:

- Identify the qualities of the experience, problem, or challenge that would be the most interesting or helpful to explore. For example, a transmedia experience creator may want to explore ways to help an audience navigate a storyworld, including entry points, maps, guides, clear exits, and how to find help.
- Brainstorm the types of spaces where people are assisted with navigation in similar ways. Observing how people enter, navigate, and engage with an in-person festival, fair, or theme park can inform ways creators can lead audiences through storyworlds.
- Consider interviewing stakeholders or users of these spaces or conduct an observation of the space.
- Document the analogous case, including photos and quotes, to help share inspiration or draw insights for later use.

(d.school, 2018, p. 36)

Business Model Canvas

The Business Model Canvas (Osterwalder & Tucci, 2005) is a tool to visualize and communicate the simple story of a business model. This business

Design Thinking and the Storytelling Goal 31

model snapshot enables entrepreneurs to communicate their vision; consider the whole; and be creative. For storytellers building elaborate storyworlds for transmedia experiences, the Business Model Canvas can force them to think about and define critical aspects of how the story is told, to whom and how they might partner with others in distributing it. This can be helpful in the early stages of the project to refine an idea for funding opportunities or pitching the project to a network or potential collaborator. The canvas features nine building blocks, and here storytelling-specific ideas that fit are added in parentheses:

1. Customer segments: the people/organizations for which value is created (audience);
2. Value proposition: products or services that create value for customers (what need this fills for the audience or what is gained);
3. Channels: touchpoints by which business interacts with customers and how business delivers value (how the audience will interact with the story and via what media channels);
4. Customer relationships: type of relationship the business is establishing with customers (the tone of the experience or the nature of the relationship with the audience);
5. Revenue streams: how and through which pricing model the business is capturing value (how will the storytelling project be funded);
6. Key resources: infrastructure of business to create, deliver, and capture value and indispensable assets (creation, storage, and distribution of storyworld assets);
7. Key activities: what is needed for the business to perform well (what is necessary to meet deadlines, timelines, and budget constraints, and how will success of the experience be measured);
8. Key partnerships: who can help leverage the business model (what organizations or individuals could help produce or promote it);
9. Cost structure: how the business will charge for the value it delivers (what will the cost to the audience be compared to the value they gain).
(Strategyzer, 2014)

In Hulme's (2010) adaptation, competitive strategy and growth strategy are added, along with techniques to visualize a model with arrows and emphasis on specific building blocks. This creates a holistic view of a model that allows for deeper engagement from interdisciplinary teams. For design thinkers, the Business Model Canvas creates an initial prototype that can then be researched, tested, and refined. The exercise of filling in the Business Model Canvas doesn't build empathy with an audience, but it can draw attention to areas where empathy research is lacking.

Prototype for Empathy

Prototypes are useful to gain valuable feedback without spending the money required to take a product, service, or story to market, but design thinkers also use this method to conduct empathy research with their end users.

Similar to how prototypes of design solutions show new information about an idea being tested, an empathy-seeking prototype can uncover insights and further understanding about people and spaces. For example, ask parents to draw themselves as comic-book heroes to learn more about their lives, values, and feelings about their roles in their families, and to flesh out a character in a story. For insight into how teens learn about the content they engage with, task them with making trading cards for the major influences in their lives. When creating a prototype, consider the people who will interact with the object or experience, and design it specifically to learn about users and their needs. Poverty simulations have been used to help people understand what it's like to live on little or no income. This same concept could be applied to understand how people would prioritize their needs and spend their money by acting out or talking about what decisions they would make with different income amounts. Compare responses to prompts or questions posted in both digital and physical spaces to see how the responses differ. Prototypes are helpful to explore user needs or probe an insight within a team or with end users.

Options for creating prototypes for empathy include the following:

- Sketching—Ask users to draw something and explain it. Users can sketch characters, create storyboards, or draw their favorite place to engage with stories.
- Gameplay—Create a game to probe specific issues to explore them in depth. A simple game can make tough questions or difficult subjects easier to tackle. Trivia games with users about their knowledge or attitudes on a topic are more fun and may elicit better feedback than a simple survey.
- Simulation—Recreate or simulate the user experience to gain a better understanding. Stage a room to recreate a scene in a story to gauge users' interest in learning more.

(d.school, 2018, pp. 18–19)

Co-creation Sessions

Designers and storytellers often create content for people unlike themselves. Co-creation sessions are a way to build empathy with end users and stakeholders by working with them directly on the design. Storytellers have many opportunities to co-create with their audience. These sessions could focus on the elements of the story or in the delivery or distribution of the aspects of the storyworld. A target demographic could offer insights into how they prefer to engage and participate in a story that could be different from another type of user.

Activities include evaluating existing solutions or generating new ideas through prototyping, sharing, and collaboration. The most important aspect of co-creation is that designers serve not as facilitators, but work alongside users or their intended audience (Lupton, 2017). Co-creation sessions can be structured depending on the team's needs, but they should be fun, stimulate creativity, and encourage people to use their hands through sketching or building a prototype.

In these sessions, it is important to involve end users in the design of the solution or story that the team is building, especially if they're going to be the ones engaging with it. A community that has contributed to the design of a story, practice, or service is more likely to adopt it, and the team will gain valuable insights into their problem or challenge and potential solution (Design Kit).

Tips for co-creation sessions:

- Start with warm-up exercises to encourage focus and creative thinking.
- Though they should be fun and stimulate creativity, activities should also be carefully planned with all required materials on hand.
- Designers and creators should work alongside their users, participating in the activity instead of simply facilitating.
- Leave time for sharing and discussion of ideas and outcomes, allowing participants to talk about their ideas or solutions in their own words; someone from the design team should take notes or record the discussion.

Engaging Extreme Users

Interviewing and observing users are critical aspects of the design thinking process to better understand the people for which a solution or story is being designed. Engaging with more targeted groups of users, called extreme users, can also elicit valuable insights. Their values, needs, and lifestyles can magnify problems design thinkers and storytellers aim to solve, revealing valuable insights, pain points, and workarounds. These users often have more knowledge, experience, or passion and play a more active role in fixing their problems, thus are more articulate about their solutions. These users would not be just the viewers of a movie from a comic-book franchise, but super fans who line up to see the movie in theaters for the midnight release while dressed as their favorite character. Extreme users of socially-concerned stories might be people on the ground—activists, nonprofit staff, or people personally affected by a social problem. Extreme users in these scenarios may also be people in positions of power—lawmakers, lobbyists, or policy wonks. Speaking with and observing these users can reveal pain points and workarounds more easily seen in this group than in the wider population.

Tips for engaging with extreme users:

- Consider the challenge, problem, or story and the users who may be on the fringe, edge, or extreme of that challenge or specific aspects of it.

- Consider where to find these users. They may have certain groups or communities they belong to or places they gather, and these can provide creators and design thinkers with ways to connect, observe, and interview them.
- Engage with super users with the same strategies employed with other users. Their experience and knowledge will inform the themes, insights, and direction of the interaction.
- Pay close attention to problems these users face and how they address those challenges. This information may provide insights into solutions or stories other users may find useful.

Photo or Video Diaries/Journals

A photo journal or video diary empowers users to tell their own stories in a visual way. With only a prompt and a few instructions, users can share their thoughts and feelings on a subject over a period of time, to prime for an empathy interview or stand alone as a way for a designer to get an understanding of the context of a user's life. This context can include the use of a product in everyday life, how other people affect and influence the user or the situation, and the journey of the user described or captured in their own words and images (Design Kit). Visual diaries or journals can encourage potential users of a story experience to think about a social problem and record their thoughts or feelings about it over time and within the context of their lives, rather than answering a question in a moment for a survey or interview. For example, asking someone to notice garbage and litter around them—in their neighborhood, on their route to work—and their relationship to it could provide insights into trash and people's attitudes about it. This method could also help storytellers better understand the lives of the people they're profiling, such as someone experiencing homelessness or addiction, without interfering or biasing interactions through their own presence. This method requires preparation and thought, materials, as well as agreement from the user or subject.

Tips for using a photo or video diary:

- Provide the person who is creating the journal with a device to capture images or video if they don't have one and a prompt to guide their entries. For example, if you're interested in learning more about when audiences engage with news articles, encourage the user to record where they are, what they're reading, and how they're feeling when they're engaging with news media or current events.
- Provide parameters around the prompt, such as a length of time or a number of entries.
- Once the time period has elapsed or the minimum criteria met, have the user send, or upload everything to a shared workspace or document.

Spend some time with what they've shared and develop questions to probe deeper.
- If conducting a follow-up interview, use the time to ask questions and encourage the participant to share their thoughts and feelings on the exercise (Design Kit).

Design Thinking for Socially-Concerned Transmedia Stories

When developing products and experiences for consumers, designers aim to trigger certain emotions to motivate consumers to take action, to buy. The same can be said for storytelling, especially socially-concerned storytelling. These stories must evoke certain emotions within the audience to motivate members to take action. Storytellers can take some cues from designers when developing transmedia stories that motivate people to make changes to address social problems.

One area within the design thinking methodology that transmedia storytellers can leverage is empathy research to better understand the audiences and stakeholders who will participate or invest in the story and the cause storytellers are championing. Many strategies exist around building empathy within the design thinking methodology and can be used to fit a variety of transmedia stories. Building empathy with audiences and stakeholders can help creators explore new possibilities or develop experiences that better resonate with audiences. And in an increasingly crowded media landscape, storytellers must continue to be creative and innovative in their delivery, narratives, and formats to engage audiences and remain relevant. In the following chapter, two case studies describe how these techniques were deployed to develop or expand transmedia stories that address environmental problems and environmental justice.

References

Beckman, S. L., & Barry, M. (2009, December). Design and innovation through storytelling. *International Journal of Innovation Science*, 1(4), 151–160.

Brown, T. (2009). *Change by design: How design thinking transforms organizations and inspires innovation*. Harper Collins.

Brown, T., & Wyatt, J. (2010). *Design thinking for social innovation (SSIR)*. Retrieved January 24, 2021, from https://ssir.org/articles/entry/design_thinking_for_social_innovation

Buchanan, R. (1992). Wicked problems in design thinking. *Design Issues*, 8(2), 5–21. https://doi.org/10.2307/1511637

Camacho, M. (2016). David Kelley: From design to design thinking at Stanford and IDEO. *She Ji: The Journal of Design, Economics, and Innovation*, 2(1), 88–101. https://doi.org/10.1016/j.sheji.2016.01.009

Chan, L., & Norris, A. (2021, May 11). Journeying to the world of possibility through the beginner's mindset. *CreativeMornings Virtual FieldTrips*. https://creativemornings.com/talks/journeying-to-the-world-of-possibility-through-the-beginner-s-mindset

Chesluk, B., & Youngblood, M. (2020). *Rethinking users, the design guide to user ecosystem thinking*. BIS Publishers.

Cross, N. (1982). Designerly ways of knowing. *Design Studies*, 3(4), 221–227.

Design Kit. (2020). IDEO.org. Retrieved March 26, 2021, from www.designkit.org/methods/co-creation-session

d.school. (2010). *Bootcamp bootleg*. Retrieved August 23, 2015, from http://dschool.stanford.edu/wp-content/uploads/2011/03/

d.school. (2018). *Design thinking bootleg*. Retrieved January 21, 2021, from https://dschool.stanford.edu/resources/the-bootcamp-bootleg

d.school. (2021). *History & approach*. Stanford d.school. https://dschool.stanford.edu/fellows-in-residence/project-fellowship-history-approach

Hulme, T. (2010, October 9). Visualise your business model (for HackFwd): StartUp Tools. *Thulme.com*. http://thulme.com/startup-tools/video-visualise-your-business-model/

Lupton, E. (2017). *Design is storytelling*. Cooper Hewitt, Smithsonian Design Museum.

Norman, D. A. (2013). *The design of everyday things* (Revised and expanded ed.). Basic Books.

Osterwalder, A., Pigneur, Y., & Tucci, C. (2005). Clarifying business models: Origins, present, and future of the concept. *Communications of the Association for Information Systems*, 16. https://doi.org/10.17705/1CAIS.01601

Pastorek, W. (2013, November 12). *Bringing design thinking to social problems, Ideo.org focuses on the people in need*. Fast Company. www.fastcompany.com/3020789/bringing-design-thinking-to-social-problems-ideoorg-focuses-on-the-people-

Phillips, A. (2012). *A creator's guide to transmedia storytelling: How to captivate and engage audiences across multiple platforms*. McGraw Hill Professional.

Pine II, B. J., & Gilmore, J. (2020). *The experience economy: Competing for customer time, attention, and money*. Harvard Business Review Press.

Saleh, S. H. (2015). *Freedom from Freedom: The beneficial role of constraints in collaborative creativity* [Doctoral dissertation, University of Colorado]. Publication No. 3704802, ProQuest Dissertations Publishing.

Schwartz, B. (2004). *The paradox of choice: Why more is less*. Harper Collins.

Strategyzer. (2014). *Business model canvas explained* [Video]. Vimeo. https://vimeo.com/78350794

4 Deploying Design Thinking for Story Design
Case Studies

Sarah Janssen

The prior chapter outlined the benefits of using the empathy research strategies of *design thinking* to create socially-concerned transmedia experiences and provided a number of options and how those might be implemented. This chapter provides more depth through two transmedia experiences that demonstrate how design thinking can shape the development and distribution of a transmedia story.

The following transmedia experiences share the common topic of water, though in different ways. One explores access to clean water as a social and environmental justice issue, and the other explores water as a climate and environmental issue. I worked on these projects in parallel—the first as an individual project I researched, designed, and performed myself, and the other in an interdisciplinary team of academics, producers, and students while pursuing graduate study. The work of each project benefitted that of the other. Through empathy research, I closely experienced very specific issues of water and the people who were affected by them. For both projects, my goal was to get people to care. The final iterations couldn't have been more different: One evolved into a global social media campaign, while the other culminated in an intimate theater performance. This highlights the flexibility of design thinking strategies. They can be used no matter the audience size, the team size, or the budget. Creators can maintain their creative vision while still asking for input from prospective audiences. Design teams can still satisfy client demands while serving an audience with a participatory experience.

Case Study 1: We're Still Here: Stories of the Flint Water Crisis

"We're Still Here: Stories of the Flint Water Crisis" (Janssen, 2017) began as a research project to explore the problem of how to relate the experiences of Flint, Michigan residents to a broader audience, and to expand the story beyond ongoing news reports. For an outsider, local and national news accounts were the primary source of information about Flint's water crisis, news of which exploded in 2014 (C-SPAN, 2016; Acosta, 2019; Lin et al., 2016). Children and adults of Flint were exhibiting symptoms of lead poisoning and other severe health problems as a result of water contamination. In an effort to save money, the city had switched water sources, from Lake Huron water provided by the Detroit water system to Flint River water treated at the city water treatment plant. Because of this switch, the degraded infrastructure of the city's pipes allowed lead-contaminated water to flow into the homes of Flint residents. Although people across the U.S. Midwest, celebrities, nonprofits, and corporations were eager to donate money and bottled water to the residents of Flint, these efforts are simply a bandage on the wounds of this community, as lead can have lasting and even permanent effects on children's cognitive development.

Flint represents a larger issue: People must be able to empathize with victims of crises like these and achieve greater social awareness around issues like water contamination; a government's representation of its people; and distrust following the mistreatment of the governed. In addition to awareness and understanding, this empathy for residents of Flint could serve as motivation to act when these issues inevitably arise in other communities.

Storytelling builds empathy and the motivation to act (Jenkins, 2016; C. Heath & D. Heath, 2007; Costanza-Chock, 2014; Russel, 2016). This is similar to how design thinking helps teams empathize with the users to create products and experiences that evoke emotions to motivate users to act. A study of both fiction and nonfiction writers shows that those in the writing profession have higher empathy scores than the general population, revealing an ability to empathize with the characters they write about. This often translates into readers being able to empathize with the characters as well. But if this connection falls short, authors employ strategies to build empathy among readers in three ways: 1) bounded strategic empathy creates a so-called in-group through shared experiences and familiarity; 2) ambassadorial strategic empathy addresses targeted individuals to build empathy for the in-group with appeals for justice, a desire to help, or recognition; 3) and finally, broadcast strategic empathy encourages all readers to feel with members of a group through common hopes and vulnerabilities (Keen, 2006).

People engage with stories in myriad ways, and storytellers have more tools at their disposal to distribute narratives that jump off the pages of a

> novel or even go beyond the movie screen. Transmedia storytelling provides a way to engage people across multiple media, ensuring a wider, more diverse audience can experience the developed narrative. It also allows for greater depth of characters, unloading some of the burdens from the central narrative to provide more information about setting or characters delivered in a different format (Phillips, 2012). Design thinking provided a process that could be applied to build empathy and offer guidance throughout the inspiration, ideation, and implementation phases of the project.
>
> These high-level theories and practices informed the "We're Still Here" project from the start. The focus of the experience was an interactive live performance created through empathy research conducted in the Flint community. Following the live performance, the audience had the opportunity to share their own messages to Flint residents and donate to a Flint foundation working with children who ingested lead-contaminated water and suffered adverse effects. These options provided outlets for the audience to take an action immediately following the performance. In addition to the performance, I published a website to curate content I collected throughout the creation of the project and add context and depth to the theater experience on a new media channel.

Empathy Interviews With Extreme Users and Stakeholders

I analyzed news stories published between April 2014 and December 2015 to get an idea of the major players in the Flint Water Crisis. They included state and local politicians, activists, doctors, biologists, and residents who shared their stories or were quoted in a news article. The analysis provided a helpful starting point to get a baseline understanding of the crisis and informed questions for in-person interviews of Flint residents.

Using publicly available data, I identified areas of the city most affected by water contamination, and then visited sites in these areas where residents could pick up free bottled water, filter systems, and testing kits. At these sites, I interviewed willing residents to ask about their personal experience with the water crisis, its ongoing effects, and their thoughts on their own futures. In total, about 50 residents shared their stories about the water crisis, in addition to a local church leader and city councilman.

Saturate and Group

Once transcribed, the interviews provided key themes incorporated into the script of the one-woman stage show. I used *saturate and group*, a design thinking exercise to unpack data in order to analyze it into key insights and findings. The findings are grouped, often by similarity, to explore themes and patterns. I chose the interview excerpts for the script from within six topics: 1) life in Flint during the crisis, 2) descriptions of the water, 3) effects on the community, 4) effects on personal health, 5) other effects, and 6) hope. These interview excerpts formed the core of the script for the three-act stage show.

Prototypes

As described in the prior chapter, designers will prototype a design at various stages to ensure that they aren't spending too much time, energy, or money on something that is not beneficial and pleasing to users. For "We're Still Here," I also developed low- and mid-fidelity prototypes before debuting the experience to a broader audience. I used aspects of Srivastava's (2013) Narrative Design for Social Impact: The Project Model Canvas, which was informed by The Business Model Canvas. By incorporating aspects of both canvases and dropping others to create my own sections, I defined the following elements:

- Storytelling: the narrative used for this experience;
- Audience: who this experience will be for;
- Resources: what is still needed to make the experience happen;
- Storyworld strategy: a plan for how users will navigate the experience;
- Content strategy: the ways in which content will be created and distributed;
- Stakeholders: potential partners and who will participate;
- Engagement: how the audience can act to affect change.

This provided a holistic view of the project and forced me to consider aspects and resources that I otherwise might have overlooked.

The second prototype was a preview of the stage show before a Flint-based audience. The final performance was held outside of Flint, Michigan, in Indianapolis, Indiana, where the local audience would be less likely to have already had a personal experience with the crisis. Though small in number, the Flint audience provided visual and verbal feedback, during and after the show. The preview show also allowed me to test the length and pacing of the script. The preview was a prototype to elicit feedback, while the canvas was a prototype in the empathy phase of the project.

Emotional Experience

This empathy research provided a foundation upon which I created the script of the stage show and influenced how I deployed other elements of the story. The script used Flint residents' own words to describe the water crisis and resulting changes, including health problems, financial struggles, and

Deploying Design Thinking for Story Design 41

other life adjustments required as a result of the contamination of the water. It highlighted how residents were made to feel after being poisoned and lied to by people who were supposed to protect them and elected to work in their best interests. Residents also described their hopes for themselves, their children, and their city. The play told a story that, though it was not that of one person, related the stories of many. It was not a traditional journalism or documentary production. Members of the audience can relate to frustration, betrayal, hope, faith, and perseverance—all of which featured in the stories of residents.

The Indianapolis show served as a high-fidelity prototype for the experience. For this iteration, I shortened the script to reduce the show's total time. I tightened the exposition, really focusing on the point of each section and what I wanted the audience to take from it. A total of 16 people participated in this prototype production in Indianapolis. At the end of the show, 13 of the 16 people submitted written messages for residents of Flint, which were used on social media to promote the experience and on the accompanying website. In addition to the messages, a total of eight donations were made to the Flint Child & Health Development Fund totaling more than $150. Many of the attendees were spouses, so the eight donations made up more than half of households in attendance. All eight households that donated had not previously donated to a cause related to the Flint Water Crisis, as indicated on the required donation form.

The audience for this high-fidelity prototype was made up of a convenience sample, mostly of people who knew me personally. Although personal connection likely deepened their response to the content and conditioned them for a favorable response, as many as four years later attendees have brought up or shared the latest news they've heard about Flint when they see me. They send me news clips, articles, or other information about the crisis and resulting criminal charges. Though it is merely an anecdotal result, the content of the show appeared to have encouraged some of the audience members to care about the crisis in a way that news articles had not before, enough so that they seek out information and converse about it years later.

"We're Still Here" could serve as a prototype for similar production strategies—particularly in the genre of documentary transmedia theater and the intimate and collective experience it provides—and for activists looking for creative ways to move an audience from understanding to action, or to drive audiences to a greater understanding of a cause.

Case Study 2: Blue Roots Project and #MyWaterStory Campaign

Circle of Blue (CoB) (Circle of Blue, 2021) is an online news platform run by journalists who inform the public about the world's freshwater resource issues from regional, national, and global perspectives. Circle of Blue stories serve a niche audience of researchers, activists, journalists, policymakers, and water experts ranging in age from 35 to 55 years old. This audience comes to CoB with knowledge of water issues on a national or global level. As climate and energy crises loom, and water scarcity already affecting people in many parts of the world, CoB is compelled to expand its reach to a more general audience.

As a nonprofit, CoB focuses its resources on providing relevant, reliable, and actionable on-the-ground information about the world's resource crises, with an intense focus on water and its relationships to food, energy, and health. With a lean central staff and funding based on grants and donations, CoB lacks the infrastructure and resources to operate outside of that mission. To expand its reach, CoB partnered with us at the Center for Emerging Media Design and Development (EMDD) at Ball State University in 2015. A team of graduate students was tasked to engage a younger audience with CoB and its content in a unique way.

We used our expertise and training in design thinking, user experience design, and transmedia storytelling to create an experience that brings CoB content to users through media forms and channels with which those users already engage, and to connect the freshwater resource crisis to their lives. The goal was to raise awareness with an audience that did not regularly engage with environmental journalism.

To achieve this goal, the team created the Blue Roots Project and the #MyWaterStory social media campaign to connect young people with the value of water and to encourage them to share their stories through works of art, photos, videos, and other digital content.

Imposing Constraints

Circle of Blue engaged with the EMDD team around a very general idea: to expose a younger age group to its content. It was critical for the team to conduct some empathy research with the Circle of Blue personnel to better define the problem. During two days of workshops, the team led the CoB team through ideation and prototyping sessions to

- identify a specific age group versus a general audience,
- brainstorm bad ideas to better define what the project should not do,
- share good ideas for inspiration about what would be possible,
- ideate ways to engage audiences and map relationships among those ideas, and
- sketch rough ideas generated in the sessions.

These initial sessions between the EMDD team and CoB proved critical to the path forward. Without these workshops, the project may have gone down a path or created a story incompatible with the goals, mission, and needs of CoB. These empathy research strategies helped us focus our design brief with a more targeted audience and provide insight into what risks CoB might be willing to take and what they had already tried.

Analogous Empathy

As university graduate students, the Blue Roots Project design team were members of the target audience and enjoyed easy and direct peer-to-peer access to its members. Through interviews and surveys, we learned members of this age group with at least some college education and living in the Midwestern United States weren't in tune with local water issues; they didn't experience serious water issues such as contamination or scarcity of water that plague other areas of the United States. Most could not name the body of water serving as the source for their municipality's tap water.

Though this population (privileged, living in a developed nation, highly educated, and not currently experiencing a water crisis) was convenient, they were exactly the kind of users Circle of Blue was hoping to engage. Though not a specific goal of this phase of the project, CoB was also looking to gain more eyes on their own content which speaks to a higher education level than most journalistic content. These users did not currently care much about water issues but might come to care, based on their involvement in other groups, causes, and organizations (Delve et al., 1990). It was this trait that made members of this group the most attractive type of user: someone who, due to a lack of awareness, did not already care about water issues, but might be convinced to care if they learned more. The solution would need to take into account this information, and we set out to learn more about how users became aware of causes they did engage with and why they decided to become engaged.

The team conducted analogous empathy attending fundraisers, group and community meetings, and other gatherings of people ages 18–24 to learn how they became involved in issues under discussion at these events and what kept the attendees active in these causes. From this research, the team learned about the motivations and influences of these young people and incorporated these into the storytelling experience.

Co-creation With the Target Audience

Once the team had identified a specific age group (millennial 18–24-year-olds who are not already activists or engaged in environmental causes), we continued empathy research. This time, however, we did this by targeting that audience more deliberately via campus clubs, student groups, and other organizations. We also focused a feedback session about our solutions with members of that age group who were engaged in their college campus community, particularly in creative endeavors such as writing, crafting, storytelling, art, and music. A university setting provided easy access to these groups. The team simply explained the challenge to them and asked, "What can we do that you would participate in?"

Through many rounds of these sessions, we developed a better understanding of what it might take to get participation from this age group. Some themes emerged about preferences for types of stories, such as imagining a future without water and an opportunity to consider the history of water in a specific region. Other themes around story delivery, such as making a movie, arose. However, engagement with the intended audience didn't end when empathy research finished. At various stages of prototyping, we returned to this audience to find out what was confusing, what was enjoyable, and what would make them scroll right past content on a social feed. We sought to develop an experience that was engaging, delightful, and meaningful, and meet this audience on the social media and other channels with which they typically engage. We then sought to elevate their understanding and appreciation of water and its value in their life or community.

Following months of moving through inspiration, ideation, and implementation phases of design thinking (Brown, 2009), we launched the #MyWaterStory campaign and accompanying websites in time for World Water Day 2017. Between then and Earth Day about a month later, the team encouraged participation and submissions from people around the world via social media and a website, while publishing blog posts highlighting submissions and recording podcasts discussing water and climate-related issues with students of this age group. By Earth Day 2017, more than 500 pieces of content were submitted from users around the world including stories, artwork, presentations, and social media posts about the value of water as part of the #MyWaterStory campaign.

This success within this specific period of time was possible after months of engagement, outreach, and activation. We began engaging in an online conversation about water issues across the globe about four months prior to World Water Day with informational and other types of social media posts. This helped establish a tone and brand of our social media accounts and build trust and engagement with other organizations, brands, and users. Beyond social media, we reached out through direct phone calls and emails to organizations around the world, sharing our story, our goal, and asking for help in promoting the experience. We created a toolkit to make it simple and easy for others to share our branded materials.

The aspects of the experience and how users might move through it had been thoroughly tested with prospective users, so we had confidence that when the social media push happened on World Water Day, people would participate. Weeks earlier, we rolled out a soft launch, asking specific organizations we had worked with during testing to participate early, priming our digital channels with content as a way to add to our credibility and show other users that participating was easy and fun. We thoroughly tested the prompts we asked people to respond to, to evaluate how we could tap into different users' motivations and different desired levels of engagement. People already engaged in water issues were more likely to spend more time on a more difficult prompt, versus a Twitter user encountering the hashtag and being able to infer from the post what the prompt is and respond without engaging any further with the experience. We went through several rounds of iteration on the prompts to ensure they were clear, concise, and reduced any barriers people might have to participate. Although the target age group was people ages 18–24, our direct outreach and the global reach of social media and its interconnected users helped us tap an even broader audience. The target audience was not engaging directly with CoB content in this stage of the project, but the goal was to encourage people to think about the value of water when in their everyday lives they are able to simply turn on a faucet in their home whenever they needed to.

Conclusion

These two storytelling experiences share some commonalities but are very different in their execution and even in their use of design thinking. For "We're Still Here," I focused the empathy research on the subjects of the story in order to bring the audience closer to the issues faced by the people of Flint. The Blue Roots Project and #MyWaterStory team conducted research with millennials in the Midwest to increase awareness of the value of water in their lives and communities through storytelling and story sharing. Each case provided its own lessons based on the goals, strategies, and constraints, but also shared some common themes: Stories can be powerful ways to connect people to issues, and although creativity and storytelling can be undervalued, they are a powerful way to influence understanding if not behavior. Further exploration could include how these strategies might be used to empower people who are often left out of conversations on socially-concerned issues. They might include the story subjects, or simply anyone without power, influence, or money. One major benefit of leveraging design thinking is that resources for how to do so abound. Built into the process is the idea that anyone can do it and can benefit from its use.

References

Acosta, R. (2019, May 20). How the Flint water crisis investigation led to manslaughter charges. *Mlive.com*. www.mlive.com/news/flint/2017/06/investigation_leads_to_manslau.html

Brown, T. (2009). *Change by design: How design thinking transforms organizations and inspires innovation*. Harper Collins.

Circle of Blue. (2021). About. *Circle of Blue*. www.circleofblue.org/about/

Costanza-Chock, S. (2014). *Out of the shadows, into the streets! Transmedia organizing and the immigrant rights movement.* Massachusetts Institute of Technology Press.

C-SPAN. (2016, February 3). *Contaminated drinking water in Flint, Michigan.* www.c-span.org/video/?404078-1/hearing-contaminated-drinking-water-flint-michigan

Delve, C., Mintz, S., & Stewart, G. (1990). Promoting values development through community service: A design. *New Directions for Student Services.* https://doi.org/10.1002/ss.37119905003

Heath, C., & Heath, D. (2007). *Made to stick: Why some ideas survive and others die.* Random House.

Janssen, S. (2017). *We're still here: Stories of the Flint water crisis.* www.westillhere.com

Jenkins, H. (2016, January 19). *Telling stories: Lina Srivastava talks about transmedia activism (Part One)* [Blog post]. Retrieved from http://henryjenkins.org/2016/01/telling-storieslina-srivastava-talks-about-transmedia-activism-part-one.html

Keen, S. (2006). A theory of narrative empathy. *Narrative, 14*(3), 207–236.

Lin, J. C. F., Park, H., & Rutter, J. (2016, January 21). Events that led to Flint's water crisis. *The New York Times.* www.nytimes.com/interactive/2016/01/21/us/flint-lead-water-timeline.html

Phillips, A. (2012). *A creator's guide to transmedia storytelling: How to captivate and engage audiences across multiple platforms.* McGraw Hill Professional.

Russell, A. (2016). *Journalism as activism: Recoding media power.* Wiley.

Srivastava, L. (2013, November 12). *Narrative design canvas.* www.slideshare.net/lksriv/narrative-design-model-canvas

5 Contextualizing the American Opioid Crisis
A Case Study in Transmedia Harm Reduction

Matt Slaby

"I bet you're pissed that I took away your ten-dollar high," he said, putting his mustache right up to the clear oxygen mask covering the face of a clean-cut young man. Two lengths of medical gauze were looped around his wrists and tied again around his thighs, restraining him so that he couldn't punch or pull at anything in the ambulance. A small, empty vial of naloxone rested on the pastel-colored Formica bench next to the rolling pram on which the man lay flat. Once administered, naloxone's contents have the simple super-power of being able to rapidly reverse the fatal effects of an opioid overdose.

It was 1998 and this was the first heroin overdose that I had seen. I was young—a new 19-year-old EMT—learning the ropes from a paramedic twice my age. At the time, overdoses were relatively rare. The moral hazard posed by needle drugs was met with the severity of a priest exorcising a demon from its host. Before administering naloxone, our protocol was to restrain the patient and use an oxygen mask to cover their face to avoid being punched or spit on when they returned to consciousness.

Contrary to popular representations, opioid drugs, like heroin or morphine, do not directly poison a person nor cause their heart to abruptly stop beating. Instead, they suppress one's respiratory drive. The lethal process takes time as the efficiency and regularity of one's respiration decreases. The heart and brain suffer from a lack of oxygen and, eventually, both cease to function altogether. Only then is a person said to have died.

Fortunately, there is a short window between when a person stops breathing and when their heart stops beating when naloxone can be administered in order to reverse the fatal effects of an overdose. As far as drugs go, naloxone is incredibly elegant and simple. Technically called an "opioid antagonist," it acts like a bouncer in the brain, pushing opioid molecules from the brain's receptors and occupying the space to prevent them from returning. Without opioids in the brain's receptors, the effects of the drug rapidly disappear, a person's respirations return to normal, and they quickly regain consciousness.

At the time, I lacked context for what I was confronted with. Even though I had just witnessed it, I hadn't fully internalized the simplicity by which an overdose could be reversed nor the ease at which a human being's death

DOI: 10.4324/9781003150862-5

could be prevented. I also had no idea that decades later I would look back on this moment as the inciting incident for an ongoing transmedia effort to educate a suspicious and often-discriminatory public (as I was then) about the value of harm reduction, its role in mitigating America's ongoing opioid crisis. My media production company Luceo has now spent more than a decade producing transmedia public service campaigns on opioid harm reduction in the states of Colorado, New York, New Jersey, Pennsylvania, and Michigan. Our work has also started from the walls of the United Nations Commission on Narcotic Drugs in Vienna, Austria and has been used to advocate at the United Nations Special Session of the General Assembly in New York. As the following context illustrates, the problem is old, massive, and seemingly daunting. As the history of this crisis shows, punishment and marginalization have failed where storytelling has been successful at reaching people who bear the largest burden of the ongoing overdose crisis.

Contexts

The circumstances surrounding the young man who had overdosed conflicted with what I had been taught about people who use heroin. This was certainly not the gritty tragedy that my generation, raised on the D.A.R.E. America (n.d.) program, had been steeled against. It was ordinary, familiar—banal, even. The man who laid before me, tied up, and muzzled by an oxygen mask cinched around his head was not what I had been told to expect. He was dressed in jeans and wore a green polo shirt with an Izod alligator over his heart, a late-1990s meld of preppiness and Brit pop and grunge. His apartment was clean and organized, part of a sprawling suburban complex of three-story cookie-cutter buildings where several of my friends lived. I knew the place and, while I didn't know him personally, I knew dozens of people just like him.

I have thought back on that call regularly and wondered at the mighty forces of socialization that had spat both of us out as unwitting students of this shared moment in time. For the young man who had overdosed, his first perceptions upon waking were the cruel taunts from the man who had just saved him. I'm sure, even if he didn't understand everything that was said in those initial moments, he must have felt the hostility and implicit inferiority. For me, in the same moments, I learned to distrust my intuition, to see someone who appeared just like me as something other and undeserving of my care. *For these people*, I thought, *the ones who do this to themselves, we do the bare minimum.*

I was wrong, though. Doing the bare minimum has had real and lasting consequences that would ultimately lead to an easily preventable public health crisis within the span of a decade. At the time, the United States had just passed sweeping crime legislation (Brooks, 1994) with sentencing guidelines and mandatory minimums that would swell America's prison population to a size roughly similar to that of the city of Chicago (Sawyer & Wagner,

2020; U.S. Census Bureau, 2010). This number is even more staggering when considered in global context: While only a little more than 4% of the global population lives in the United States, one in four inmates are held in American prisons (Travis et al., 2014; Walmsley, 2015). The War on Drugs that underpinned much of this carceral prerogative was a ubiquitous and moral force in the country's perception of itself and its role in policing its own citizens. Kicked off in earnest by President Richard Nixon in 1971, it treated drugs as "public enemy number one" (Barber, 2016) and backed efforts to eradicate drug production, trafficking, and use with an annual budget estimated at 51 billion dollars (Drug Policy Alliance, n.d.). The prevailing view treated drugs as a moral hazard and their use as a consequent moral failing.

Under the color of this ideology, a new approach to policing materialized. Deborah Peterson Small, the Executive Director of Break the Chains, an advocacy organization committed to addressing the disproportionate impact of punitive drug policies on poor communities of color has spent much of her life as a thought leader on the matter. She explains that for most of its history, policing has been a reactive affair. That is, when a crime occurs, it is reported. The police then respond and try to solve the crime. The drug war, however, created a new kind of proactive policing. "Drug users don't call the police on themselves," she explains.

> The police have to go and search for them. So, where they decide to search, where they decide to focus, where they decide to look, is going to have a big impact on our perceptions of who's committing the crimes. [Consequently], the War on Drugs empowers police to use their discretion, to decide which drug users they go after [and] which communities are going to be the ones that they focus on.
> (Personal communication, April 2019)

Demographic statistics on rates of incarceration bear out this thesis. Taken as a whole, drug use permeates all strata of society yet the bulk of the enforcement of drug laws are markedly saddled to poor people and people of color (*2015 National Survey on Drug Use and Health: Detailed Tables*, 2016, p. 239; Fellner, 2009). One in nine Black children living in the United States today has at least one parent who is incarcerated, compared to one in 57 white children (Western & Pettit, 2010). Black people are incarcerated at a rate of five to seven times that of white people and account for almost half of all prisoners incarcerated with a sentence of more than one year for a drug-related offense (Carson & Sabol, 2012). One in 13 Black people of voting age finds themselves stripped of the franchise because of state restrictions following a felony conviction. Of 2.3 million people currently incarcerated in the United States, an estimated one in five are locked up for drugs; additionally, 1.5 million people are arrested each year on drug charges (Sawyer & Wagner, 2020; *The Drug War, Mass Incarceration and Race*, 2018).

"The thing about the language of war is that it sets up an enemy. You don't have wars with friends. It implies maximum force," explains Peterson Small (Personal communication, April 2019). The advent of modern mechanized warfare and commensurate economic siege tactics, she explains, have caused battlefield casualties to skyrocket. Civilians, though, have borne the brunt of 20th- and 21st-century conflict (Marc, 2016). What that means is that battles, whether fought in an actual battlespace or prosecuted at the end of a police battering ram, necessarily result in civilian casualties. They are to be expected as a necessary product of the undertaking. "And that can be tolerated because we're at war," says Peterson Small.

In addition to a multi-decade-long drive to fill our prisons, the casualties can also be counted in a staggering number of overdose deaths. In the years that have intervened between when I saw my first heroin overdose and this writing, more than 750,000 people have died from drug overdoses in the United States making it the leading cause of death for Americans under the age of 50 (*CDC's Response to the Opioid Overdose Epidemic*, 2021; Reynolds, 2017). Stated in numbers that are less abstract, that is roughly the equivalent of 2,050 Boeing 747s crashing in the same span of time—more than a crash every four days. This number, calculated using an average seating capacity of 366 for a Boeing 747 from 1999 to 2020, notably does not account for other manners of drug-related death, including disease, infection, and trauma that results from drug use. It also begs one very important question: Given the scope and scale of this tragedy, why are we not treating it with the same sense of urgency that we would treat the frequent occurrence of air disasters?

Ruth Kanatser, the Syringe Access Director for the Harm Reduction Action Center, an agency in Denver, Colorado that provides services to people who inject drugs, believes she knows the answer. Kanatser is a bright, articulate, and outwardly caring person. In her professional role, she is also a vociferous and incisive proponent for advancing public health interventions for people who use drugs without preconditioning those services on abstinence. She argues that society has a schizophrenic relationship with how we address the issue. Because it is never fixed to a solid ideology, it whipsaws between a punitive and a medical model. "When a person is considered good or deserving then we use the medical model. But if they're poor or a criminal or in jail, then we use the crime and punishment one" (Personal communication, May 2013). Kanatser believes that, in failing to address the gray area between total abstinence and chaotic drug use, we miss an important opportunity to make significant positive changes to the health and welfare of people who use drugs and, consequently, to the benefit of communities in which they live. Kanatser, a person who formerly used heroin for many years, knows firsthand that the dry numbers reflected in morbidity and mortality data are also sons, daughters, brothers, sisters, mothers, and fathers. Their losses are not isolated but rather ripple outward from one person to the next.

"What ends up happening is an immeasurable loss of human potential and life."

What sets drug use apart from many other disease pathologies is that many of its consequent harms are imminently preventable. Whereas heart disease, diabetes, or cancer often weave winding roads of causation and equally complex roads to recovery, fatal opioid overdoses are simply preventable and easily reversed. Likewise, communicable diseases endemic to populations of people who inject drugs—things like viral hepatitis and HIV—are largely within reach of a solution given a handful of cost-effective, humane, and fundamental changes to how we view the problem and what tools we are willing to bring to the table. The most significant barriers to these interventions are not scientific; they are political.

In 1988, a young man named Kurt Schmoke, then the mayor of Baltimore, found himself testifying on a balmy September afternoon before the House Select Committee on Narcotics Abuse and Control in Washington, DC. The hearing room was packed. Its chair, congressman Charlie Rangel, had earlier declared Schmoke to be "the most dangerous man in America" (Schmoke, 2007, p. 95). Schmoke was seated on a panel of American mayors who were staking claims to a variety of alternative approaches to the question of drugs. His particular view was a message of sweeping drug decriminalization. Being the messenger of decriminalization in the shadow of Nancy Reagan's "Just Say No" campaign was something that he would later recall as a "very lonely experience" (Personal communication, 2016). Schmoke was a pragmatist, though, and he had become disillusioned with the idea of using the blunt tool of law enforcement to address a complicated and entrenched problem that he believed could not be solved by simply ratcheting up penalties.

Schmoke did not come to this conclusion easily. Years before he became mayor, he served as Maryland's State's Attorney. It was the early 1980s and he, like most of his colleagues, was rank-and-file adherent to the ethos of the drug war. When it came to the question of drugs, Schmoke believed wholeheartedly in a decidedly punitive model. He accepted the conventional wisdom that drugs were a choice and that legal punishment could be applied to condition people against making that choice. In fact, in his role as State's Attorney and, before that, as Baltimore's City Attorney, Schmoke had been instrumental in prosecuting his fair share of Baltimore's drug cases.

For the young prosecutor, everything changed on December 3, 1984. At the time, a 36-year-old colleague of Schmoke's, Detective Marcellus Ward, was working undercover as part of a DEA task force. Ward had spent months infiltrating a network that was bringing heroin into Maryland from neighboring New York State. Just as the winter sun disappeared, slipping low beyond the streets of West Baltimore, Ward trudged up the steps of a three-story rhyolite brick row house situated atop a storefront called the Kandy Kitchen in city's Booth Boyd neighborhood. Ward was wearing a wire to record a heroin deal, while a team of officers waited outside, prepared to make an arrest at its conclusion. Then something went wrong. For inexplicable reasons, the officers waiting outside rushed into the building too early, clamoring into its narrow stairwell before they were supposed to. Ward, knowing that the man he was dealing with was armed with a .357 Magnum, tried to distract him. Nervous after hearing the commotion, the man pushed Ward onto a couch and shot him four times. The shots, and Ward's last agonal breaths, were broadcast to police listening in on the wire that he wore from the street below (Baltimore Police Historical Society, 2019). The tape of the killing would haunt Schmoke for decades.

As State's Attorney, it fell to Schmoke to prosecute the case. He had to make a critical determination at its outset. If the shooter knew that Ward was a cop when he pulled the trigger, he'd face the state's gas chamber. Killing a cop was one of several crimes that could invite Maryland's most extreme penalty. Schmoke and his staff turned to the tape to better understand the shooter's frame of mind, to look for evidence of what he knew—and what he didn't—at the moment when he pointed the pistol at Detective Ward and pulled the trigger. The toll of the killing and the grim task of reviewing its recording was immense. Ultimately, Schmoke determined that the shooter was unaware that Ward was a cop.

As he played and replayed the tape, something else had happened to Schmoke. He began to come to terms with the inadequacy of the criminal justice system to remedy the malaise that cost Detective Ward his life. "I had to reflect on what it really meant. I kept coming back to the view that this man who did the shooting was doing it because of a profit motive in distributing drugs" (Personal communication, 2016). He quietly concluded that drug prohibition had a lot in common with alcohol prohibition of the 1920s and early 1930s. Namely, drug usage remained constant, though the effect of forcing it into the shadows primarily served to create a perverse, violent, and tragic black market.

Schmoke became Baltimore's mayor in 1987, taking the helm of a city that had suffered two decades of blight following the closure of its steel mill and the middle-class flight that occurred in the wake of the riots following Dr. Martin Luther King Jr.'s assassination. The city's population had shrunk from 950,000 to 750,000, bleeding off the value that its formerly diverse blue-collar workforce had once built up. As the city's diminishing educated elite carried on as-usual in jobs tied to institutions like Johns Hopkins, work for its lesser educated citizens had dried up. Surplus housing left in the wake of urban flight had drained real estate of its value, and huge swaths of the city's working class found refuge in both sides of the drug trade. In his prosecutorial years, Schmoke had wrung his hands at the violence that would backfill any meaningful drug bust as rivals jockeyed for the territory that had just been cleared out by the police. Now, as Mayor, he began to speak out on the subject of drugs, advancing an idea that would soon earn the scorn of Rangel's House Select Committee on Narcotic Abuse and Control.

"I would go to organizations and I would ask them three questions," says Schmoke (Personal communication, 2016).

> I would say, 'Do you believe that we have won the war on drugs? Do you think that we are winning the war on drugs? Do you think that doing more of the same for the next decade will win the war on drugs?' Generally, even skeptical audiences, answered no to all three of those questions. Then I said, 'Well, would you be willing to consider a different approach?'

Denver

I first met Lisa Raville at a coffee shop in the winter of 2011. Raville was—and still is—the Executive Director of the Harm Reduction Action Center, a Denver organization that provides direct services to people who inject drugs. I had been encouraged by a friend of mine to do a story on the organization and had begrudgingly agreed to the meeting. The meeting seemed almost foolish to me as the lessons that I had been taught in my younger years about people who used drugs had crystalized into a categorical black and white. Drugs were bad. Enabling people who use drugs to persist in using them was an even harder sell. I privately believed that providing anything that decreased the risks of drug use seemed tantamount to encouraging it. After all, we were engaged in a war on drugs; providing comfort to the enemy was something not to be blithely undertaken.

At the time, Raville's nascent organization was based in a single-story red house built at the turn of the 19th century in a working-class neighborhood butting up against an enormous rail yard just south of downtown Denver. The Harm Reduction Action Center served people who injected drugs with safe syringe disposals, health education, and bleach kits to help clean used syringes in a primitive attempt to stop the spread of blood-borne pathogens like HIV and viral hepatitis. Visitors to the house could also clean their clothes, take a shower, and get something to eat. In those early years, syringe programs and access to naloxone, the drug that reverses the fatal effects of an opioid overdose, were prohibited by state law under the rationale that access to those things would encourage drug use. After explaining what her organization did, Raville broke down some of the local statistics. About three out of every four people in Denver who injected drugs had hepatitis C. One in ten had HIV. Most had experienced at least one near-fatal overdose. Many more were dying.

The numbers were stunningly bleak.

As she spoke, the depth of Denver's crisis struck me in a way that I had not previously considered. The number of people who would contract otherwise preventable diseases was far from marginal. Among people who injected drugs, it was a clear and underreported epidemic. I struggled to dissociate the stigma of injection drug use from its consequence before settling on an apt comparison. If people who drank beer were contracting hepatitis C or HIV at similar rates because they had shared a mug or drawn beer from an unsanitary tap, the public outrage would be so severe that the problem would be solved before sundown on the same day. The problem, it seemed, had roots that drew nourishment from social norms that delineated acceptable drug use from the *verboten*. That hierarchy meant that, in Denver alone, many thousands of people would get sick and die from things that were preventable. It also meant that the public health system would carry the cost—both financially and also in terms of the allocation of limited resources. Compared side-by-side, the decision seemed obvious. A sterile syringe, the primary vector for the spread of HIV and viral hepatitis among people who inject drugs, costs less than ten cents; lifetime treatments for hepatitis C or HIV generally range from the low hundred-thousands upward of a half-million dollars. "Why would we not try to fix this?" implored Raville.

The weeks that followed were much like the beginning of any journalistic project. I spent a lot of time listening to people talk about the circumstances of their lives. I listened as people told me about how they learned that they had contracted hepatitis C or HIV and heard about the shame and the stigma that followed. I listened knowingly to people who recalled hostility and abuse at the hands of medical professionals upon waking up from an overdose. I met a woman whose son was friends with many of my own. He had died from an overdose in the bathroom of a house where I had been on dozens of occasions to visit other friends who lived in the same house. As the subject and the people that it affected came into clearer focus, I began to recognize that the lines which I had carefully drawn to distinguish myself from the subjects of my work were disintegrating. I started to feel more like a reporter in the midst of war who becomes disillusioned with the notion that the carnage is in any way noble, antiseptic, or productive. I saw what Deborah Peterson Small meant when she said that civilian casualties are a necessary condition for the war on drugs.

In the spring of 2011, I produced a short series of portraits and stories about several people from the Harm Reduction Action Center who had suffered preventable overdoses or who had contracted preventable diseases. The work paired portraits in diptych with another image of the place where the subject had overdosed, contracted HIV, viral hepatitis, or had died (Figure 5.1). Each diptych was accompanied by long captions explaining the importance of harm reduction practices in reducing the occurrence of what was rapidly becoming a national crisis. At the conclusion of the project, *Mother Jones* published it (Slaby, 2013).

The work somehow still felt incomplete. The project had challenged my assumptions about people who used drugs. The sheer magnitude of needless suffering and preventable loss weighed heavy on my conscience. Even with the work behind me, I was still nagged by the question that Raville had asked when we first met: *why would we not try to fix this?*

Contextualizing the American Opioid Crisis 55

Figure 5.1 Two overdose diptychs

Project and Methods

Since the publication of that first body of work, I have veered from the rote parameters of objective journalism and have now been part of the development of dozens of media campaigns focused on this historically minimized issue. Most of this work has been aimed at reducing the stigma faced by people who use drugs while advocating for material changes to the public health and criminal justice systems. These projects have all been undertaken in partnership with Luceo, a strategic media firm that was originally created by a small group of editorial photographers. While photography has been a significant and important element to most of this work, we have iterated stories about harm reduction across media forms and channels with the goal of reaching new and unlikely audiences. In short, our work has aimed to drive change by amplifying the voices of people who are affected by the war on drugs and its preventable collateral consequences.

Specifically, our work on this subject is built on three core beliefs that are informed by our journalistic roots. First, when it comes to speaking about harm reduction practices, we believe that authenticity counts. Most of the materials that we produce place value on personal narrative and allow real people to tell their own stories, in their own words. Second, we believe that when these stories are delivered on-target they provide an effective catalyst for action. We see developments in the rapidly changing mediascape as an opportunity to reach new audiences with content that is specifically tailored to their preferences. Third, we believe that harm reduction-focused campaigns are best measured by incremental shifts in perception and behavior. We know that building support around harm-reduction-based interventions requires both large-scale social transformation and individual changes in behavior. Simply put, our work aims to normalize and destigmatize harm reduction on a societal level while simultaneously encouraging incremental positive changes on an individual one. Over the last decade, our work has been used to advocate for changes to state and local laws, promote changes in the administration of public health services to people who use drugs, and engage with community stakeholders on the topic of how harm reduction serves the broader public interest.

In August 2020, we began developing a public health campaign rooted in the principles of harm reduction for the Michigan Department of Health and Human Services. Michigan, like many other states, was in the throes of an overdose epidemic. To make matters worse, Michigan's Black population was disproportionately shouldering the worst of it. Although harm reduction services existed throughout Michigan, they were often shrouded in secrecy and stigma and had not been widely publicized to the state. Our challenge was to develop materials to reach Michiganders at risk of overdose in order to educate them about the importance of harm reduction and to encourage the utilization of harm reduction services throughout the state.

Contextualizing the American Opioid Crisis

Unlike traditional advertising, where campaigns are carefully scripted and cast with professional actors, we began work in the spirit of journalism by searching for real people whose stories would also help advance the State's goals. The resulting media would appear as posts and paid advertisements on social media platforms, as video on YouTube, as digital advertisements, and on billboards and posters throughout Michigan (*Opioid Resources*, 2021). We also developed a web tool that allows people who click-through on the advertisements to geolocate nearby harm reduction and treatment services. Far from abstinence-based anti-drug-use ads which frequently employ fictitious hyperbole and scare tactics, we recommended that the campaign be direct, unfiltered, earnest, and produced in documentary fashion. The state government agreed.

Drawing on contacts from a decade of similar work, we located four Michiganders—as locals are called—with stories that highlighted the life-saving role of harm reduction for people who use drugs. The subjects were representative of the demographic that the state wanted to reach with the campaign. Our plan was to spend time with each of them, filming and photographing their lives and work under the campaign slogan that we had developed to explain the incremental nature of harm reduction: "Change. At Your Own Pace."

The campaign's four subjects were drawn from a larger pool of people who had been recommended by stakeholders from around the state. We conducted interviews with people in the larger pool, looking specifically for those whose stories were superlative, representative of the targeted demographics, and, most important, whose retelling of their own story would lend to the documentary aesthetic of the campaign. Earnestness, authenticity, and emotive recall were prioritized in our selection process and each subject's story was outlined in conjunction with key messaging pillars that we had drafted to support campaign.

Unlike scripted testimonials, our production process relies on interviewing subjects using active listening to elicit responses that approximate key messages—but in the vernacular of each subject. Accordingly, we favored people who were well versed in the principles of harm reduction and whose lived experiences would help connect with targeted demographics as they would be natural and authentic messengers for the campaign. We then presented the full array of potential subjects to the state along with our recommendations. Four subjects were selected, including two Black men, a white woman, and a Latino man. Each subject had a history of past drug use with experience providing vital harm reduction services to people who use drugs.

Once the campaign's subjects had been selected, we created a brief that outlined each person's story along with a film treatment describing the beats that we hoped to document. For example:

> **Jesse, 66-year-old grandparent, MSW [Master of Social Work], harm reduction service provider, and former heroin user.**

"When I'm handing out syringes, I like to tell people to stay hydrated. It reminds each person that I care about them." Jesse provides harm reduction services from the back of a van throughout the Downriver area of Detroit. As a person who has survived multiple overdoses and hepatitis C, he believes that it is important to treat people with dignity and respect regardless of their drug use. "I do a lot of listening. I meet people where they are at and help them stay alive," he says explaining that harm reduction is focused on the grey area between chaos and complete abstinence to help people improve their lives and health. After decades of heroin use, Jesse recalls that he finally stopped because "somebody treated me like a human being." That's why he provides things that people need for their health, like sterile syringes and naloxone, and also things like socks, underwear, and water. Those extra items remind people that they are human and that someone cares about them. "That's the secret of harm reduction," he says. "This is how we build trusting relationships. We help people make small changes that add up to something big."

We then paired each story arc with a film treatment. Jesse's read:

> Jesse provides mobile direct services and outreach from his vehicle for an area harm reduction organization. Unlike a fixed brick and mortar site, Jesse really meets people right where they are at. It is personal for him and the viewer should see that as he drives around providing care with his limited resources. We will focus on his story being told while he's inside of his van driving through the neighborhoods. The viewer will see him as compassionate, informed, and committed to helping others as he engages with people who rely on him for the things and support that they need to stay healthy.

We then went to Michigan and began the process of documenting the stories of each of our subjects. We joined Jesse as he delivered naloxone to a young man at risk of overdose. We are filming as he pulls into neatly kept single-family suburban home in Downriver Detroit. The man had called Jesse minutes earlier to request it. He is inquisitive, soft-spoken, and interested in being prepared. Jesse encourages his proactivity, speaking kindly to him as he explains the signs of an overdose and how to administer naloxone using the intranasal dispenser that he is holding in his hand. As a harm reductionist, Jesse believes that working with people who use drugs is a realistic and pragmatic way to improve public health and to give people who use drugs an opportunity for a better and healthier life. "Drugs are a fact of life here in America," he explains. "We have to find a way to help folks not die because of their use. With naloxone, we're able to provide that."

We photograph and film Jesse's interactions along with our three other subjects, moving our small crew between each subject and setting

Contextualizing the American Opioid Crisis 59

Figure 5.2 Michigan opioid harm reduction billboard
Source: Courtesy of KT Kanazawich.

throughout the day and late into the night. Our work in Michigan is filled with similar anecdotes, bits, and pieces from the lives of the three other people who we have been entrusted to document. We film a former sex worker who now leads a team of volunteers, including doctors and public health administrators, as they provide harm reduction and medical services for people who use drugs along vast corridors of Detroit's blighted and vacant tracts. We spend time with a young Black man in recovery whose family was drawn from the South during the Great Migration after the turn of the 19th century to a suburb that Henry Ford built to house Black Americans. They had come to a segregated Motor City, lured by the promise of good paying work. He is a rapper who has amassed a loyal local following with sing-song lyrics narrating his personal struggles. He speaks candidly about the importance of harm reduction and of treating people who use drugs with dignity and respect. We ride around with another older Black man who comes home several nights each week from his day job as a healthcare worker to pull a second shift volunteering as a harm reduction service provider. He loads his iguana-green muscle car with sterile syringes, naloxone, and other supplies to make rounds to people whose lives and health depend on the materials that he provides.

Having spent two decades of his life on the streets using heroin, he's empathetic and clearly invested in helping others in the same way that someone once helped him.

> There's a lot of people out there that's hurting, man. I really feel for them people. That's the reason why I go out there—if I can just help save one person. To me it's like the angels rejoicing in heaven.

We logged our film and transcribed interviews from each subject. We also selected quotes from each subject to be utilized on the other print and digital materials that the campaign called for. The media plan included 30- and 15-second YouTube spots that tell each person's story as well as a laundry list of digital and mobile banner advertisements, social media placements, convenience store posters, and billboards. While all four stories were united under the common theme of promoting harm reduction to people who use drugs, each story was presented as authentic to its subject. Accordingly, each print and digital asset that we produced included additional quotes and context from each subject reiterating the common message in their own words.

The campaign was launched in March 2021 and remains live at the time of publication. In four short months, it has garnered 43.2 million impressions, 6.3 million video views, and 77,500 click-throughs to the campaign's service-finder microsite. These quantitative metrics are the benchmarks that advertisers use to justify their bottom line and tell their clients how many people were exposed to the media that they produced. It's a quantitative game—often a cynical one. For me, though, the most meaningful measure of success is qualitative. It's less easy to pin down in terms of dollars-and-cents but clear-as-day in terms of value when you see it. For this campaign, that measure was met one morning as I scrolled through my Instagram feed to find a post featuring a video of a middle-aged Black woman standing in front of an enormous billboard along a Michigan highway. A gray sky hangs low and the winding sound of traffic whizzing by punctuates the soundtrack. The post is written by her son, one of the subjects of our campaign, speaking about how Black people need to see a familiar face in harm reduction and recovery. His mom holds a notebook, clutching it to her chest as she smiles, clearly elated. Her son's 14-foot-tall image stands over her on the billboard next to a quote which reads, "We help people who use drugs make healthier choices." His aunt, off-camera, narrates:

> This is my sister's son, Bryce, on a billboard—look! I love it, I love it! And he's making a difference in the world, yes he is! That's so freaking on-point. And this is his mom. She's so proud, look at her!
>
> (brycethethird, 2021)

References

2015 National Survey on Drug Use and Health: Detailed Tables. (2016). Substance Abuse and Mental Health Services Administration. www.samhsa.gov/data/sites/default/files/NSDUH-DetTabs-2015/NSDUH-DetTabs-2015/NSDUH-DetTabs-2015.pdf

Baltimore Police Historical Society. (2019, November 1). *Detective Marcellus Ward.* https://baltimorepolicemuseum.com/en/bpd-history/roistering-past/item/797-det-marty-ward.html

Barber, C. (2016, June 29). *Public enemy number one: A pragmatic approach to America's drug problem.* www.nixonfoundation.org/2016/06/26404/

Brooks, J. B. (1994, September 13). *Violent Crime Control and Law Enforcement Act of 1994* (1993/1994) [Legislation]. www.congress.gov/bill/103rd-congress/house-bill/3355/text

brycethethird. (2021, March 27). *World class starts at the crib* [Social Media]. Instagram. www.instagram.com/reel/CM8qRfEFYa_/

Carson, E. A., & Sabol, W. J. (2012). *Prisoners in 2011* (Bulletin NCJ 239808; p. 7). U.S. Bureau of Justice Statistics. https://bjs.ojp.gov/content/pub/pdf/p11.pdf

CDC's Response to the Opioid Overdose Epidemic. (2021). [Data Overview]. Centers for Disease Control and Prevention. www.cdc.gov/opioids/data/index.html

D.A.R.E. America. (n.d.). *The history of D.A.R.E.* https://dare.org/history/

Drug Policy Alliance. (n.d.). *Drug war statistics.* Drug Policy Alliance. https://drugpolicy.org/issues/drug-war-statistics

The Drug War, Mass Incarceration and Race. (2018, January 25). [Resource]. Drug Policy Alliance. https://drugpolicy.org/resource/drug-war-mass-incarceration-and-race-englishspanish

Fellner, J. (2009). *Decades of disparity: Drug arrests and race in the United States* (Backgrounder No. 1-56432-450-8). Human Rights Watch.

Marc, A. (2016). *Conflict and violence in the 21st century: Current trends as observed in empirical research and statistics.* World Bank Group. www.un.org/pga/70/wp-content/uploads/sites/10/2016/01/Conflict-and-violence-in-the-21st-century-Current-trends-as-observed-in-empirical-research-and-statistics-Mr.-Alexandre-Marc-Chief-Specialist-Fragility-Conflict-and-Violence-World-Bank-Group.pdf

Opioid Resources. (2021). Michigan.Gov. www.michigan.gov/opioids/

Reynolds, D. (2017, June 6). Overdoses now leading cause of death of Americans under 50. *CBS Evening News.* www.cbsnews.com/news/overdoses-are-leading-cause-of-death-americans-under-50/

Sawyer, W., & Wagner, P. (2020). *Mass incarceration: The whole pie 2020* [Press Release]. Prison Policy Initiative. www.prisonpolicy.org/reports/pie2020.html

Schmoke, K. L. (2007). Guest editorial: Dark cloud over education: A personal perspective on the drug war. *The Journal of Negro Education,* 76(2), 93–102.

Slaby, M. (2013, August). Photos: Heroin users revisit where they overdosed. *Mother Jones.* www.motherjones.com/media/2013/08/xanadu-heroin-users-overdose-photos/

Travis, J., Western, B., & Redburn, F. S. (2014). *The growth of incarceration in the United States: Exploring causes and consequences.* National Academies Press.

U.S. Census Bureau. (2010). *U.S. Census Bureau Quickfacts: Chicago city, Illinois.* www.census.gov/quickfacts/chicagocityillinois

Walmsley, R. (2015). *World prison population list*. Institute for Criminal Policy Research.
Western, B., & Pettit, B. (2010). *Collateral costs: Incarceration's effect on economic mobility* (p. 44). The Pew Charitable Trusts. www.pewtrusts.org/~/media/legacy/uploadedfiles/pcs_assets/2010/collateralcosts1pdf.pdf

6 Storylines and Conceptual Lineage
Tomas van Houtryve and the Contextualization of History

Matt Slaby

One of the things I noticed when I look at old pictures from my own family, are these stunning visual echoes through time of specific features that people have. Like, you'll look at a photo of a very old uncle or aunt or whatever, and you'll notice the same ears or eyebrows, or cleft, some little genetic feature that makes its way through time.

—Tomas van Houtryve

Introduction

Tomas van Houtryve (n.d.) is an accomplished photographer and transmedia documentary producer whose work has appeared in a long list of well-known magazines, galleries, and is held among some of the most prestigious collections in the world. The conceptual nature of van Houtryve's work is what sets him apart from many of his colleagues. He is thoughtful in his approach and deliberate about his process and message. In many ways, he also blurs the boundaries between technical surveillance images and those which serve an additional aesthetic purpose. In van Houtryve's world, those two categories often intersect. He uses a variety of media and processes to accomplish this, from contemporary technologies such as drones and thermal imaging, to 19th-century wet-plate photography. In recent years, his *Blue Sky Days* project (Open Society Foundations, 2014) asked viewers to imagine themselves behind the robotic eye of military drones looking down as life plays out far below, oblivious to the technology that surveils them from high above. Following on the heels of this project, van Houtryve produced *Lines and Lineage* (Leica Oskar Barnack Award, 2019), a series of wet-plate photographic diptychs that explore a collective amnesia around the pre-1848 border between Mexico and the United States. In this work, van Houtryve implores viewers to imagine an era of American history that occupies a limited space in our popular imagination. He believes that this is at least partially because indigenous and European history in the region long predates the arrival of photographic equipment to document it. His work attempts to fill in gaps in the photographic record by depicting people

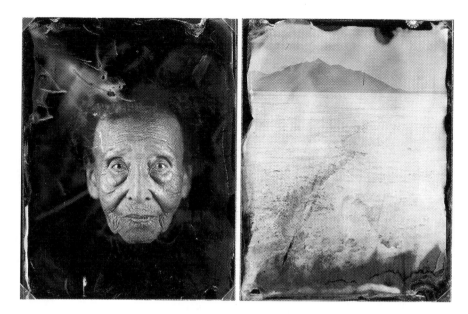

Figure 6.1 Anna Maria Gallegos de Houser and the Bonneville Salt Flats diptych

Note: Anna Maria Gallegos de Houser was born in 1912, the year New Mexico became a U.S. state. The Bonneville Salt Flats in Utah lie ear the early-nineteenth-century border between the Mexican territory of Alta California and Oregon Country, which was then jointly claimed by the United States and Great Britain.

Source: © Tomas van Houtryve.

whose lineage is drawn from populations that existed there long before border lines were drawn. *Lines and Lineage* is now a book, exhibitions at world-class galleries, has been excerpted in editorial publications, and exists as a series of artifacts in the work's original wet plates. A television documentary film is in production at this writing. What follows is a lightly edited version of an April 2021 conversation between transmedia documentary producers Matt Slaby and Tomas van Houtryve in which van Houtryve contextualizes the story he tells in the *Lines and Lineage* project, evokes the historical echoes he sees in today's socio-political landscape, and describes the ethos and process he used production.

Conversation

MATT SLABY: Tom, your background—your actual lineage—is a little revealing in terms of how you may think about nationality, place, and ownership. I wonder if that's had any influence on you and your *Lines and Lineage* project?

TOMAS VAN HOUTRYVE: My dad was a diplomat. My mom has roots in California. We have family records going back to the 12th century in the same area of Belgium. I'm the only one not born in that area of the world in the last 800 years. Now I live within spitting distance of it again. It's interesting. It's like, do you want to identify with a historical story? Do you want to identify with DNA? Do you want to identify with a nation? Do you want to identify with a tribe or a race or a language? I think about all these things a lot and it's . . . I don't really fit in here in France, I'm not a French citizen. I always felt a little bit out of place in American society, too, even though I felt a connection to the land.

MS: This reminds me of a radio piece I just heard about identity and place. It was about a woman who has identified as black all of her life. Then she took a DNA test. The first test that she got back identified her as only 2% of African origin. And then subsequent tests would show her genetic racial makeup anywhere from more than half into the low single digit percentages. It threw the whole question of her identify into the air.

TVH: Well, the U.S. is so . . . it's the one drop rule. In Latin America, or just even in Mexico, we could say the idea of blackness doesn't exist in the same way. You being from Colorado or me having roots in California—we had a black president already. It was the Mexican President Vicente Guerrero. He was of mixed African and indigenous ancestry. While he's not even necessarily seen as a black person in Mexico in the U.S. he certainly would be. The last Mexican governor of California was Pío Pico. He's not celebrated as black in Mexico—or even in California. He was just considered a Mexican. But if he had been a U.S. citizen, he definitely would have been considered black. His grandmother was black so [he would have satisfied the one drop rule].

MS: The tools of oppression remain powerful.

TVH: Long lasting formula.

MS: see that you've highlighted a quote from Albert Camus about the role of government in your biography. It's compelling. It says: "By definition, a government has no conscience. Sometimes it has a policy, but nothing more."

TVH: It never has a conscience. It's just policies. As a result, a lot of what government produces in Camus's eyes—and in mine too—is really absurd in the sense that it can seem like a good idea in the machinery of keeping the state alive or protecting the elite or any other objectives that [preserve] power. But it's obviously not a compassionate force. It's not human in any way.

MS: Why choose to highlight this particular quote? I mean, it seems to illuminate something about your work.

TVH: It's just a red flag, something to keep in mind and keep U.S. on our guard. It's just to raise our hands and say, "Hold on a second. Let's

Figure 6.2 Nathan Alexander Steiner and Green River diptych

Note: Nathan Alexander Steiner is a descendant of Pío de Jesus Pico, the last Mexican governor of California. Pico was of mixed African, indigenous and Spanish ancestry. After U.S. conquest, non-whites were stripped of their legal, property, and voting rights. Previously named El Rio de San Buenaventura, the Green River, which flows through Wyoming, Colorado, and Utah, was first mapped in 1776 by Spanish explorers Domínguez and Escalante. The image was made near the early nineteenth-century border of Alta California, Mexico, and unorganized territory of the United States.

Source: © Tomas van Houtryve.

listen to the voices of real people. Let's look out for the little guys, let's see who's being crushed in the role of progress."

MS: Would you say that your instinct to look at who's being crushed in the role of progress plays a role in your *Lines and Lineage* work?

TVH: A little bit less. I was really attracted to that quote when I was working on [my projects related to] communism and also the drone war stuff. That quote really resonated me with those projects. I think it would also resonate with me if we were to talk about the specific policy of the U.S.-Mexican border wall, the contemporary one. But *Lines and Lineage* is more about amnesia and that old saying about how the victors write history. It's a little bit more about memory than it is about policy.

MS: Can you explain what you mean by that specifically? What do you mean by historical amnesia?

TVH: Since I grew up in California, I was exposed to the American education system and how it taught history. The way that history was taught to me, the story of where I came from, started with Columbus and then skipped to the Mayflower and the pilgrims, and then to the founding of the United States, then to western expansion. The way that that story was told was as if some plucky, enterprising, individualist pioneers came into a (mostly) virgin territory, encountered (mostly) native people and set up an industrious new civilization.

What was skipped over to a large extent is that there was already a new civilization set up by [another group of] plucky pioneers in the West before they ever arrived. [In my schoolhouse telling of this story] the role of the Spanish conquest of the Americas was heavily downplayed. There's a long running theme of native Americans either being ignored or over-idealized as the noble savages. And Mexico's role was [largely ignored].

MS: Can you give me an example of one of these disparate historical narratives?

TVH: Well, if you live in a western state, Barack Obama wasn't your first black president. It was Vicente Guerrero. If you live in the West, slavery wasn't abolished in 1865, it was abolished in around 1824 or 1821, depending on [if you take the view that its abolition] was in the Mexican constitution or when [the ban on slavery began to be better] enforced. As somebody who lives or grows up in a place like Colorado or California or New Mexico, you would think that those dates would be taught. [What appears to happen, though, is that] only English-speaking history is taught and Spanish-speaking history of equal weight and importance—like history of emancipation and important firsts—is ignored.

MS: Your *Lines and Lineage* work focuses primarily on what takes place after the Treaty of Guadalupe in 1848.

TVH: It focuses on is an interesting coincidence. It was 1848 when the treaty of Guadalupe Hidalgo was signed [ending the Mexican-American War]. And so that's when the border changes its position to [what we now know as the Mexican-United States border]. That's a huge inflection point for the West. I was really interested in California, because a year later, in 1849, the gold rush begins. [California history is only really taught to school children] from that moment forward. You learn about the railroads, the gold mines, the different pioneers who arrived, and the institutions that they set up—things like Stanford University. But before 1848 there's this eerie silence.

Even the NFL [National Football League] team is called the 49ers. [The year is] a big deal. But as a photographer, I was trying to fill in that vacuum and saying, "Okay, what happened before the gold rush?" I've seen the pictures of the gold miners. I've seen early daguerreotypes of them. I've seen the pictures of the golden spike, the spike that was driven in the railroads to connect east and west. These kinds of pictures show up in museums all over the place. But I was really curious about what Mexican California looked like before 1848.

Photographic technology didn't really make its way to the West until after the U.S. conquest, even though it had already been invented about ten years earlier. Because the West was difficult to travel to, and isolated in a sense that there was no Panama Canal, cameras didn't seem to make it to the West [before 1848]. There are no surviving [photographic] plates [found in] all the research that I've done from before the American conquest of the West.

Not only do you have the victors and the people who conquered the West writing the story, but you also can't even look back at photography to get a visual of it either. So I said, "Okay, as a photographer, that's the visual archive that I wished that I had had when I was growing up." Or that I wish that I could walk into a museum and see. That would help me imagine the Mexican past and have it live in my imagination as vividly as the Wild West that is celebrated by western movies or other things that are very alive in our historical imagination.

MS: The Wild West really just spanned ten years. I think people think that it lasted for a century.

TVH: It's so popular and it plays an outsized role. Conversely, the Mexican period [predating 1848] occupies so little space. Mexican California did not last long. The period of New Spain before Mexican independence, however, was an extremely long period. In fact, the amount of time that colonial Spain was in New Mexico is longer than the span of time that the United States has been an independent nation. We're talking two and a half centuries of history. If you're actually in Santa Fe or you're a New Mexican or have family links back to that, it seems pretty present, but that doesn't play a big role in the way American history is taught.

I saw a map that was published in the Economist magazine in 2014 that showed current Hispanic census data. Then I overlaid that map with the pre-Guadalupe-Hidalgo border. It lines up like 95%. So 95% of the Spanish-speaking communities, whether it's from immigration or legacy Hispanics, fall within the old borders.

MS: This is really interesting. I wanted to follow that but, I mean, with 1848 being the year that you described as the year of interesting coincidence, did anything prior to that play into your thinking about how to conceptualize this? I'm thinking particularly like, Texas secession or the Gadsden purchase?

TVH: Yeah, the Gadsden purchase [of a tract of Mexico by the U.S. in 1854] is a teeny bit afterwards so that's like the very final piece of the border. And that's got an interesting story too. At that point, it looked like the South could break free from the North, and it wanted access to the Pacific Ocean. If it didn't have the Gadsden purchase, it couldn't run a railroad from the deep-South states to the Pacific Ocean. It was like a little extra bit of land that was bought with that in mind. Because agriculturally (or otherwise), it's useless—fairly useless—land in an extremely arid, harsh desert. It opens up an interesting part of the story that was

Storylines and Conceptual Lineage 69

also downplayed in the way it was told to me—that there were these industrious, freedom loving pioneers, who rolled west because eastern America was energetic, industrious, and expanding, and it needed more space.

That's a typical narrative of manifest destiny. But actually, I would argue, most of the Western expansion was really driven by politicians from the South and for the express purpose of the expansion of slavery. After having studied more about Texas, that's the feeling that I have about Texas, too. That is to say that, as much as slavery was the cause of the U.S. Civil War, it was similarly the main cause of Texan secession from Mexico. It was basically the exact same factors of the Civil War playing out a couple of decades earlier [in a place] where you had slave-owning plantation owners like Austin with their slaves. And you also had Mexico, which had recently abolished slavery and was little by little starting to enforce [the ban]. Those plantation owners didn't want to lose their slaves and it was worth it for them to break free from the government in order to keep them.

MS: But then they initially were rejected by the United States, right? Didn't they want to join right away?

TVH: Yeah. They wanted to join right away. I think it was always a project of the Texans to become an American state. But the problem is, in the U.S., you had control of government and Congress and the presidency that was flopping back and forth between northerners and southerners. And so at the moment—if I'm correct—the moment that they wanted to join the United States, you had a northern abolitionist president. And then it was Polk, who was himself a slave owner from the South. Right after he became president, he accepted Texas [to the union]. That tipped the balance, adding one more slave state than free states in the union. It's very linked up with the politics of that time, which had to do with slavery and abolition. So, I would really say the annexation of Texas was not just about Texans wanting their freedom. It's also linked to the geopolitics of the South wanting to expand slave territory.

MS: It's interesting when you talk about this in terms of amnesia—I mean, circumstances are somewhat different, right? It's history rhyming, it's not repeating itself, but it seems like some of those dynamics are set up right now just in terms of talking about [statehood for the U.S. territory of] Puerto Rico or D.C. [District of Columbia], or . . .

TVH: Totally, totally. There's a lot of echoes. I mean, the Texans tell themselves a story of the Texas revolution really being all about freedom and a fight against tyranny, the tyranny of the Mexican dictatorship of Santa Ana. When they tell the story, if you go to the Alamo [historic site] and see how the story is told, they just totally ignore the part about slavery. They just leave it out as if it wasn't a factor at all. That seems like selective amnesia because it's embarrassing that people were not just fighting for one thing that seems noble. They were also fighting for something that seems completely despicable today (and seemed despicable at the time to the abolitionist). That part is left out of this story.

TVH: The story of how California became a state [is also really compelling] and another historical echo. It's not taught in California schools. I dare you to ask any of your friends from California, where did that bear on the flag come from exactly? Extremely literate, smart people—people with degrees from Stanford and Berkeley and UCLA—they don't know the story. So, I was just so shocked when I found out the story myself and it has a very historical echo with what just happened at the U.S. Capitol [violent attempt to stop the tally of presidential votes on January 6, 2021].

MS: It's a dark story.

TVH: Yeah. Well, after Mexican independence from Spain—Spain had a relatively closed immigration policy. When Mexico took over, they opened up immigration. They wanted both people from southern Mexico and other people, including Americans and Europeans to come in as colonists and immigrate to California. [These people] were given land grants. The condition for doing that is that you had to become naturalized as a Mexican citizen. Then you had to occupy the land for a certain amount of time, otherwise you would lose it. And so there were quite a few Anglo-Americans that came from the East [and many] British people that came from British territories. They were given land grants in northern California around Sacramento and Redding and that area.

Then you had another character, Captain Fremont, who was given a mission by the U.S. military to map the Rockies. He went freelance and decided to break with his orders and to sneak into Mexican territory. When he got there, he came across some of these land grant recipients who were Anglophones but had naturalized as Mexican citizens. He did not have orders to invade Mexico or to snatch Mexico and put it in American hands. So he came up with a ruse. He decided that he would spread a false rumor, a big lie among these Anglophone land owners that the Mexican army was coming up from the South, that it would kick them out, that it would burn down their ranches and that they would lose everything. The people freaked out, formed a posse, combined into a mob, and then stormed into the Mexican army barracks in Sonoma and into the house of Mariano Vallejo who was the highest-level officer at that point in Northern California.

Some of these people were dressed like the "QAnon Shaman" [conspirator Jake Angeli] at the January Sixth capitol invasion. They were described as shoeless, shirtless hillbillies that were running on this wild lie, a cooked-up rumor that wasn't true. Apparently, the accounts at the time said there was a moment of hesitation when Vallejo talked to them and said, "What are you talking about? I granted or supported many of your land grants. We're not sending out the army to clear you out." But by the time they had gotten to Vallejo's house, they'd already murdered a few people and stolen quite a few Mexican horses. And so there was a speech by one of the insurrectionists where he said, "Either we're stopped now and we're murderers and horse thieves, or we continue and will be revolutionaries."

So, they continued and they took Vallejo hostage. They stormed into the neighboring barracks and they drew an image of a bear on a bed sheet. It was apparently so badly drawn that it looked more like a pig, and they wrote the words "California Republic" on it and hoisted that flag. The California Republic lasted about a month. Unbeknownst to them, over in Texas, the Mexican-American war had actually broken out and the U.S. had declared war on Mexico. So, months later, an American ship finally came into the Mexican [provincial] capital (which, at the time, was in Monterrey) and took control of California from the bear flaggers, much to the relief of many of the Mexicans who were sick of the marauding and mistreatment that [they had suffered under their brief rule]. California changed hands and changed governments based on a false rumor that incited an insurrection.

The state uses the same flag that was created by those insurrectionists to this day. That's the birth story of California. For me, once you learn that, I find it to be deeply embarrassing and morally vacant. It's not a proud origin myth for a state.

MS: No. When you frame this in terms of interesting coincidence, I mean, that's another. I don't know whether you'd call it a coincidence or not, but it's certainly a phenomenon.

TVH: Yeah. I mean the bear flag is basically the Trump flag in the 19th century—it's not that different. Then you go to a place like [the University of California at] Berkeley where their symbol is the bear. It's the exact copy of the bear, is a silhouette of the bear on the bear flag. Every football player and every basketball player for UC Berkeley wears the bear logo. And Berkeley is probably the most hardcore identity in campus politics on the face of the earth—or at least on the U.S.—and there's just complete amnesia about this.

MS: I mean, I don't mean this to be insulting, but you can't be the only person that knows this right? Somebody at UC Berkeley knows this.

TVH: No, no. I came across it from the writer Rebecca Solnit [who wrote about it] back in the late 90s. I'm not the only one to know, but it is not popular history. Your average student that goes to UC Berkeley does not know it. And your average person that's an informed person in California that thinks of themselves as informed and progressive does not know it either. It's interesting.

MS: It is. Switching gears to technical stuff: How did you conceptualize this body of work as a diptych showing a landscape and a portrait?

TVH: Some of the first work I saw of the [California] Gold Rush and of the period were diptychs. It was very common at the time to have two plates in a folding case, like a velvet protected folding case. The diptych was the common form of the time. That was my inspiration. I initially thought about using daguerreotype, but instead I ended up using wet plate collodion, which is a slightly later photographic process. I was put off by the fact that you have to boil mercury to develop your daguerreotype. I didn't want to put myself at-risk. Also, the point wasn't to be a complete technical purist, I wasn't into the pure reenactment part of it. But I wanted the common viewer, when they see these pictures, their instinctual reaction to it is, "Oh, this is an archival picture. This is an old picture. This could be a picture from that time period."

MS: Can you describe the subjects that you selected and why you selected those subjects for this project?

TVH: One of the things I noticed when I look at old pictures from my own family, are these stunning visual echoes through time of specific features that people have. Like, you'll look at a photo of a very old uncle or aunt or whatever, and you'll notice the same ears or eyebrows, or cleft, some little genetic feature that makes its way through time. I find that to be one of the most amazing things of looking at old photos of one's own family. [This] similarity of look through time that is transmitted through generations meant that if I were to photograph the direct descendants of people who've been living in the West before U.S. conquest, they would look like the people that had been there before. Using both the process from the time and the descendants of those who lived during that time, you would actually get something that looked more or less like the people would have looked [pre-1848].

I selected families that trace [their roots to] the West from before 1848—whether they are indigenous people or Hispanic people or many mixed people, also.

MS: Yes. How did you find the specific people? Did you draw from people who had already put themselves out as having some relationship to this pre-1848 history that you're telling?

TVH: Yeah, some of them. There are some associations. There's a group called the *Californianos* in California that are some of these old families that had land grants and things. They get together for lunches and conferences. Within that group, there was one woman that was really into genealogy, and she'd been doing genealogy for other group members. She had also been hired by native tribes in California to do genealogy for them also to try to sort out missionized Indians and things like that. I photographed members of this association and then this woman helped set me up with many more people. I also contacted Kevin Moloney [the editor of this book] in Colorado, because he's a direct descendant of a legacy Hispanic family, the Salazars, who've been living in San Luis and before that in Santa Fe for many centuries.

In Santa Fe, I also hired somebody who had been working specifically on a documentary project linked to genealogy. He's half Navajo himself, so he was able to connect me with all kinds of people in New Mexico.

MS: What about your video work along the divided San Diego border—is that related to this?

TVH: It's related in the sense that, when I first started turning my gaze to the border I thought it'd be interesting to do something comparing the contemporary border and the historical border. The historical border project just became so rich and self-contained that it didn't really need so much of the contemporary border. I think it also weakened it to do something really too direct, like side-by-side the old border/the new border. In my initial thoughts that was part of it, and when I looked at the contemporary border, one of the interesting elements to it was the way under Obama and the Bush administration—before Trump—they'd already been building what they'd been calling a virtual fence. Like a border built out of surveillance technology, sensors, and aerial drones and things like that.

I was thinking about looking at the contemporary border with some of those tools, because I'd done that with my drone war thing. That's what brought me to the contemporary border, that's how I ended up at the border with my drone. But while I was there photographing that idea, I just kept having this vision in my head of the waves in the Pacific viewed from above. I didn't even bring my drone to shoot video. I brought it to shoot still photos.

A few days before I got to that area, I kept having that vision in my mind. And so I had three batteries with me for the drone, and used two of them to take still photos. And then I saved the last battery, switched out the camera, put on the video camera and shot the waves crashing into the barrier in the Pacific Ocean. And I find that that image is so much more simple, but so much more profound, than the original idea that I had. I just find the contrast between the eternal time of waves and the political timeline of building a border wall. Once those two things are visible in the same frame and hitting against each other, it's a very powerful message and a very powerful visual in and of itself.

MS: Yeah, I agree. I was driving through the middle of Wyoming a few years ago. The eastern part of the state is an old ocean bottom. It was late and the moon was out and I was watching all these barbed wire fences that delineated plots of private property. I was really compelled by the foolishness of the fence when viewed on any longer scale of time. Like, are there ghost dinosaurs that see the fence and can't make any sense of it? The fences would appear foolish or alien to anything living there before the modern era.

TVH: In geological time it just seems totally, totally ridiculous. But if you take a satellite view of that part of the West, you'll see these perfect square tiles everywhere, because different grass has been planted in different people's private property. So it's crazy. Really, the little teeny pieces of fence have changed species and nature over an even longer period.

MS: Europe, obviously has its own . . . a longer history of controlling pieces of land, too.

74   Matt Slaby

TVH: Yeah, it's weird when you go to the Alps, which are mountains even higher than the Rockies or the Sierras, it's just been inhabited by people for so many hundreds or even thousands of years that almost nothing is natural left. Every pasture has been grazed by sheep and goats for the last 1,000 years and every forest has been cut and then replanted. It's the wild areas, the so-called wild areas of Europe, that have been living in human stewardship for so long. It's totally different.

MS: You started with a very archaic format, relatively speaking. Do you have plans to expand the channels where you show the project or what mediums that you may choose for future work on this particular topic?

TVH: *Lines and Lineage* is, for the most part, finished. There will be a TV documentary about the project, too. I feel like that medium is the perfect amplifier for the story that I want to tell. That's the way that I choose photographic or visual processes these days is try to feel like, "what is the right visual tool that fits this story?" I like to let the story decide. I feel like that was really the right one. So I don't have plans for another photographic process, but video [can certainly supplement it]. It allows people to express their voices in a different way and to have different pacing and reach different audiences, too.

The way that I've brought motion to those things is I've done some filming of the actual process, the chemicals. It is very beautiful and tactile in a way, seeing a piece of glass suspended or in a developing tray is visually interesting when it's filmed with the right lighting and things like that.

MS: What do you expect the TV documentary will add to what you've already done?

TVH: First, it reaches a different audience. Unfortunately, still photography is either [on a digital] platform or [often reaches a declining] audience—especially for the kind of still photography where people linger on images. [That kind of photography is so much different from] the kind where someone swipes through in less than a second. The reason that I got into still photography is that it is a little bit slower as a medium than to flick through your cell phone screen. [I hope that] the television audience will be able to bring it to different people and to tell the story in a different way.

MS: Are there other venues where the work may be shown? If I understand, there is the book, the exhibition, the plates themselves—are you using the plates themselves?

TVH: The exhibitions that I've shown so far tend to also include the video work of the waves. The divided video installation tends to be shown sometimes in the same room, sometimes in a separate room, but the curators that have selected the work are often are attracted to that video, too. The plates themselves can be used as an actual art object and displayed in their own way. Right now, I just haven't really had the space or venue to do that. That's something that I'm open to, and that

I've thought a little bit about. There are ways that I have in mind that could work really well. But it hasn't actually happened yet.

It also depends on the commercial life that the work has left in it, and what venues open up to it as time goes on. It's hard to say, because I launched the book in November, 2019. The U.S. has a different relationship with history today than it did when I started the work. Although I wouldn't say that extends yet so far to the history of the West, it has a different relationship to black history. It has a different relationship to Confederate history than it did when I started the work in 2017. But that relationship seems yet to evolve when it comes to the history of the relationship to the West and Hispanic culture.

MS: One last question for you: is there anything that we didn't talk about today that you think, especially in light of the varied channels and media in which your work appears?

TVH: Well, it's certainly a transition to come from the still photography world where, at the time I entered it, all the pieces were in one place. Like the whole chain of production between creating the work and then distributing it was all encapsulated in the same thing. Now, that's not the case. The chain of production has been broken. Video and social media are so easy to add. That is freeing. I'm not a digital-native person. I did start my career when photography had its own life chain from production to publication and the economy that went with it. But I think that this particular kind of work does lend itself to being outside of that closed chain of photography production and being and seen in different ways. And so probably the limiting factor on it is not the story itself, but it's my own open or closed mindedness to seeing different ways to tell the story.

References

Leica Oskar Barnack Award. (2019). *Lines and lineage*. Tomas van Houtryve, Lines and Lineage. www.leica-oskar-barnack-award.com/en/series-finalists/2019/tomas-van-houtryve.html

Open Society Foundations. (2014). *Blue Sky Days*. Open Society Foundations. www.movingwalls.org/moving-walls/22/blue-sky-days

van Houtryve, T. (n.d.). *About—Tomas van Houtryve photography*. Tomas van Houtryve. https://tomasvh.com/about/

7 Challenging Hegemonic Narratives
Power of Story-Based Design Strategies in Activating Sustainable Social Change

Francesca Piredda and Mariana Ciancia

Claiming a Narrative Turn in Design for Sustainable Social Change

Emerging sustainable and inclusive ways of living generate a constellation of small grassroots initiatives that "require visions, strategies and co-design tools to move from ideas to mature solutions and viable programs" (*DESIS Network*, n.d.). Co-design is about the meaningful involvement of end users and stakeholders in the design process, and about participatory processes driven by design discipline (Sanders & Stappers, 2008). Although co-design and design for social innovation are valuable practices that have long driven social change (Ehn, 2008; Mulgan et al., 2007), the alternative perspective of giving media and content design the central role in social inclusion processes can be developed further within the design discipline. This perspective has emerged, thanks to the discussion promoted by the DESIS Network, an international design community that has explored and discussed how designers experiment with many different ways of using storytelling for social innovation (Bertolotti et al., 2016, 2014; *DESIS Philosophy Talks*, n.d.). Many of the projects developed within the DESIS Network have used storytelling in an instinctive way, without outsourcing specific types of competencies from the disciplines that have traditionally dealt with the topic of narratives, such as narratology and media studies.

In this chapter, we address the power of stories to activate change processes and to promote the construction of a collective imagination. We outline the importance of narrative in situating, shaping, and assessing the worldbuilding techniques that underpin transmedia practices for social change. We also describe the three design phases and related creative activities—collecting, crafting, and reframing—that we have identified and developed over the years, and that can be taught in a design school.

Mainstream Versus Margins

Contemporary Western society is influenced by the misleading idea of progress toward a better future. The progressive perspective of capitalism

DOI: 10.4324/9781003150862-7

proposes a rhetoric of the future and of innovation in which the future is seen as a continuation of what has already been. In this scenario, technology and science support the coveted elimination of problems and limits in the human condition. Wellbeing is conceived as boosting human capacity to produce and consume products through owning and devising personalized sets of products. The past is regarded as a straight line that goes toward the future—a future that will inevitably be better than the past. Today, even though this rhetoric attracts deep doubts because of the traumatic ongoing COVID-19 pandemic, it is still present to some extent in our contemporary society. Neoliberalism, consumerism, and individualism can be viewed as examples of hegemonic narratives still present in our contemporaneity. Crises that crack them—such as the 2020 coronavirus pandemic—reveal that the traditional way of planning in linear time is a rigid, fragile paradigm (Tassinari et al., 2015; Tassinari & Staszowski, 2020). The contemporary socio-economic perspective obsessively tries to fix them by developing socio-technical mechanisms and progressive narratives that shape and legitimize the idea of a linear trajectory.

In this study, we develop these observations further by adopting a narrative framework. Big narratives promote a univocal imagery of reference that relates to large-scale universal and confirmative certainties about the changes needed for a better future and for wellbeing. However, we claim that multiple storylines can coexist, leveraging the presence of multiple characters within the main story, who can be the heroes of many possible narrative journeys. We begin with the idea that every story can be told from different viewpoints, and that secondary characters can become the protagonists of narratives stemming from "the leftovers," the remains of the failure of linear progress (Tassinari et al., 2015, p. 417). They face specific challenges in everyday life, becoming the main protagonists of grassroots actions that are different from mainstream ways of living. They rediscover and reinvent the taste and enjoyment of finding alternative ways to live, to create things, to share, to collaborate, to grow, and to nurture (Meroni, 2007). Thus, they are the main agents of sustainable change at the margins of the mainstream—what Walter Benjamin (2006 [1936]) defined as "fragments," the result of the failure of the big narratives (Tassinari et al., 2015, p. 417).

Next, we present two key twofold concepts connecting the contribution of design narratives for social innovation. The first is that of "fragments" as both 1) spontaneous, small-scale, short-term initiatives of social inclusion outside of the mainstream and 2) alternative secondary stories that are nodal plot points of sustainable, inclusive narrative worlds. The second concept is that of "everyday heroes," as both 1) agents of inclusive change processes—activators, protagonists, and participants—regardless of whether they are professional designers or citizens finding solutions to everyday problems and 2) people who enact specific narrative functions to implement the action, and embody alternative values within the story ("actants"; Propp, 2010 [1928]; Greimas, 1983 [1973]).

From this perspective, it is possible to conceive that local actions of "acupunctural" planning (Jégou, 2010; Manzini, 2010) and situated knowledge (Haraway, 2016) coexist with large-scale processes. Together they represent the engine and infrastructure for social change. Citizens and designers both play a meaningful role in co-designing solutions for tackling quick and recurring breaks in routine, and for finding new meanings. Both citizens and designers can reimagine themselves within the real-life context by playing the role of fictional characters, inspired by real people from the local community (*everyday heroes*). They weave together the fictional and the real worlds (Piredda, 2018). In particular, designers can play several roles in a project: They can provide design and co-design tools for envisioning and sharing a better future, mediate the relationships between stakeholders by using a narrative framework, or also be part of the narrative with the citizenry (Tassinari et al., 2017).

Everyday Hero: Agent of Individual and Collective Transformation

De Certeau (1984) avoided the counterculture versus mainstream debate and depicted three types of practices defined by the relationships between users and production tools and devices: usage and consumption, everyday creativity, and forms of practice. Those relationships refer to tactics (behaviors) and rhetoric (representations) as "secondary images" produced by, and from, a society's margins, through a process of continuous transformation and trans-codification of meaning. For example, in the media design and communication field, repertoires, contents, and artifacts are edited and used by people to foster identities and disseminate knowledge among people who share interests and practices.

The idea of daily life as the opposite of specialized activity was born in the social sciences. What about the art field? According to the *Situationist International*, it represents the alienation of individuals and has a negative nuance. However, it also refers to the potential and richness of everyday will and imagination that enable one to feel the subversive power of the political and collective dimension (Bandini, 1999). Debord (2005, 2020) revealed and practiced the *trivialization of art*, or the end of specialized acts and the integration of a revolutionary and social creativity into daily life: Aesthetics defined as art is politics (Bandini, 1999). The Situationist critique of daily life is conducted through a critique of modern society, proposing politics as a realization of the imagination, the integration of the "marvelous" in everyday life. The political approach to art practice is linked to the concept of utopia (Bourriaud, 2002). Based on that, design can contribute to eliciting creativity as the art of everyday lives, thus setting a common ground in terms of expressive and communication tools for sharing knowledge (Tassinari et al., 2017).

This discussion brings us to the idea of design as a strategic asset for managing the aesthetic value of social practices and addressing the idea of human social interaction as an aesthetic phenomenon. The aesthetics of everyday lives can be derived from people's experiences and stories toward a symbolic dimension that enables them to unlock and spread new meanings—a mythology of everyday life. In that sense, narratives could evolve from the multiple perspectives of the users who take part in a collective meaning-making process.

According to Walter J. Ong (2013), heroic figures with virtues—leaders who can save the planet—come from basic noetic motive "to organize experience in some sort of permanently memorable form" (p. 63). Oral memory works effectively in remembering extraordinary people, but not colorless personalities because they are not memorable enough. To assure weight and memorability, heroic figures tend to be typecast figures in epics. Consider fairytales about fantastic figures that are narrated to children: "The heroic and marvelous had served a specific function in organizing knowledge in an oral world" (p. 63).

According to the cognitive approach to narrative studies, the character and storyworld are both mental models—incrementally constructed as shared models between recipients and authors or between the audience and creators—in which other narratives can be built, starting from characters' expectations, desires, and goals.

In Western culture, these ways of transmitting knowledge and preserving stories have increasingly separated from real life, causing an irreversible break between the fantastic and the factual genres. In this sense, the building of transmedia narrative worlds allows the coexistence of the *primary* (factual) and *secondary* (fictional) *worlds* (Wolf, 2012). Moreover, transmedia projects make the narrative worlds unfold in a situated context, letting them be accessible through digital touchpoints and creating immersive experiences.

Building the characters and the world often pushes the designer toward fiction, while usually, the ordinary participants involved in this process prioritize "entrenched actual-world models" (Herman et al., 2010, p. 55) to the extent that they need to recognize or compare themselves and their life experiences with those in the story. According to the principle of minimal departure (Ryan, 1980), individuals readily reconstrue the unfamiliar using the familiar, and they reconstruct this possible world as something close to the world they already know. In this sense, the art of storytelling should not be viewed exclusively as an entertaining activity, but as a key tool for building identity, either individual or collective. In addition, it should be viewed as a way to organize and share collective knowledge and personal experiences (Venditti et al., 2017).

According to the communication theories in classical narratology, any communication-oriented model of narrative should answer the question about what its truth-functional status or reliability is (Herman et al., 2010). Shall designers question their role, then? Shall they ask themselves how to avoid stereotypes?

Narrative worlds are mental constructs shared by the narrator and the narratee that continuously generate brand new storylines and elements according to their various wills, desires, and expectations (Pinardi & De Angelis, 2006; Wolf, 2012). Habits, values, and beliefs conflict both at the level of the characters (micro) and at the level of the narrative world (macro). Anthropologist Carlo Tullio Altan (1995) analyzed the process of national identity formation and defines the ways in which people come to recognize themselves in that identity. Borrowing from Altan's reflections, Davide Pinardi and Pietro De Angelis (2006) defined the generative elements of the narrative world as the factors through which the world takes on identity and consistency; it becomes the background for a reliable story and fueling its construction. These elements are *topos* (the territory), *epos* (the historical memory), *telos* (the aims; the community's aims), *ethos* (the dominant values), *logos* (the languages), and *genos* (the relationships of kinship and lineage). To these, Pinardi and De Angelis (2006) added *chronos* (time): As long as narrative worlds are dynamic and generative, they will always change in line with the changes in imagery, culture, and society.

Each narrative world can be composed of the so-called *Overworld* (society, planet, etc.), *Underworld* (specific contexts), and *Internal world* (character) (Pinardi & De Angelis, 2006). From the scale-based view, as the world changes, characters change too. Narratively speaking, we would refer to the structure of the myth and to the Hero's Journey (Vogler, 2007), which starts when the hero gets the *Call to the Adventure*, which makes the hero leave the *Ordinary World* and face manifold adventures in the *Special World*, engaging in fights with the *Enemies*, and meeting the *Mentor* and the *Allies*, until the hero can return to a renewed *Ordinary World*. At that point, the hero would have grown and many things would have changed, resulting in a new equilibrium. Many stories from contemporary Western culture (movies or novels) are based on this narrative structure. Moreover, it represents a model based on ancient archetypes that restore themselves over and over again and inform most narratives across times and cultures (Campbell, 2008).

The narrative worlds included in a tale can be in conflict, generating the dynamics of the stories themselves. The German philosopher Hannah Arendt (2013) referred to Aristotle's definition that man is a political animal, *zoon politikon*. To participate in constructing the common realm and to be an active component of societal life is what defines the most profound human vocation. Arendt sees this as the meaning of the word *hero*—not a superhuman being, but rather, one who contributes to the construction of the public sphere. In the classical Greek theater, it is the choir that tells the stories of those heroes and allows the role of the hero—the individual in the society who assumes responsibility—to emerge. Through those enacted stories, citizens in ancient Greece were also able to recognize their own vocation and happiness within the common sphere (Tassinari et al., 2017).

Moreover, from a narrative standpoint, people are fundamentally agents, insofar as their identity is shaped by their actions. In designing communication as a process, the designer should always consider the oral character of language. In particular, some characteristics of orally based thought and expression remain and represent an opportunity for change-oriented, narrative-based projects: They should be *agonistically toned, empathetic and participatory*, and *situational*. The agonistic dynamics of oral thought processes and expression have been central to the development of Western culture, which institutionalized them through the "art" of rhetoric (Ong, 2013).

Narratives have a transformative power: Stories offer examples of how to face and manage conflicts in everyday life and generate change processes. Transmedia storytelling should be designed as a participatory process in which professional designers and non-designers collaborate within a *transmedia practice* to avoid the risk of totally and automatically equating people with the characters of their life stories. Designers should avoid limiting the extent of self-reflection, self-awareness, or self-control they are willing to grant the individuals they aim to represent. People should be able to take part as narrators or perhaps even as authors of these stories. This approach would be consistent with the audience's role in the contemporary media landscape characterized by the technological development of media channels and devices that empowers people to participate in political and social life, starting intervention at the grassroots level.

Regardless of its disciplinary context, the narrative perspective on identity recognizes the need to account for both the transformation and the stability of individuals and uses stories as the ideal medium for balancing change with sameness.

Fragments: Micronarratives as Drivers of Change

Behaviors and grassroots actions related to social innovation can be considered fragments resulting from the crisis of the hegemonic Western culture. These leftovers have emerged again, and it is to them that we can turn when the big narratives begin to fail—fragments of the mainstream that require a different narrative to be told, an alternative micro-story. For example, during the first lockdown in Italy in spring 2020, mainstream storytelling was about the fear of transmitting COVID-19 through human contact. The *social distancing* and *Io resto a casa* (I stay home) messages spread throughout the media. Suddenly, however, different kinds of images went viral on social media and started to colonize broadcast channels. Spontaneous, grassroots actions emerged as diffused flash-mobs: having lunch together, sharing the same table across different but contiguous balconies, and singing and playing music together from windows overlooking courtyards across different neighborhoods. These alternative micro-stories contributed to delivering an alternative and positive message: *distanti ma vicini* (distant, but close).

On a social level, a crisis can help people acknowledge what is potentially present in reality but missed at the margins. The possibility to keep on being close was still there, even though it could not have become factual without the creativity and marginal practices of very local and situated social groups. Crisis can fuel the embrace of reimagined possibilities and turn them into alternative actions that can challenge hegemonic narratives. Thus, the role of the designer in the field of social innovation is that of mediator and a provider of tools and processes for envisioning and co-creating micro-stories that can promote positive societal change. Specifically, the role of the designer of narratives is to recognize these fragments among the remains of the mainstream stories, and to collect and spread them in innovative ways (Bertolotti et al., 2016). To do so, designers need to

- work with communities to develop in-field activities;
- design and make available tools and processes for co-designing stories in order to elicit the stakeholders' agency and emancipate nonexperts;
- assume the meanings of both the words "fragment" and "micro-story," as we propose: (a) as good practices on the margins of the mainstream to be used to break the dominant story and (b) as narrative contents, which when connected using an articulated plot (multistrand and transmedia narratives), enable designers to reconstruct and feed a narrative world as an alternative to the dominant, hegemonic one.

In our work, *fragments* are small-scale and short-term social inclusion initiatives that can be amplified through alternative stories and storytelling strategies distributed across media (online and offline). Combined, they can create inclusive narrative worlds. Therefore, fragmentation can be intended as a specific property of digital media narratives, in which contents are characterized by interactivity and are constructed to enhance the user's ability to interconnect them.

In digital narratives, interactivity is configured not only as of the physical actions that users perform (e.g., click, comment, or share) but also as a cognitive process that the extradiegetic narratee carries out. It is a process through which people can treat micro-contents as autonomous since each fragment has its own meaning although connected to a wider narrative. Therefore, the ability of the audience to recognize autonomous chunks as a narrative relies on the way the content is designed.

According to Ryan (2004), the design of narrative content on digital media should consider formal aspects (the syntactic level of the narrative discourse), content aspects (the semantic level of the autonomous contents conveyed through channels), and interactive aspects (the pragmatic level of narrative). Moreover, a designer should take into consideration two more concepts that affect the way in which users can create connections between dispersed micro-content—the principle of minimal departure and the concept of narrativity. The principle of minimal departure (Ryan, 1980, 1991) warns that individuals' interpretation of a message is influenced by the reality they know, and vice versa, establishing a bidirectional connection between the real and storyworld. This means that designers of distributed content must consider these information-process rules that frame sense-making activities (Liveley et al., 2021). The concept of narrativity (Ryan, 2007) refers to the characteristic of a media text to be constructed as a narrative by the reader regardless of whether all of the traditional narrative structures and elements are present in the text: Examples of this are social media posts leading people to grasp complete stories starting from a small number of narrative elements (such as short sentences and images). We can consider the singular posts as a proto-narrative fragment that—combined with other content from the news or popular culture—can be read as parts of a complete narrative (Murphet, 2005).

In light of these premises, micro-stories and small chunks of content can be considered fragments of bigger narratives, letting people activate meaning-making processes and a sense of belonging through cognitive processes: what we defined "aesthetics of micronarratives." Media contents should (a) possess some degree of narrativity, (b) be composed of autonomous media texts that are scattered across media and distribution channels, and (c) enable users to use their cognitive ability to read the contents as part of a bigger narrative. In fact, designers can elicit the cognitive effort of their audience by structuring micronarratives within a whole storyworld. This can reinforce the relationship between media texts and people, and promote a shared mental image among audience members (Venditti et al., 2017). The phenomenon of memes on social media represents an interesting example: Current events usually trigger the production of these amatorial contents made up of modified and remixed images (usually frames from movies, paintings, or pieces of art) which everybody can easily interpret as references to news, media coverage, and popular culture. Digital manipulation and memes become tools for escaping from real mundane life, leading to new collective imagery. Audiences are used to contents as fragments of a bigger meaning-making system. The risk is that they do not care about the opportunity of exploring and diving into the overall complexity of the meanings conveyed.

Challenging Hegemonic Narratives

Narrative change is a complex, nonlinear process, but it has the potential to drive social change in powerful ways. Designing for social innovation and sustainability involves radical changes in the present to encourage short- and long-term outcomes. It inserts conflicts into people's everyday lives by challenging their well-established habits and ethics, visions, and personal agendas. According to Cameron Tonkinwise (2018), "Non-designers tend to suffer from confirmation biases and endowment effects that over-valorise what currently exists, discounting the possibility of betterment" (p. 75). Conversely, designers are committed to perfectibility, always looking for changing existing situations into preferred ones (Simon, 1996). However, what is better and what is worse? What is preferable? And for whom?

Recalling the beginning of this chapter about progress and linear time, we exploit the contribution of Tonkinwise (2018), who discussed the prevalent notion that what is preferable is progress. He declared that, in line with the concept of progress, "the creative act of designing is inherently destructive. Designers . . . destroy what currently exists by replacing it with a preferable one" (Tonkinwise, 2018, pp. 74–75). Designers' and non-designers' visions may differ. The actors involved in innovation processes often are from different backgrounds, have widely varying expectations, and speak different languages (Bertolotti et al., 2016). Moreover, Manzini (2015) distinguishes between diffuse design, performed by everybody, each person and each collective subject—from enterprises to institutions, and to communities—that must define and enhance a life project; and expert design, performed by those who have been trained as designers, describing how they interact. Some of them may be "prepared to unlearn and relearn modes of interaction . . . mostly because the latter are, in the end, easier and more convenient, and hopefully more effective and pleasurable" (Tonkinwise, 2018, p. 76). Tonkinwise (2018) argues that radical innovation needs some form of destruction of the traditional narratives we are used to. Designers should more clearly recognize their creativity as a destructive practice against the unsustainable ways of living that are destroying our societies.

We prefer to move away from the nihilistic vision of the designer as "destroyer." In fact, assuming the concept of "adversarial design" (DiSalvo, 2012), we propose "agonism" as the political perspective of design practice, and we warmly recall "its roots in the Greek *agon*: a public celebration games; a contest for the prize at this games; or, a verbal contest between two characters in a Greek play" (DiSalvo, 2012, p. 2). In particular, we focus on the dramatic meaning that emerges from ancient rhetoric (the second part of the oration, after the preface and before the epilogue) and theatrical agon, which Enciclopedia Treccani (Agone, n.d.) defined as follows: "scenes from Greek tragedy and comedy that result in a contradiction between two actors; . . . the dispute between two adversaries, with the participation of the chorus, usually inserted between the *pàrodos* and the *parabasis*."[1]

Then, the notion of agonism is interesting because it refers to a particular kind of conflict as relationship and experience with proper social and material consequences. These conflicts enable and shape the practice of questioning, challenging, and reframing the ongoing conditions of life.

Further, "Narrative is not a regulatory and prescripting apparatus which tends to build a higher abstract order, but it is instead a dialectical system based on human intentionality" (Mattana, 2016, p. 67). Without the conflict, a narrative is reduced to a simple statement, a mere record of facts. Conflict is the fundamental element that can trigger a story, to activate the dialogic relationship with the narrative world. "Worldly" thinking, for Haraway (2016), is a "risky game of worlding and storying; it is staying with the trouble" (p. 13). This means that transmedia design has the complex role of building shared meanings for sustainable and inclusive change.

A transmedia design process should include *situated* heroes who embody a system of shared values that develops a dramatic relationship with the narrative world. Transmedia storytelling should activate the abductive processes of interpretation by connecting the fragments and building micronarratives as the plot points of alternative narrative worlds.

Story-Based Design Strategies

While in the next chapter, we will describe in detail the method and tools we have developed and used in field experiments, in this section we present the practice of *Transmedia design*, our contribution of theoretical reflections about inclusive and collaborative processes, and the role of aesthetics within the processes of co-designed storytelling. Over the years, we have activated a process of community engagement for experiments on coproduction and sense-making with people in the community. Thus, we identified three design phases and related creative activities that can be taught in a design school—collecting, crafting, and reframing.

Collecting materials is the inspirational basis for narrative design. Listening to testimonies and collecting visual materials as sources of inspiration are two activities that designers typically experience. Design schools teach these as the first exploratory activities that students must perform before they design anything. Within the communication design field, this exploration can be conducted on a specific theme, situation, or space and is aimed at gathering as many fragments as possible to produce an archive of raw material that can be used to build the narrative artifact.

The second phase—*Crafting*—is devoted to the creation of storyworlds, characters, and storylines and is aimed at allowing the audience to cognitively reconstruct narratives. In doing so, the designers should be able to master the theoretical foundation of narratology to create and craft the narrative elements (character, event, conflict, causality, and point of view).

Last, *Reframing* is the phase in which the designer needs to subdivide the story into key points, combine different aesthetic languages (e.g., text, image, drawing, sound, video, meme, gif), and transform and format them into content across multiple media and distribution channels. In this design process, the autonomous fragments collected at the beginning of the design activity are reframed with new meanings, and—according to the concept of narrativity (Ryan, 2007)—can be mentally connected to form a fuller narrative in the audience's mind (Venditti, 2017).

Reflections on Representation

Narrative productions (video or other types of languages) in the field of social innovation design are often characterized by an aesthetic quality that is inconsistent with the content they represent. Both ongoing and completed experiences related to local social innovation actions often remain inaccessible, and since they are not shared with the wider audience, they remain unknown outside of their original publication context. A visual uniformity in communication productions also reveals a lack of visual culture and of consideration of the effectiveness and meanings conveyed. These narratives often seem to be characterized by a *naïve* over-positivity and a "happy ending." In our opinion, this is often because storytelling techniques are used to eliminate any narrative conflict, which means removing "the dark side" of the matter. Consequently, these stories tend to seem overly reductive and deny real-world complexity (Bertolotti et al., 2016).

The tools that designers traditionally use are oriented toward problem-solving rather than starting a dialogue and allowing meaning-making. Even when designers carry out rapid prototyping, their aim is usually to verify solution efficiency, and not to verify communication effectiveness or to reflect on the generated meanings. The result is a flattening of the representation. The tools and technologies designers use for developing design projects and processes affect both the artifact's outcome and the process itself.

In contrast, if we adopt the "adversarial design" ethos (DiSalvo, 2012), we engage the conflict as the driver of the narrative; it is not just a problem to be solved but is mainly a generator of questions—the flint of change. The "storytelling qualities" (Bertolotti et al., 2016) may vary according to awareness of and accountability to the conflict: Does the narrative represent the conflict(s) that the characters and the world are dealing with ("conflict-based")? Or is the conflict completely missing? Is the conflict already solved ("suspended conflict"), as is typical in advertising in which the presented situation simply shows the uses of a product, describes the product itself, or demonstrates certain small actions and feelings related to an experience in progress? Ryan (2017) questioned whether "'worldness' can be considered a scalar concept, realized to different extents in narrative texts, and what it takes for a narrative to evoke a world to the imagination" (p. 31). *Story-dominant* narratives, we argue, emphasize the story or plot and may largely leave implicit the world that contains events, objects, and characters.

In the case of collaborative processes, other types of storytelling qualities must be considered. The storytelling qualities mostly refer to the designers' role in choosing what to tell and how: They can develop and realize the project by translating topics and issues that emerged from a participant in the listening phase or, conversely, can facilitate the process by providing storytelling tools to an individual or a group without contributing their own competencies in producing the transmedia project. The elaboration and crafting of the collected materials and narrative elements may strive toward a complete representation (Wolf, 2012) by being close to (realistic) or distant (fantastic) from, the actual reference world (Ryan, 2017).

To support the integration of narratives into design processes, we developed and tested specific tools that designers and non-designers can use in the collaborative processes of story creation and worldbuilding. We discuss these tools in the next chapter.

Final Remarks: Worldbuilding and Social Change

We presented a theoretical framework and our unique approach to social change through narrative. We highlighted the synergy between the different scales of intervention that the design perspective should adopt on worldbuilding and transmedia narratives. These scales include the small-scale, short-term design and production of narrative artifacts (fragments as micronarratives) and, by contrast, the large-scale, long-term processes of collaboration and shared change (narrative worldbuilding). The concept of time (*chronos*; Pinardi & De Angelis, 2006) was proposed as a multidimensional perspective that informs processes of change, both in terms of transforming the actual society and the narrative elements representing it. The practice of transmedia design—a combination of techniques derived from transmedia story production (Dena, 2009), and the research-through-design approach (Frankel & Racine, 2010; Frayling, 1993) that specifically uses workshop and design activities as a source of knowledge—was articulated earlier in a three-phase design process with the aim of engaging various actors and many stories as parts of a classical Greek choral narrative. Collecting, crafting, and reframing the materials available from participants activates a circular generative process that can transform diverse imagery into a shared, complex, dynamic narrative world.

Once an experience has been related, it enters the collective discourse, and multiple participants determine the meaning it acquires. The authority of others (designers, audiences, or others playing different roles in the design process) in shaping the story by connecting and producing fragments of the complex transmedia projects can be misleading. Translating and conveying meanings this way can become oppressive. Therefore, transmedia design should make room for opportunities and activities of self-reflection for the audience via storytelling. This empowers designers and overcomes the dependency on hegemonic discursive practices.

Transmedia design makes mentally constructed worlds concrete by establishing tangible rabbit holes and touchpoints in the physical world, connecting them to the possible solutions we can imagine, engaging stakeholders and audiences in their daily activity, and keeping them alive like a compass that guides our choices through a wider, complex perspective. In this regard, Bourriaud (2002) was interested in utopia as a "device" to move away from the abstract and locate the concrete. The original concept of *micro-utopias* is still useful to describe art and design projects that create temporary, small-scale, convivial experiments. The interpersonal relationships this creates within communities and *networked micro-utopias* (Wood, 2007) are the plot points of a transmedia change system.

Acknowledgment

The authors would like to thank the colleagues who have shared their reflections about storytelling and design practice over the years: Elisa Bertolotti, Heather Daam, Virginia Tassinari, and Simona Venditti.

Note

1 *Pàrodos* is the first choral passage in an ancient Greek drama. *Parabasis* is the point in the play when the chorus addresses the audience directly.

References

Agone (n.d.). *Enciclopedia treccani*. Retrieved November 15, 2021, from https://www.treccani.it/enciclopedia/agone
Altan, C. T. (1995). *Ethnos e civiltà: Identità etniche e valori democratici*. Feltrinelli.
Arendt, H. (2013). *The human condition: Second edition*. University of Chicago Press.
Bandini, M. (1999). *L' estetico e il politico: Da Cobra all'Internazionale Situazionista 1948–1957*. Costa & Nolan.
Benjamin, W. (2006). The storyteller: Reflections on the works of Nikolai Leskov. In D. Hale (Ed.), *The novel: An anthology of criticism and theory 1900–2000* (pp. 361–378). Blackwell Publishing.
Bertolotti, E., Daam, H., Piredda, F., & Tassinari, V. (Eds.). (2016). *The pearl diver*. DESIS Network, Dipartimento di Design, Politecnico di Milano.
Bertolotti, E., Federica, D., & Piredda, F. (2014). Interferenze digitali: Un'estetica dellepratiche digitali a supporto del discorso di design. In C. Coletta, S. Colombo, P. Magaudda, A. Mattozzi, L. L. Parolin, & L. Rampino (Eds.), *A matter of design: Making society through science and technology*. STS Italia Publishing.
Bourriaud, N. (2002). *Relational aesthetics*. Les Presses du réel.
Campbell, J. (2008). *The hero with a thousand faces*. New World Library.
Certeau, M. de. (1984). *The practice of everyday life*. University of California Press.
Debord, G. (2005). *Panegirico: Tomo Primo-Tomo Secondo*. Castelvecchi.
Debord, G. (2020). *The society of the spectacle*. Princeton University Press.
Dena, C. (2009). *Transmedia practice: Theorising the practice of expressing a fictional world across distinct media and environments* [Doctoral dissertation, University of Sydney].
DESIS Network. (n.d.). DESIS Network. Retrieved February 9, 2021, from www.desisnetwork.org/
DESIS Philosophy Talks. (n.d.). DESIS Philosophy Talks. Retrieved February 9, 2021, from www.desis-philosophytalks.org/category/events/storytelling/
DiSalvo, C. (2012). *Adversarial design*. Massachusetts Institute of Technology Press.
Ehn, P. (2008). Participation in design things. In *Proceedings Participatory Design Conference 2008*. Participatory Design Conference (PDC). http://muep.mau.se/handle/2043/7196
Frankel, L., & Racine, M. (2010, July 7). The complex field of research: For design, through design, and about design. In *Proceedings of the Design Research Society (DRS) International Conference*. DRS2010–Design and Complexity, Montreal, Canada. https://dl.designresearchsociety.org/drs-conference-papers/drs2010/researchpapers/43
Frayling, C. (1993). *Research in art and design*. Royal College of Art.
Greimas, A. J. (1983). *Structural semantics: An attempt at a method*. University of Nebraska Press.
Haraway, D. J. (2016). *Staying with the trouble: Making kin in the Chthulucene*. Duke University Press.

Herman, D., Jahn, M., & Ryan, M.-L. (2010). *Routledge encyclopedia of narrative theory*. Routledge.
Jégou, F. (2010). Social innovations and regional acupuncture towards sustainability. *Strategic Design Scenarios*. https://www.strategicdesignscenarios.net/social-innovations-and-regional-acupuncture-towards-sustainability/
Liveley, G., Slocombe, W., & Spiers, E. (2021). Futures literacy through narrative. *Futures*, *125*, 102663 . https://doi.org/10.1016/j.futures.2020.102663
Manzini, E. (2010). Small, local, open and connected: Design research topics in the age of networks and sustainability. *Journal of Design Strategies*, 4(1), 24–30.
Manzini, E. (2015). *Design, when everybody designs: An introduction to design for social innovation* (R. Coad, Trans.). Massachusetts Institute of Technology Press.
Mattana, W. (2016). Storytelling or: How I learned to stop worrying and love the conflict. In E. Bertolotti, H. Daam, F. Piredda, & V. Tassinari (Eds.), *The pearl diver* (pp. 66–70). DESIS Network, Dipartimento di Design, Politecnico di Milano . http://archive.org/details/ThePearlDiver_DESIS
Meroni, A. (2007). Creative communities: People inventing sustainable ways of living. *Polidesign*.
Mulgan, G., Tucker, S., Ali, R., Sanders, B., University of Oxford, & Skoll Centre for Social Entrepreneurship. (2007). *Social innovation: What it is, why it matters and how it can be accelerated*. Young Foundation.
Murphet, J. (2005). Stories and plots. In R. Huisman, J. Murphet, & A. Dunn (Eds.), *Narrative and media* (pp. 47–59). Cambridge University Press.
Ong, W. J. (2013). *Orality and literacy: 30th Anniversary edition*. Routledge.
Pinardi, D., & De Angelis, P. (2006). *Il mondo narrativo: Come costruire e come presentare l'ambiente e i personaggi di una storia*. Lindau.
Piredda, F. (2018). Il territorio come mondo (narrativo). Il confine fra mondo reale e mondo finzionale come luogo del progetto. In M. Parente & C. Sedini (Eds.), *D4T: design per i territori: Approcci, metodi, esperienze*. LISt Lab.
Propp, V. (2010). *Morphology of the folktale: Second Edition*. University of Texas Press.
Ryan, M.-L. (1980). Fiction, non-factuals, and the principle of minimal departure. *Poetics*, 9(4), 403– 422. https://doi.org/10.1016/0304-422X(80)90030-3
Ryan, M.-L. (1991). *Possible worlds, artificial intelligence, and narrative theory*. Indiana University Press.
Ryan, M.-L. (2004). *Narrative across media: The languages of storytelling*. University of Nebraska Press.
Ryan, M.-L. (2007). Toward a definition of narrative. In D. Herman (Ed.), *The Cambridge companion to narrative* (pp. 22–35). Cambridge University Press.
Ryan, M.-L. (2017). The aesthetics of proliferation. In M. Boni (Ed.), *World building: Transmedia, fans, industries*. Amsterdam University Press. https://library.oapen.org/handle/20.500.12657/25975
Sanders, E. B.-N., & Stappers, P. J. (2008). Co-creation and the new landscapes of design. *CoDesign*, 4(1), 5–18. https://doi.org/10.1080/15710880701875068
Simon, H. A. (1996). *The sciences of the artificial*. Massachusetts Institute of Technology Press.
Tassinari, V., Bertolotti, E., Daam, H., & Piredda, F. (2015). Telling the stories of design for social innovation: Towards an ecology of times. In L. Collina, L. Galluzzo, & A. Meroni (Eds.), *The virtuous circle design culture and experimentation*. McGraw Hill.

Tassinari, V., Piredda, F., & Bertolotti, E. (2017). Storytelling in design for social innovation and politics: A reading through the lenses of Hannah Arendt. *The Design Journal*, *20*(S1), S3486–S3 495. https://doi.org/10.1080/14606925.2017.1352852

Tassinari, V., & Staszowski, E. (2020). *Designing in dark times: An Arendtian Lexicon*. Bloomsbury Publishing.

Tonkinwise, C. (2018). 'I prefer not to': Anti-progressive designing. In G. Coombs, A. McNamara, & G. Sade (Eds.), *Undesign. Critical Practices at the Intersection of Art and Design* (pp. 74–84). Routledge.

Venditti, S. (2017). *Social media fiction: A framework for designing narrativity on social media* [Ph.D. Thesis, Politecnico di Milano]. http://hdl.handle.net/10589/132153

Venditti, S., Piredda, F., & Mattana, W. (2017). Micronarratives as the form of contemporary communication. *The Design Journal*, *20*(S1), S273–S282. https://doi.org/10.1080/14606925.2017.1352804

Vogler, C. (2007). *The writer's journey: Mythic structure for writers*. Michael Wiese Productions.

Wolf, M. J. P. (2012). *Building imaginary worlds: The theory and history of subcreation*. Routledge.

Wood, J. (2007). *Design for micro-utopias: Making the unthinkable possible*. Gower.

8 Teaching Transmedia Practice in a Design School
The Plug Social TV Experience

Mariana Ciancia and Francesca Piredda

Introduction

For several decades, people have been moving through a mediascape in which storytelling has been influenced by technological developments and new modes of distribution and consumption. The result is what Fisher (1984) defined as the "narrative paradigm," claiming that people best comprehend information and complex social interactions through a narrative logic. This media scenario contributes to disseminating transmedia phenomena and allows people to actively create messages as authors (agents) and co-authors (audience members).

Since transmedia storytelling has been a narrative and a social practice for many centuries (Scolari et al., 2014), today's transmedia practice—a framework for the production of transmedia stories defined by Dena (2009)—adopts design practices that utilize and overcome the challenges of a mediascape that is in continuous evolution. It is possible to define the transmedia phenomenon as a *design practice* precisely because it is an activity composed of tacit knowledge, conducted by practitioners who operate according to knowledge gained through the everyday experience. The process of designing storyworlds and distributing them on multiple channels follows a *learning-by-doing* approach in which practice is experienced as knowledge creation (Ciancia, 2018).

In light of such premises, if we seek to apply the potential of transmedia storytelling and the design discipline to areas beyond entertainment, it is necessary to develop a model of the practice of *transmedia design* that is derived from the professional world.

Acknowledging the paramount role of transmedia practice in the current mediascape, it becomes necessary for communication designers to explore new frontiers of storytelling and to understand the theory, processes, and tools of transmedia design. This type of design must be understood as a media and communications discipline that involves the development of multichannel communication systems based on narrative worlds that are able to engage audiences with fictional and socially-oriented stories.

DOI: 10.4324/9781003150862-8

The ImagisLab research group at the Department of Design of the Politecnico di Milano has been working on transmedia design since 2010, with the aim of defining processes, methods, and tools for experimentation with transmedia practice, and to extend such practice to areas beyond entertainment (Ciancia, 2018; Ciancia et al., 2018; Piredda et al., 2015). ImagisLab is a design research and teaching group focused on building brands, stories, and communication experiences. Research and education are strongly integrated into hands-on and in-field activities for building audiovisual content, communication strategies, gaming experiences, and transmedia storytelling for branding and social innovation. Our passion is shaping and disseminating stories, working collaboratively in various contexts and experimenting with narrative experiences and interactions. Since 2013, we have been developing a design methodology for conceiving transmedia communication strategies through a research and teaching project named *Plug Social TV*.

Plug Social TV: An Example of Situated Narrative Practice

In this chapter, we present *Plug Social TV*, a project developed in a suburban area of Milan (the Bovisa and Dergano neighborhoods). For three years (2013–2016), the project involved not only the university (Politecnico di Milano) but also the zoning board of the suburban area of Milan (Zona 9, which is now known as Municipio 9), citizens, artisans, retailers, and neighborhood associations. The project is an experiment in collaborative design that involves multiple participants (i.e., students, researchers, citizens, and associations) and is configured as a design studio that aims to test the use of transmedia practice as an engine of identity and engagement processes to support the new needs of these two neighborhoods of Milan.

Dergano and Bovisa are two working-class districts located in the northeastern outskirts of Milan. At the beginning of the 20th century, this area was the location of the first two Italian film institutes (SAFFI Comerio, later named Milano Films[1] and Armenia Films[2]). The end of the century signaled the beginning of an era distinguished by continuous planning activities in the two districts. These began with the dismantling of factories and involving the building of the university complex of the Politecnico di Milano in 1994. What remains constant in Dergano and Bovisa are activities related to the human and social relations of the neighborhood, with small specialty shops, workshops, restaurants, and several cultural and social associations becoming a distinguishing feature of the area. Students from the School of Architecture and the School of Design at the Politecnico di Milano add to a local population composed of elderly workers, artisans, professionals, and immigrant populations from several countries (mostly China, Egypt, and the Philippines[3]), who have settled in Dergano and Bovisa over the past 30 years. These two suburbs of Milan continue to undergo profound social, economic, and urban transformations, remaining an excellent ground for testing the ability of communication strategies to support community building, construction of collaborative networks through transmedia practice, and experimentation with new production processes (e.g., sustainable business models, crowdsourcing, and crowdfunding).

Since 2013, action research and in-field education activities that occur on and off the School of Design's campus of the Politecnico di Milano have included multiple participants and perspectives. Within the *Plug Social TV* project, more than 100 design students, approximately six design researchers, citizens, and local associations meet each other in academic or urban contexts to develop social dialogue and collaboration, weaving factual and fictional worlds to express a shared vision of a better future (Anzoise et al., 2014; Piredda & Fassi, 2015). *Plug Social TV* is a multichannel communication system based on storytelling that has four principal aims: to create a shared imagination through the power of story; to provide dialogue and enhance engagement among citizens, local associations, and students; to support the repossession of the area on behalf of the citizens to encourage a greater degree of cohesion; and to experiment and teach transmedia practice in a design school within a social innovation field.

The *Plug Social TV* project has produced a bespoke multichannel communication system distributed across various social media platforms and developed according to a situated process of listening to and collaboration with the local community. This activity of listening to the community is an important attribute of social TV, as highlighted by using the word *social* in the name of the research project itself. In the context of the project, the term *social* refers to the fact that the main distribution platforms are social media—Facebook (www.facebook.com/plugsocialtv), YouTube (www.youtube.com/plusocialtv), Twitter (twitter.com/plugsocialtv), and Instagram (@frammenti_plug/@Adam_Plug)—and to the fact that social networks and social television are recognized by researchers as playing a pivotal role in the processes of self-representation and self-narration (Anzoise et al., 2014). In fact, storytelling has become the core of the project because of the ability of stories to define a rich and common ground for discussion and involvement of people. It becomes a catalyst for growth and change.

Students from the Master of Science in Communication Design program develop the *Plug Social TV* project and the transmedia content it spreads. We employ a research-through-design approach where hands-on activities encourage students to experience the use of transmedia practice and the power of storytelling in their design practice. This leads us toward defining a methodology for transmedia design.

To define the process of transmedia design and the set of tools used to support the student designers in conceiving and developing transmedia communication projects, we tested them in three different editions of the course *Final Design Studio*:

1   Fuoricampo#1. From October 2013 to January 2014, a class of 45 master's students developed transmedia storytelling projects and distributed

them through *Plug Social TV*. This built a shared mental image of the neighborhood to support the local citizens reclaiming the urban space. In this process, the students were guided by a guiding document: the *Paper Format* (detailed in the following).

2   Fuoricampo#2. From October 2014 to January 2015, a class of 53 students designed and developed transmedia content for *Plug Social TV* in reference to four subjects: food, work, culture, and green urban spaces. To develop this transmedia content, the students were equipped with the *Transmedia Building Model*, an early-stage instrument developed during a Ph.D. research (Ciancia, 2018).

3   Fuoricampo#3. From October 2015 to January 2016, a class of 17 students unpacked and reframed storyworlds that were selected from the first and second editions of the course. In this year, the students were equipped with the final version of the *Transmedia Building Model* (Ciancia, 2018) and the following set of tools developed by the Imagis-Lab research group to support both storyworld and character creation: *Storyworld Canvas, Character Wheel,* and *Story Map* (Ciancia et al., 2018; Mariani & Ciancia, 2019; Piredda et al., 2015; Venditti, 2017).

We conducted participant observation (DeWalt & DeWalt, 2010) of students designing their transmedia works in order to understand and compare the effectiveness of the processes and provided tools, and to explore their potential within the design of transmedia curricula. The School of Design also created statistical reports and gathered qualitative feedback from students through formal questionnaires at the end of each course for the assessment of the teaching effectiveness. These data allowed us to evaluate the processes and narrative apparatus we had been employing. After two iterations, we arrived at the definition of the *Transmedia Building Model*, and the set of tools for designing narratives.

First Year of Experimentation—Fuoricampo#1: Identity, New Media, and Storytelling for Social Innovation

In the first year (2013/2014 academic year), the design studio Fuoricampo#1 aimed to test and prototype the use of stories as an engine of identity processes and community engagement. There were two main objectives: to inform the inhabitants of the two neighborhoods of Milan (Dergano and Bovisa) of the existence of the social innovation initiatives, and to design new initiatives with their involvement. In this process, a core aim was to use storytelling activities to create awareness around existing social innovation best practices (local, national, and international), and understanding of the stakeholders through the use of design thinking and co-design approaches. The final result was the launch of a social television (TV) system that collected and published all the student-designed transmedia content.

The entire design process was composed of three phases: 1) the exploration of eight parks and public greens in the neighborhoods; 2) the development of transmedia content for the social TV; and 3) the audiovisual production of the content.

The first phase aimed to explore the local areas and collect visual documentation, audiovisual content, and oral histories to create a repository of stories and contents. The activity of *flânerie* (the art of strolling and looking through the urban landscape as a spectator) and the critical technique of the *dérive* (Debord, 1958) (the rapid unplanned drifting through the physical space of the city) were followed by the co-design workshop named *In a Garden* on October 26, 2013. Small groups of students consisting of an interior designer and two communication designers interacted with the citizenry. The workshop required the students to identify the narrative that would become the core of the transmedia concept through the use of photos, sketches, mind maps, interviews, notes, and keywords collected by the young designers and the citizens. The main output of this activity was a narrative braid, created from the combination of narrative threads derived from the testimonies of the citizens collected during the workshop. This narrative braid was required to include at least the following narratological elements: two characters, one object, one place, and one main action.

Over the following month, the materials collected during the exploration of the neighborhoods were developed and transformed into minidocumentaries (Galbiati et al., 2013), which were later shown to the local citizens during an exhibition at the Dergano-Bovisa library on December 14, 2013. The exhibition aimed to activate a discussion between the students and the community, particularly given that some of the citizens were also the characters of the collected stories and audiovisual works. The exhibition was also an opportunity to launch *Plug Social TV* using Facebook (as the main platform), YouTube, and Twitter (the Instagram profile was to be added in May 2015) to present to the community the social TV as the collector of their future transmedia narratives.

In the second phase, the students were engaged in the development of transmedia content with the objective of encouraging community-based storytelling, activating the involvement of stakeholders, and helping to build an active community. Starting from the material collected and the stories gathered during the neighborhood explorations, the students were asked to build storyworlds and develop story arcs that could be primarily disseminated online as a web series, as well as in offline media. To sustain the process of designing a transmedia project, we provided student designers with the *Paper Format*, which is a project description document defined from existing project management tools that had been developed previously by practitioners in the transmedia field: the *Project Reference Guide (Bible)* by Pratten (2011) and the *Transmedia Production Bible* by Hayes (2011). The *Paper Format* document consisted of the following four sections:

1   Storyworld: This contained data about the narrative context, synopsis, and storylines, and their plot points, characters, and project tagline.

2 Media Structure: This referenced the description of the channels and platforms involved in the distribution of the storylines, the possible modes of interaction, and the user journey with touchpoints for the audience.
3 Business and Production: This focused on the business model of the designed system, pushing students to include crowdfunding and crowdsourcing processes in content production, and to create tentative partnerships and collaboration with local stakeholders.
4 Format Description: This referenced the description of the narrative, the art direction, and the production indications. This section was added by us specifically for the design of the web series.

Despite the short duration of the design studio (4 months), in the third and final phase, the students produced audiovisual content designed to promote the transmedia format, populate the editorial plan of *Plug Social TV*, and continue to maintain the engagement of the community that we began to build in the first phase of the project. The results of this first experimentation were nine projects designed by different groups of students, each of them characterized by its own genre, language, tone of voice, media structure, and level of audience involvement.

The positive aspects of the course highlighted by the students were the application of storytelling and communication strategies to social issues (e.g., green urban spaces, food culture, sustainable cities and communities, and safeguard of the cultural heritage) and the relationships they built with local associations. The young designers described the interaction with real stakeholders as frustrating but highly valuable training before they would enter the professional world. Often the production plan of the projects should be re-organized according to the availability of the stakeholders, provoking a delay in the development of the content. However, it let the students have an authentic work experience (valuable for their future). The main negative aspect highlighted by the students was the short amount of time dedicated to developing this transmedia project.

While the lectures and the learning-by-doing approach worked well to provide students with general knowledge about designing transmedia projects, the proposed *Paper Format* was not fully functional. Integrating the two documents, the *Transmedia Bible* and the *Paper Format*, which are usually used separately, led students to focus immediately on the single storyline of the web series, rather than on the narrative world. This led to the design of nine projects that were well developed from a narrative perspective, but that made little use of the potential of multichannel distribution that is typical of transmedia practice; they had essentially linear stories (and were not real narrative worlds).

As a consequence, we decided to expand the possible topics during the following experimentation in an attempt to increase the degree of creativity of the students. We provided them with a revised and updated version of the strategic document for designing transmedia systems: the *Transmedia Building Model*.

Second Year of Experimentation—Fuoricampo#2: Identity, Transmedia, and Storytelling for Social Innovation

Throughout 2014, *Plug Social TV* stayed active in communicating the social initiatives of the neighborhoods, such as events, workshops, and activities carried on by the local associations. One year after the launch of the project (October 2014), *Plug Social TV* presented nine web-series promos, nine minidocumentaries, and a series of extra content such as interviews, snippets of collected stories, and citizen anecdotes that had been gathered by the students of Fuoricampo#1 and archived and distributed by a small editorial staff composed of the researchers involved. The goal of the second year of experimentation (2014/2015 academic year) was to develop new transmedia content for *Plug Social TV*. The aim was to create narrative worlds and disseminate these worlds through different media (analog and digital) in order to engage the community of the Bovisa and Dergano districts through processes of engagement, collaboration, and co-creation that would catalyze action there. The continued profound social, economic, and urban transformations of these districts make the area excellent for testing the ability of communication strategies to support community building. Through the construction of collaborative networks through transmedia design and experimentation with new production processes, the students were challenged to design transmedia projects that would connect local communities and their cultural relative values with the universal values recalled by shared stories. This created narrative worlds with the involvement of stakeholders to experiment and promote diverse models of content generation (such as co-branding, product placement, and branded content). In this edition, we decided to give students the opportunity to choose the project focus from among the following four topics: food (connected to the theme of the Expo Milan 2015: *Feeding the Planet, Energy for Life*), work, culture, and green urban spaces. We proposed a process with two phases: 1) listening (citizenry) and strategizing, the main objective of which was to define a digital strategy for the social TV and 2) transmedia content development and audiovisual production.

As in the previous year, the designers undertook an exploration of the territory, gathering stories, interviews, and visual material. The goal was to build an archive of narrative content about the neighborhoods to keep the social TV active while waiting for the editorial plan to be created by the students. The outputs were semi-finished products (e.g., photos, videos, sketches, interviews, keywords, video sketches) distributed across the platforms to tell a story about Dergano, Bovisa, and their inhabitants. These semi-finished products are unfinished, deliberately rough communication artifacts that illustrate a project still in process and engage the audience in the act of completion (Piredda et al., 2013). This process allowed us to use this content for nurturing and activating socially-constructed imagery to produce new knowledge (Durand, 1999). In parallel to the collection of narrative contents, the students were asked to rebuild a strategic setup for *Plug Social TV*, and to plan the distribution of the narrative content, referring to data coming from Facebook Insight and YouTube Analytics. The results were two documents: the digital strategy for *Plug Social TV* and the editorial plan describing the online content management.

As in the previous edition, the results of the first phase were introduced with a neighborhood launch event of the renewed social TV, the aim of which was again to draw the local community's attention to the content designed and produced by the design studio Fuoricampo#2.

The second phase developed transmedia content about the subject chosen by each team of students from among the four topics. This resulted in story-based systems about food, work, culture, and green urban spaces created to enhance community engagement. In this edition, ten transmedia projects were designed, all of which were characterized by a coordinated and complementary connection among the different analog and digital channels of *Plug Social TV*, rather than representing simple duplication of content. These ten narrative worlds considered the affordances of the chosen channels. They were hybrid experiences in which the overlapping of real and virtual activities encourages new forms of interaction and participation, providing for the active involvement of the identified audience. Indeed, the design studio course produced ten transmedia projects shaped as distributed stories on social media and situated storytelling experiences (exhibitions and workshops).

Working on correcting the problems that had emerged in the previous edition, we equipped the students with a revised and updated version of the strategic document to guide the design and description of the project in its entirety. This document, named the *Transmedia Building Model*, was composed of the following four sections:

1 Storyworld: This contained descriptions of the narrative world, characters, storylines, and their connections within the real world.
2 Functional Specification: This was the strategic development of the transmedia content for achieving the project's objectives. This section was devoted to defining the target users and personas, media channels, devices involved, multichannel structure, and the rules of engagement (i.e., touchpoints, entry points, and the rabbit hole). The suggested tools were those coming from the design field, such as user personas and user journey maps (tools with which design students are commonly familiar).
3 Productive Specification: This concerned the specifications that enable designers to proceed with the project's implementation and sustainability (i.e., business model, production team, partnerships, and sponsorships).

4   Promotion and Communication Strategy: This section entails creating the communication strategy for the project's launch.

Students were asked to create a short film designed as a cornerstone of the transmedia project to be distributed on YouTube and promoted through a teaser distributed on Facebook.

This second experimentation demonstrated to us how that the narrative worldbuilding activity is a design issue that requires a systemic approach of ideation, planning, and production. The ten transmedia projects designed prove to be more mature than the nine projects in the first edition: The former were well-developed storyworlds, leading to great possibilities in terms of multichannel distribution, while the latter were mainly linear stories focused on a single media channel. This confirmed that the prototype project description document (*Transmedia Building Model*) and the developed methodology fulfilled their purpose. However, some difficulties arose in the worldbuilding and scriptwriting activities. According to the students' feedback, the main challenge of the projects was to build the storyworlds in the allotted time given that the first part of the course (2 months) was dedicated to the exploration of the territory, leaving only a month and a half to complete the media production phase of project.

An interesting result of this second edition was that we obtained fascinating audiovisual artifacts that did not completely succeed in conveying the narrative world. As a consequence, we decided to begin the third experimentation from some of the storyworlds developed in the previous two editions, thus providing the future students with a set of design narrative tools to support them in the worldbuilding and scriptwriting activities

Third Year of Experimentation—Fuoricampo#3: Everyday Heroes

To push forward the research in the third edition (2015/2016 academic year), the challenge presented to the design students was to develop transmedia projects that expand upon the narrative worlds built over the previous editions. The process consisted of the following two phases: 1) worldbuilding and story creation and 2) transmedia project development. In both phases, students were supported by the *Transmedia Building Model*, a tool for designing and managing the complexity of multichannel projects, whose final form was consolidated and enhanced, thanks to the observations and feedback of students who had used preliminary versions of the document. The information we gathered from the students in the first two editions allowed us to reflect on the methods and tools used in the course, and to revise the *Transmedia Building Model* document. The final model was composed of four main sections, each of them accompanied by the indication of specific steps, tools, and existing platforms to support the conception of transmedia content:

1 Storyworld: This is the first point to be dealt with in transmedia design, whether it is created from scratch (top-down crafting) or inferred from an existing story (bottom-up creation) (Dowd et al., 2013).
2 Narrative Content: This refers to the definition of the main narrative, the so-called cornerstone of the transmedia project, the starting point to which all the other possible and multiple story threads will be referring. To develop this definition, it is necessary to identify characters, storylines, plot points, and art direction.
3 Functional Specifications: This is the strategic distribution of the narrative content across the media involved.
4 Production Specifications: This concerns the elements that enable designers to proceed with the project's implementation (business model) and management (audience building strategies and community management).

During the first phase, the students were divided into teams which chose one of the five storyworlds selected from the previous editions. After the analysis of the imaginary world, the students highlighted the pivotal values of the world created, involving the neighborhood stakeholders for designing and developing new story braids. To achieve this, the young designers were provided with the following tools for designing and describing the fictional world, characters, and their storylines: *Storyworld Canvas*, *Character Wheel*, and *Story Map*. *Storyworld Canvas* is a narrative design tool for the qualitative description of a narrative world based on the elements identified by Pinardi and De Angelis (2006): *topos* (environment), *epos* (background story), *ethos* (value system), *telos* (life goals and objectives), *logos* (language), *genos* (system of relations), and *chronos* (the world evolution through time).

To assist the students in designing robust characters and their storylines, we developed the other two tools: *Character Wheel* and *Story Map*. As with narrative worlds, we derived from narratology some reference descriptors to support character design: the tool named *Character Wheel* allows characters to be described according to their inner world (age, gender, ethnicity, nationality, physical and mental skills, and personality) and their external world (environment—where they live, social class, civil status, religion or other beliefs, education, work experience, habits, physical appearance, and favorite activities). A description of the characters through the psychological area, the physical area, and the sociological area allows us to depict not only the inner and outer worlds of the characters but also some specific traits connected to the identification of personal *telos* (i.e., the motivations that drive them to act, becoming the engine of the character arc through which their background stories are developed). Then, to sustain and feed the writing process, we provided students with the *Story Map* tool, which is a canvas for guiding the students in creating the character's storyline and developing a basic narrative structure according to the theory of equilibrium

(Todorov, 1971; Todorov & Weinstein, 1969), which states that a story must involve equilibrium, disruption, resolution (recognition, and the attempt to repair the damage), and a new equilibrium.

Once the narrative framework was defined, students moved on to the second phase in which they focused on developing the transmedia system, specifically using the third and fourth sections of the *Transmedia Building Model* (Functional and Production Specifications). In addition to the design of the content, the students were asked to promote the storyworlds and subsequently *Plug Social TV*, building participation in the neighborhood through the events named the Plug Social Workshops. The results were an exhibition (*7minutes, The Prodigious Event*[5]) that aimed to gather the Bovisa community, projecting into the real world the community's stories, characters, and atmosphere of the imaginary built world. Workshops organized with partners in the area launched the service designed by students (*I Dolci di Ettore*[6]), to allow new audiences to discover the realities of the artisan history in the neighborhood (*Artigianni*[7]), or to involve citizens in foreseeing the future of the neighborhood (*Bovisa 2116: Postcards from the Future*[8]).

According to the students' feedback, the Plug Social Workshops were a very positive element of the edition of this course. Indeed, the implementation of projects, in which citizen participation was crucial in assessing the actual impact of the work developed, encouraged students to reflect on the importance of the evaluation and measurement process in strategic communication.

Final Remarks

In the contemporary mediascape, the use of narrative structures deliberately in all genres of communication is of increasing importance. This mediascape also demands distributed narratives that allow for participation from the audience, qualities answered effectively through transmedia storytelling techniques. That is, communication designers must now adopt an approach to communication design that allows listening to and understanding the audience's needs, designing and managing the resulting storytelling strategies, building the narrative worlds, and developing robust characters that inhabit such worlds.

The 3-year experience of the *Plug Social TV* project allowed us to develop an approach to teaching transmedia design that includes theory, process, and tools for designing courses and workshops. These three aspects of the course are summarized in the following.

Theory

From a theoretical perspective, *transmedia design* is a discipline at the intersection of media studies and design culture that concerns the analysis, development (design, production, and distribution), and management of multichannel communication systems based on narrative worlds. This is a complex media field that requires the versatile skills of the transmedia designer, which include not only creativity, imaginative ability, and digital literacy but also managerial aptitude. Thus, it is of great importance to create teaching methods that can ensure the acquisition of such skills. Understanding the relationship between the transmedia phenomenon and the design field has allowed us to identify a dual role of transmedia design. Although this type of design is a practice that operates as a problem solver, it is above all a sense-maker.

Transmedia design acts as a problem-solving practice in relation to the process of developing complex narrative systems. Transmedia design works toward the optimization of content production not only from an artistic perspective but also from an economic perspective. Transmedia design is a discipline that allows the development of projects for multiple audiences with content spread through various media channels, providing consistency throughout the experience. In so doing, these projects can ensure a return on investment even though we live in a scenario characterized by audience fragmentation in which people consume content on different channels. In this sense, the design discipline is useful to transmedia practice because it allows the modeling of processes for the multichannel production such as design, development, and distribution processes of content. An example is the *Transmedia Building Model*: a tool for designing and managing multichannel projects that we developed and tested within the *Plug Social TV* project.

Transmedia design also acts as a sense-making practice. That is, it allows projects to become potent carriers of new meanings and knowledge because they are based on the activity of constructing worlds. The design discipline can support transmedia practice through the formalization of tools for managing the complexity of projects, and transmedia practice can enrich design activity. It enables the designer to go beyond simple storytelling and become a worldmaker. This makes it possible to create narrative-based projects to promote social change, giving spaces to the audience for self-expression, creativity, and community building. For example, the *Plug Social TV* experience was created with the aim of experimenting with the use of transmedia practice in the field of social innovation. The development of projects based on co-created fictional worlds as representations of reality and audience engagement made users discover existing activities and realities in the neighborhood, becoming part of an active community.

What has emerged with *Plug Social TV* experience is the ability of transmedia practice to activate processes in which the distribution of story-based strategies allows people to interpret and participate in the narratives that surround us every day. Thus, communication, storytelling, and design move from audience engagement to real processes of narrative change (ORSIMPACT, 2019).

Process

The evidence that emerged from the experimentation conducted in the three editions of the course is that the design process does not change, whether you are developing brand communication or social responsibility projects. The theoretical definition of the transmedia design discipline has allowed us to experiment and develop a process of action research and in-field education activities that included multiple participants and perspectives. The *Plug Social TV* project tackled aspects of communication design that are particularly pertinent in the current communication and design landscape. The contemporary mediascape mature professional designers capable of proposing concrete solutions, identifying emerging needs, guiding engagement processes, and managing the complexity of narrative artifacts distributed through multichannel strategies. From the perspective of design education, this has meant structuring a design studio course that integrates lectures with hands-on practice and co-design activities. This mode of learning is common to all courses provided by Politecnico di Milano's School of Design, where students are offered authentic challenges that allow them to develop the required skills through direct application of the tools and theories presented.

The transmedia design teaching activity described in this chapter consisted of three principal aspects: introduction and discussion of theoretical foundation for the disciplines involved; group work using existing tools and new instruments that were developed by the researchers to support the design process; and presentation and discussion of projects with the local community involved in the project, and collecting feedback from peers and stakeholders. The lectures took an active learning approach and applied strategies typical of active learning classrooms. The main topics of the lectures were transmedia storytelling used as a lever of innovative communication projects; digital strategy applied to the fields of corporate social responsibility and communication for social change; and audiovisual language used as a fundamental element in designing content for analog and digital media. However, the greatest specific value of the design studio Fuoricampo was the highly collaborative, team-centered approach it took. In fact, students enrolled in the courses have always worked in teams organized according to strategic and creative skills that are highly complementary. They incorporated the professional practices of the most traditional and established communication agencies and integrated skills and structures that design introduces into the marketplace. Lastly, the strongly collaborative approach was beneficial in the interaction with the stakeholders in the neighborhoods; the citizens understood as the audience of the projects, as well as the institutions, associations, and merchants who often acted as our sponsors or partners.

Tools

The experimentation conducted through the *Plug Social TV* project allowed us to work not only on the design process but also on providing students with specific tools aimed at empowering the conception and production of transmedia projects. Since 2013 we have conducted hands-on experimentation aimed at observing how the proposed methodology and the developed instruments affected the students' transmedia design practice. The result is a set of tools aimed to support and instruct in different design activities. The *Transmedia Building Model* is an instrument for designing and managing multichannel projects; *Storyworld Canvas*, *Character Wheel*, and *Story Map* are used to support building storyworlds, characters, and storylines. Each of these tools was developed through both teaching and research, and tested by more than 100 students in a period of three years.

In conclusion, the process for conceiving transmedia communication strategies developed by ImagisLab not only includes tools coming from the design thinking methodology but also introduces an ad hoc apparatus for the strategic design of narratives and collaborative story construction. We began with the idea that stories can be considered an intangible heritage of societies and that the dimension of sense-making is strictly connected to storytelling, both in relation to individual or collective creative processes and expression, and in relation to managing real narrative conflicts that trigger a need for change, a mediascape in which a close relationship between the real world and the fictional world has emerged. Design can make this relationship explicit by developing narrative systems that are capable of activating change and that create an impact on real life.

We believe that teaching transmedia design is essential in the curriculum of a design school, giving students the methods and tools to operate within contemporary society and enabling them to promote effective narrative change.

Acknowledgment

The authors would like to thank all the students from the School of Design, Politecnico di Milano and the colleagues who participated in the Plug Social TV project over the years: Gabriele Carbone, Marisa Galbiati, Katia Goldoni, Marco Ronchi, and Simona Venditti.

Notes

1 Milano Films is one of the main Italian film production companies. It was founded in 1909 by a previous company (SAFFI Comerio, which was founded in 1908), thanks to 20 financiers of the Milanese nobility who were interested in investing in the new industrial movie reality. Milano Films remained active until 1926. Among the films it produced was *L'Inferno* (1911), the first feature film in the history of Italian cinema.
2 Armenia Films was founded in 1917 on a plot of land owned by Milano Films. This was a film production, rental, purchase, and sales company owned by Johannes H. Zilelian.

3 These data are retrieved from the Milanese Integrated Statistical System at http://sisi.comune.milano.it/ (January 4, 2021).
5 The exhibition was designed and produced by Elena Corbari Verzelletti, Francesca Di Vito, Mario Martinasco, and Huiling Li.
6 The workshop was designed by Elisa Di Nofa, Pieralberto Faggian, Giuseppe Esposito, and Luca Raschi, and took place on January 30, 2016.
7 The workshop was designed by Umberto Dolcini, Zhang Ge, Simone Pietro Romei, and Riccardo Schito, and involved the collaboration of Fablab Milano and the local forge La Fucina di Efesto, and took place on January 23, 2016.
8 The workshop was organized and conducted by Gabriele Clemente, Rossella De Vico, Elisa Pintonello, Lorenzo Rizzoni, and Giulia Valentini and took place on January 30, 2016.

References

Anzoise, V., Piredda, F., & Venditti, S. (2014). Design narratives and social narratives for community empowerment. In C. Coletta, S. Colombo, P. Magaudda, A. Mattozzi, L. L. Parolin, & L. Rampino (Eds.), *A matter of design: Making society through science and technology* (pp. 935–950). STS Italia Publishing.

Ciancia, M. (2018). *Transmedia design framework: Design-oriented approach to transmedia practice*. FrancoAngeli.

Ciancia, M., Piredda, F., & Venditti, S. (2018). The design of imaginary worlds: Harnessing narrative potential of transmedia worlds: The case of watchmen of the nine. *Facta Ficta: Journal of Theory, Narrative & Media*, 2(2), 113–132. https://doi.org/10.5281/zenodo.3515110

Debord, G. (1958). Theory of the dérive. In K. Knabb (Ed.), *Situationist international anthology* (Revised and expanded ed., pp. 62–66). Bureau of Public Secrets.

Dena, C. (2009). *Transmedia practice: Theorising the practice of expressing a fictional world across distinct media and environments* [Doctoral dissertation, University of Sydney].

DeWalt, K. M., & DeWalt, B. R. (2010). *Participant observation: A guide for fieldworkers* (2 edizione). Altamira Pr.

Dowd, T., Niederman, M., Fry, M., & Steiff, J. (2013). *Storytelling across worlds: Transmedia for creatives and producers*. Focal Press.

Durand, G. (1999). *The anthropological structures of the imaginary*. Boombana Publications.

Fisher, W. R. (1984). Narration as a human communication paradigm: The case of public moral argument. *Communication Monographs*, 51(1), 1–22. https://doi.org/10.1080/03637758409390180

Frankel, L., & Racine, M. (2010, July 7). The complex field of research: For design, through design, and about design. In *Proceedings of the Design Research Society (DRS) International Conference*. DRS 2010–Design and Complexity, Montreal, Canada. https://dl.designresearchsociety.org/drs-conference-papers/drs2010/researchpapers/43

Frayling, C. (1993). *Research in art and design*. Royal College of Art.

Galbiati, M. L., Ciancia, M., Piredda, F., & Vezzoli, C. A. (2013). Integrating audio-visual communication into system design for sustainability. In Kirsi Niinimäki & Mira Kallio-Tavin (Ed.), *Dialogues for sustainable design and art pedagogy: The AH-Design project*. Aalto ARTS Books.

Hayes, G. P. (2011). *How to write a Transmedia Production Bible: A template for multiplatform producers*. Screen Australia. www.screenaustralia.gov.au/funding-and-support/feature-films/tools-and-insights

Mariani, I., & Ciancia, M. (2019). Character-driven narrative engine: Storytelling system for building interactive narrative experiences. In *Proceedings of the 2019 DiGRA International Conference: Game, Play and the Emerging Ludo-Mix* (pp. 1–19). www.digra.org/digital-library/publications/character-driven-narrative-engine-storytelling-system-for-building-interactive-narrative-experiences/

ORSIMPACT. (2019). *Measuring narrative change*. www.orsimpact.com/publications.htm

Pinardi, D., & Angelis, P. D. (2006). *Il mondo narrativo: Come costruire e come presentare l'ambiente e i personaggi di una storia*. Lindau.

Piredda, F., Ciancia, M., & Bertolotti, E. (2013). Animation as boundary object: Promoting cultural changes through audiovisual design. *2CO Communicating Complexity—2013 Conference Proceedings*, 234–243.

Piredda, F., Ciancia, M., & Venditti, S. (2015). Social media fiction: Designing stories for community engagement. In H. Schoenau-Fog, L. E. Bruni, S. Louchart, & S. Baceviciute (Eds.), *Interactive storytelling* (pp. 309–320). Springer International Publishing. https://doi.org/10.1007/978-3-319-27036-4_29

Piredda, F., & Fassi, D. (2015). In a garden: Designing gardens through storytelling. In L. Collin, L. Galluzzo, & A. Meroni (Eds.), *The virtuous circle design culture and experimentation* (pp. 119–129). McGrawHill.

Pratten, R. (2011). *Transmedia project reference guide (Bible)*. www.slideshare.net/ZenFilms/transmedia-project-reference-guide-bibl

Scolari, C., Bertetti, P., & Freeman, M. (2014). *Transmedia archaeology: Storytelling in the borderlines of science fiction, comics and pulp magazines*. Palgrave Macmillan.

Todorov, T. (1971). The 2 principles of narrative. *Diacritics*, *1*(1), 37–44. https://doi.org/10.2307/464558

Todorov, T., & Weinstein, A. (1969). Structural analysis of narrative. *NOVEL: A Forum on Fiction*, *3*(1), 70. https://doi.org/10.2307/1345003

Venditti, S. (2017). *Social media fiction: A framework for designing narrativity on social media* [Ph.D. Thesis, Politecnico di Milano]. http://hdl.handle.net/10589/132153

9 Transmedia Action Research
Progressive Pedagogy and Community Engagement

Leslie L. Dodson

This chapter posits *transmedia action research* as a new methodological construct fusing transmedia storytelling with action research theory and practice. This progressive practitioner and pedagogical approach is grounded in participatory community engagement practices that are informed by a transmedia action research logic. I examine the adoption and application of transmedia action research at Worcester Polytechnic Institute (WPI), a science, technology, engineering, and mathematics (STEM) university in Massachusetts, specifically in the context of the mandatory Interactive Qualifying Project (IQP). Each year, approximately 1,000 WPI students participate in the IQP, an interdisciplinary team-based social science research project in one of 50 project centers—from Bangkok to Cape Town and Cuenca to Yerevan—where students investigate and address global challenges. In 2017, various WPI faculty advisors interested in pursuing novel approaches to engineering education and global engagement at the intersection of STEM and society began introducing the new transmedia action research paradigm into domestic and international IQP projects. We found transmedia action research to be an effective engagement strategy in which stakeholders, students, and researchers share in the translation, composition, production, and distribution of storyworlds that bolster social change.

Creative Scholarship

The transmedia action research paradigm builds on previous community engagement scholarship, including participatory action research (PAR) and participatory learning and action (PLA). It expands those concepts to include the collaborative generation of multi-stakeholder, multi-platform storyworlds informed by research to create numerous entry points for community engagement. The goal of transmedia action research is to support deep participation by stakeholders and researchers in creating actionable information by and for community members using entertaining, embodied, and experiential storyworld logics. The transmedia action research described here involved the production of story assets that frame and articulate climate resilience, resulting in the development of storyworlds that encourage

DOI: 10.4324/9781003150862-9

both personal responsibility and community action. At their core, each storyworld project involved the co-creation of immersive, facilitated climate games with community members that, in concert with other transmedia assets, supported the necessity to know, act, and make evidence-based decisions at all levels of society. Central to transmedia action research, each storyworld was informed by the lived experiences of vulnerable community members. Thus, the approach challenges stakeholders and STEM students to think critically and imaginatively about assumptions, approaches, and possible solutions.

Action Research for a Better World

The Global Lab (the Lab) at WPI is committed to creative scholarship in service of global engagement. As co-director of the Lab, I conceived of and introduced transmedia action research—research with a social change agenda facilitated by innovative storytelling—into the IQP, which is a graduation requirement. The immersive social science IQP research project occurs at one of 50 global project centers where student teams work with faculty advisors on open-ended, community-centered research projects sponsored by civil society organizations, public agencies, or government sponsors.

Each year, the Lab introduces approximately 500 IQP students to the principles and practices of transmedia storytelling. Training is grounded in Henry Jenkins' acknowledgment that "in the ideal form of transmedia storytelling, each medium does what it does best" (Jenkins, 2003, p. 4). The Lab's definition of creative scholarship for social change adopts a "somewhat fluid" definition of transmedia storytelling that allows for "wide-ranging application" to catalyze social change (Hancox, 2014). This is consistent with Jenkins' recognition that:

> we are still in a period of experimentation and innovation. New models are emerging through production practices and critical debates, and we need to be open to a broad array of variations of what transmedia means in relation to different projects.
>
> (Jenkins, 2011, p. 14)

At the Global Lab, "storyworlding for the greater good" involves developing participatory practices that support community engagement informed by research and a transmedia action research logic.

Transmedia Action Research: A New Construct

As a new methodological construct, transmedia action research integrates transmedia storytelling with action research theory and practice to produce new knowledge and to co-generate "knowledge for action" (Cornwall & Jewkes, 1995). Transmedia action research asks researchers to be active participants in creating storyworlds with and for community members and stakeholders. With its explicit research and learning goals, transmedia action research differs from transmedia activism—although both seek positive social change as a desired outcome (Hancox, 2017).

With its emphasis on story-gathering and storytelling, transmedia action research acts to amplify social change by catalyzing new conversations between researchers and local stakeholders and between community members and institutional actors, thereby connecting formal sites of power with local communities. Transmedia action research stimulates co-creation and the coordination of storyworld assets to raise awareness, educate, and support decision-making and action. By amplifying extant media (through translation and reinterpretation) and by coproducing new media with community members, transmedia action research is centered at the nexus of research, storyworlding, and participatory community development.

This emergent concept is grounded in user-centered design principles and the tenets of participatory research (PR). It is also informed by insights from the fields of transmedia storytelling, creative science communication, decision science, community-based adaptation (CBA), and progressive pedagogy. Transmedia action research embraces participatory storytelling and story-gathering in all their manifestations as central to both the research endeavor and the social change agenda.

Theoretical and Methodological Considerations

Of the numerous action research approaches, transmedia action research is most closely aligned with participatory action research (PAR) and participatory learning and action (PLA) (Kemmis et al., 2014). Both PAR and PLA are members of a family of "approaches, methods, attitudes, behaviours and relationships, which enable and empower people to share, analyse and enhance their knowledge of their life and conditions, and to plan, act, monitor, evaluate and reflect" (IDS, n.d., p. 1). PAR and PLA both "promote the active participation of communities in the issues and interventions that shape their lives" (Thomas, 2001, p. 1).

Distinct from other qualitative research methods, participatory action research acknowledges that "local knowledge forms the basis for research and planning" (Cornwall & Jewkes, 1995, p. 1667). PAR generates intertwined relationships between researchers and stakeholders where "local people are involved in a process through which they are empowered to take charge of the research process and to organize to implement potential solutions or to take action" (Cornwall & Jewkes, 1995, p. 1671). Participatory learning and action does not have the same research demands but is nevertheless an approach where "communities are supported to analyse their own situation, make decisions about how to best tackle their problems, and, as a result, feel empowered to take action" (INTRAC, 2017, p. 1).

Furthermore, PLA examines the role of teaching as a force to understand and strengthen processes of civic engagement (Taylor & Fransmann, 2003).

Respect, Social Energy, and Storytelling

Creating or unblocking social energy is an explicit research outcome of participatory research. This is achieved by elevating local perspectives and personal experiences, which "support self-development and mobilise social energy and capacity for self-organised, often collective development/learning processes" (Hagmann et al., 2003, p. 21). Mobilizing social energy requires researchers to develop "a deep understanding of what 'drives' people . . . and how development is linked to the personal and collective potentials of people" (Hagmann et al., 2003, p. 21). Furthermore, initiatives that consider community values are more likely to be implemented, and stakeholder cooperation can help generate trust in organizations implementing the strategies (Vanderlinden et al., 2017).

Participatory and transmedia action research strategies share an appreciation of innovative methods "in new contexts with local people" where "research activities are expanded to encompass performance, art and storytelling" (Cornwall & Jewkes, 1995, p. 1671). Thomas (2001) notes that PLA "combines an ever-growing toolkit of participatory and visual methods with natural interviewing techniques" to facilitate collective analysis and learning (p. 1), as does transmedia storytelling. Furthermore, the transmedia action research approach to community engagement and participatory research echoes Sundin's observation that storytelling "has the potential to give evidence meaning, motivate and engage audiences and give relevance to their realities" (Sundin et al., 2018, p. 2). Additionally, enabling stakeholders to represent their own perspectives using visual and experiential tools such as photography, video, formal and informal text, analog media, and embodied play encourages all community members to participate regardless of age, ethnicity, or literacy (Thomas, 2001, p. 1; Cornwall & Jewkes, 1995).

Creative Climate Communication

Health, environment, and climate change initiatives (to name a few) rely on effective science communication to inform evidence-based decision-making (Joubert et al., 2019). Yet often, science communication does not "contain the information recipients need, in places where they can access it, in a form they can comprehend" (Fischhoff, 2013, p. 14037). Innovative communication tools, such as those incorporated in creative climate communications and transmedia storytelling, can help "transfer evidence and communicate it to multiple audiences (decision-makers, environmental managers, the public, etc.)" (Sundin et al., 2018, p. 3). Scholars and practitioners recognize that storytelling is a powerful form of science communication in that stories and contextual narratives link evidence and emotion, logos, and pathos to increase people's willingness to respond and act (Sundin et al., 2018). "When an audience becomes emotionally receptive of facts, chances increase that they will respond and act on the knowledge" (Sundin et al., 2018, p. 1).

Transmedia action research processes and products recognize story-gathering and storytelling as separate endeavors that yield both qualitative data and media for community engagement. Specifically, transmedia story-worlds aim to increase stakeholders' engagement with scientific information to support the implementation of evidence-based decisions: "By placing knowledge into context, stories are easier to process and generate more attention and engagement than traditional logical-scientific communication" (Sundin et al., 2018, p. 2). Of particular relevance to transmedia action research is scholarship on the role of experience in decision-making, often shared through stories. "Experience, because of the emotional pathways it triggers, can be a more effective means of knowledge-sharing than mere exposure to information" (Boycoff & Osnes, 2014, p. 5). Story-gathering by community members and action researchers showcases the importance and impact of lived experiences and stakeholders' understanding of the issues. Together, contextualized transmedia story assets, in concert with formal media, can motivate a willingness to act and improve decision-making.

Community-Based Adaptation and Climate Games

Transmedia action research is also consistent with the goals of community-based adaptation (CBA) in that both are "multi-dimensional, collaborative, inclusive approaches" (Boycoff & Osnes, 2014, p. 5; Koelle & Annecke, n.d.). Beneficial CBA, and arguably, effective transmedia action research, "is community-driven, empowering, and strengthens local capacity" (Ashley et al., 2009, p. 5). Scholars have observed that CBA initiatives featuring facilitated, analog climate games "help communities analyse the causes and effects of climate change, integrate scientific and community knowledge about climate change, and plan adaptation measures" (Reid et al., 2009, p. 13). As Boycoff and Osnes (2014) note, immersive games for children and adults that are "accessible, dynamic, adaptable, promote learning and dialogue" (p. 1) can effectively raise awareness and stimulate behavior changes. Crookall (2013), too, highlights the important role that "simulation/gaming and debriefing should play in educating people to combat climate change" (p. 195).

Educators, practitioners, and scholars recognize that educational games can help speed up the learning process and foster understanding at every age (Bachofen et al., 2012). Facilitated serious games are increasingly used as critical learning and behavior change tools for social and humanitarian efforts, enabling greater disaster resiliency and encouraging stakeholders to take action based on what they gained from the game (Clerveaux & Spence, 2009). "Purpose-driven playful environments" encourage better decision-making and the development of new behaviors in daily life (Boycoff & Osnes, 2014, p. 15). They can also inspire participants to discover common interests as well as differences in climate-risk-management priorities. As research tools, games provide opportunities to study community understanding of issues, evidence, and adaptation measures. By "acting out" what people would do in emergency situations, it is possible to identify misunderstandings or misconceptions—information that can feed back into game design (Clerveaux & Spence, 2009).

The Red Cross Red/Crescent Climate Centre is a leader in the development of serious games designed to speed up learning, dialogue, and action on climate risks (*Climate Centre*, n.d.). By enabling players to "inhabit" the reality of climate-risk-management strategies through embodied play, players are able to test plausible futures in a captivating and fun way (Bachofen et al., 2012).

Case Studies in Transmedia Action Research and Serious Climate Games

In each WPI Interactive Qualifying Project case study discussed in the following, transmedia story products addressed climate change knowledge gaps by connecting formal "top-down" information with "bottom-up" personal narratives (Ashley et al., 2009). These storyworld assets sought to enhance individual and community capacities to deal with complex, dynamic climate conditions by "meeting people where they are" while inspiring and enabling new considerations, meaningful learning, and sustained climate-risk-management behaviors (Boycoff & Osnes, 2014).

Each case study explores challenges and opportunities to improving disaster risk strategies (i.e., climate awareness, risk management, and readiness) at short-, medium-, and long-range decision-making timeframes. Each examines the role of student scholars as "transmediary" agents of change. This is a complex and dynamic role in which students served as media-makers and information mediators brokering content by and between policymakers, civil society organizations, scientists, engineers, activists, and under-and-unserved community members. These simultaneous endeavors are the foundation of transmedia action pedagogy.

While in the field, student teams pursued deliberate and less-planned approaches to composing and recomposing climate awareness storyworlds by repurposing media and adapting Climate Centre games to amplify adaptation awareness and action. It is important to note that in transmedia action research, the existence of media assets alone does not constitute a sufficiently robust social-action storyworld. Transmedia action storyworlds are actively constructed through the creation of new relationships between extant and new media, as well as between formal institutions and affected communities, to explicitly drive social change informed by social science research. The transmedia action research approach required researchers and collaborators to curate and rescale existing institutional (i.e., organizational or government) media to make it relevant to community stakeholders, and it required the coproduction of new, tailored media products by, with and for community members into comprehensive storyworlds for research and social change. The main locus of co-creation remained at the community level where students and stakeholders worked and played together to design, adapt, iterate, refine, and evaluate climate games and other storyworld products.

Teams collected and coproduced storyworld assets such as audio interviews and video vignettes to inform campaigns while simultaneously conducting research on user-centered design principles applied to game dynamics and mechanics. Project research questions focused on how transmedia assets improve, promote, or scale up adaptive thinking and action and how a transmedia action research approach contributes to more effective community engagement.

Albania: Storyworld for Marginalized Communities

> Making outreach a cooperative process can help build trust in both the overall plan and the organizations implementing the plan. Allowing for feedback increases personal investment in the risk mitigation projects.
> —(Dickinson et al., 2017, p. 31)

The 2017 "Reducing Flood Risk in Shkodra Through Community Engagement" transmedia action research IQP explored the production of a transmedia storyworld to reduce exposure to flood-related risks in northern Albania. Working with members of marginalized communities, including the Roma population, rural farmers, and women's organizations, along with emergency responders, this project addressed short-term planning, preparation, and decision-making in the flood-prone Drin-Buna River Basin.

The lowland Shkodër Region is part of an extensive waterway spanning Albania, Macedonia, Kosovo, and Montenegro. Moderate flooding occurs annually, but the area faces increasing risk of flood frequency and intensity due to climate change (Deutsche Gesellschaft für Internationale Zusammenarbeit (GIZ), 2015). In 2010, a catastrophic flood inundated the area, displacing 14,500 families, endangering 16,500 animals, and swamping nearly 25 square miles (15,000 acres) (IFRC, 2011). As of 2017, the poorest families still had not recovered from the flood.

The student research team assisted the Climate Change Adaptation in Flood Risk Management, Western Balkans (CCAW) project of Deutsche Gesellschaft für Internationale Zusammenarbeit (GIZ), the German development agency. GIZ, along with researchers from Albania's Institute for Geosciences, Energy, Water and Environment, government ministries, and the meteorological agency had previously produced various climate and flood management media including an elaborate 138-page Flood Risk Management (FRM) report, flood maps, scientific papers, printed evacuation routes, and alerts. While useful, these institutional assets did not reach or address the needs of people marginalized by social stigma (e.g., the Roma) or geographic isolation (e.g., farmers). Unidirectional media were often not available, understandable, or actionable by residents and much of it was not suitable for low-literate populations. Furthermore, the extant media did not constitute a storyworld: it was structured, logical, formal, and top-down, rather than expansive, iterative, and nonlinear. Pursuing a transmedia action research approach, researchers and stakeholders co-created accessible and actionable flood risk tools to complement mono-logic scientific and institutional media. The Albania climate transmedia storyworld ultimately included a bi-lingual facilitated climate game, photographs, a video, and a family emergency planning toolkit that featured easy-to-understand illustrations as well as text, all of which harmonized with other decision support tools.

User-Centered Design

Fieldwork revolved around "meeting people where they are," listening to stories of vulnerability, trauma, and loss in various areas, including farmhouses in Obot and Dajç, a Shkodër fire station, an Illyrian Village warehouse, and a restaurant in Zus. Over the course of seven weeks, the student research team collected 21 oral histories (contextual narratives) and conducted six key informant interviews that generated data and community engagement. Focus groups were sites of participatory, user-centered design and co-creation of a suite of analog and digital storyworld assets on flood risks, flood preparation, and evacuation procedures. Walking tours (embodied research) and community-supplied photos and videos (photo-elicitation) informed a "Voices of the 2010 Flood" video, which stimulated conversations about how to better prepare for floods.

> We sought to understand the gap between the expert knowledge expressed in the GIZ plan and local perceptions of floods and flood risks. To do this, we collected information on people's experiences in

past floods and then used these insights to identify vulnerabilities based on people's preparation for and responses to flooding. We developed tools to facilitate the transfer of information from the comprehensive FRM plan presented by GIZ to those who are actually at risk.

(Dickinson et al., 2017, p. 40)

Before the Flood Game

Interviews and fieldwork with firefighters, women's groups, farmers, and Roma people led to the creation of the "Before the Flood" game, modeled on one designed by the Climate Centre (*Climate Centre*, n.d.). In this multi-stakeholder sorting game, players share past experiences about floods and devise steps to reduce risks by ranking preparation action cards such as untying animals or clearing ditches, coupled with weather forecast and time cards. The highly visual game better aided those who could not read text and was accompanied by a *Family Fill-In Emergency Guide* synthesizing information from GIZ brochures. (Material was produced in both Albanian and English.) In a sign that the storyworld approach had value, those living with the specter of flooding suggested additional storyworld features that might help them prepare for future floods, including a children's flood readiness song, cartoons, flood art, a graphic novel, bracelets, stickers, and (informed but informal) brochures.

Climate Grief

Immersive community engagement, which is central to transmedia action research, helped promote agency at the individual, family, and community levels. Supporting personal and community agency through "serious" games can help offset what Climate Centre researchers call climate grief:

> Climate change may often be accompanied by "climate grief" which happens when people feel defeated by a sense of inescapable doom. However, games give people an outlet to express their concerns in a fun and welcoming environment, without undermining the seriousness of the issues.
>
> (Cuendet et al., 2020, p. 24; Suarez, n.d.)

Indeed, the "Before the Flood" gameplay "created a momentary sense of community, sparked discussion and debate, and kept people's attention" (Dickinson et al., 2017, p. 96). The *Family Fill-In Emergency Guide* helped define and support personal responsibility in flood preparation by framing participants as owners of a plan reflecting their family's needs, while the video, with images and voices of neighbors and relatives, stimulated discussions about the need to prepare for floods.

The Shkodra transmedia action research storyworld set out to help stakeholders protect themselves from economic loss and physical danger by affording "a group of people who describe themselves as hopeless an opportunity to take action" (Dickinson et al., 2017, p. 11). Student researchers, though, came to understand that action research involves more than action. The storyworld, with its formal and informal media, serious game, and community input, helped "people to live life with a little less fear of the next flood, a little more confidence that their efforts can change the outcome of a flood, and the knowledge that people do care about their experiences and situations" (Dickinson et al., 2017, p. 111).

New Zealand: Business and Serious Play

In addition to educating business leaders on the effects of sea-level rise, playing a serious game detaches them from their own experiences. This allows them to learn about the issues in the context of a playful perspective.
—(Cuendet et al., 2020, p. 57)

Seaview Gracefield is an industrial hub of marine services, light industry, waste processing, and machine shops in a low-lying coastal area near Wellington, New Zealand. The 2020 transmedia action research IQP, "Adapting to Rising Sea Levels in Seaview Gracefield, New Zealand: Developing the *Seaview Sea-Level 'Sea-narios'* Climate Game" focused on adult learning and shared decision-making to mitigate an array of impacts from rising seas and a rising water table, which are projected to intensify with climate change.

The fragile and critical industrial area employs approximately 7,000 people in 700 businesses, some of which are hazardous facilities (Cuendet et al., 2020). When intense rainfall events occur, Seaview Gracefield is prone to several types of flooding including inundation due to poor drainage capacity; storm surges; overtopping of embankments; and flooding from surface runoff (GWRC, 2017). The Greater Wellington Regional Council (GWRC), a government agency, works to mitigate flood risk in the area. Along with partners in the science, policy, and planning arenas, the GWRC had previously produced policy briefs, emergency response directives, and climate projections. Nevertheless, the GWRC identified the need to better understand how owners of small- and medium-sized enterprises plan, prepare, and make decisions over a medium-term horizon (up to 50 years).

To understand business priorities and gauge knowledge of climate change and sea-level rise, student researchers conducted 20 interviews with business leaders, chamber of commerce members, and local politicians. These contextual narratives revealed that many business leaders were unaware of educational resources available to them. Interviews also revealed a lack of awareness of climate risks accompanied by a lack of urgency to make business contingency plans. Student researchers determined that "without a baseline of knowledge of the effects of sea-level rise on infrastructure and business operations, we determined that it is premature to expect businesses to be planning for something they do not understand" (Cuendet et al., 2020, p. 60).

To galvanize decision-making in response to rising seas, the STEM students simplified climate models and other scientific information into a climate scenario fact sheet highlighting flood risks and vulnerabilities in the Seaview Business District. The *Climate Change Fast Facts: How Will it Affect You?* brochure featured information on urban infrastructure vulnerabilities and insurance implications. The image-rich fact sheet and other visuals served as both data and discussion tools, used as educational aids in interviews and as tools to help researchers and GWRC understand business leaders' current understanding of climate change. The fact sheet was enhanced by photo-elicitation, a social science research method in which stakeholders provide personal media.

> Visual aids such as maps communicate vulnerability quickly and clearly. Short textual facts supplement the visuals. By showing rather than telling what will happen due to climate change, we were able to both educate business leaders and gain their perspectives on how sea-level rise was, or might, affect their businesses.
> (Cuendet et al., 2020, p. 27)

The Sea-narios Game

Serious gameplay for adults was a core component of this transmedia action research project. The *Seaview Sea-level "Sea-narios" Climate Game* (adapted from the Climate Centre's "Act to Adapt" game) highlighted specific risks to Seaview businesses, informed by walkabouts and interviews with business owners. The game featured localized industrial flood hazards such as groundwater inundation, susceptible gas pipes, and water-damaged industrial equipment. It was designed to spark conversations about the effect of sea-level rise on business owners in Seaview Gracefield while also exploring self-interests and community interests. During gameplay, players are directed to collectively decide which vulnerable shared assets to prioritize while also protecting business-specific assets.

GWRC advised researchers on learning outcomes for the game, which centered on creating a cognitive experience of the impact of flooding and sea-level rise in Seaview. Specific learning outcomes focused on the ability of business owners to identify infrastructure vulnerable to different types of flooding and to recognize the importance and urgency of proactive planning in the context of climate uncertainty. By integrating extant media from GWRC and other sources with new, co-generated storyworld elements, the transmedia action research team amplified the reach of institutional media, making it more accessible and relevant to small- and medium-size businesses. Furthermore, in projects that address adult decision-makers, transmedia story elements are effective dialogic instruments inspiring meaningful discussions about measures that individuals and communities can take. Transmedia action research methods also created linkages "from the ground" up to the sponsoring agency with the expectation that "this information, and the perspectives of nearly two dozen business leaders in Seaview Gracefield provide the sponsor with material and insight they can use for additional community engagement" (Cuendet et al., 2020, p. 60).

Greece: Educational Climate Games

> *We are in the process of growing up, but we still love to play games.*
> —Greek Student at KPE

The 2019 "Educating Greek Students about Climate Change through Serious Games" IQP was designed with and for 13- to 15-year-old Greek students in Thessaloniki, Greece's second largest city. The transmedia action research project resulted in the creation of an extensive educational toolkit of 14 climate games and related media, many of which were tested with 185 schoolchildren. Sponsored by the Environmental Education Centre of Eleftherio Kordelio (KPE), the project focused on long-term, generational change.

KPE Thessaloniki is one of 54 centers established by Greece's Ministry of Education to educate local communities about the environment and sustainable development (*KPE*, n.d.). KPE had incorporated games into prior programs, and for this WPI project, the organization sought new ways to help students recognize the impacts of climate change on individuals—and the effects of individuals on climate change (Gulezian et al., 2019). As Cordero et al. (2008) note, "effective climate change education should emphasize the personal connection between the student, energy, and climate change using active learning methods" (p. 871).

Urban Resilience

In Greece, climate change is projected to have wide-ranging detrimental effects. Climate models project that between 2045 and 2065, Greece may face up to 20 more heat-wave days per year. These are expected to be accompanied by a 12% decrease in rainfall and a sea-level rise of up to 59 cm—an array of climate shocks and stresses driving the need for education on urban resilience strategies (Georgakopoulos, 2017). KPE's educational initiatives are part of a large-scale action plan that includes Thessaloniki's membership in the "100 Resilient Cities" network, along with the city's 2030 Resiliency Plan, considered to be components of a civic-scale transmedia storyworld.

IQP students pursued a mixed-methods transmedia action research approach to developing game content and gameplay mechanics. They developed story-gathering and storytelling tools to gauge teenagers' climate knowledge, including surveys that revealed a knowledge gap about climate science, carbon dioxide contributions to the greenhouse gas effect, and how climate change drives changes in habitable land. Researchers piloted, tested, evaluated, and published a portfolio of 14 climate games with and for students and KPE faculty. Some games, including *Answer with your Feet, Before the Storm, Sinking Island, Extreme Weather Tag,* and *Race for Resilience,* were adapted from Red Cross Red/Crescent humanitarian games. Each game was supported by visualizations, and each included a climate change lesson plan.

The Greek students helped design and field-test six games, including the *Sinking Island* teamwork and strategy game where groups compete to stay on their shrinking (paper) island threatened by rising sea levels, and the *Before the Storm* card game that addresses extreme weather events and resilience strategies.

Game Mechanics

Student researchers found that blending entertainment with information was paramount. The most effective climate games were simple, flexible, and featured continuous challenges. The suite of games included "physical action, collaboration, and competition while being informative, fun and short" (Gulezian et al., 2019, p. V). Having fun while learning made the experience memorable and the information durable. Furthermore, local contexts and stakeholder input were reflected in all steps of storyworld production, from preproduction (brainstorming game content, identifying learning abilities, maturity levels, and experiences), gameplay (game mechanics), and post-play evaluation and feedback (Gulezian et al., 2019). The transmedia action researchers also "gamified" post-game assessments to evaluate how effectively the games stimulated learning. These assessments informed improvements to the games.

Student researchers also developed a facilitator's guide featuring the portfolio of games, tips for playing, and debriefing questions. A digital booklet included video interviews with KPE staff advising Greek educators on how to incorporate games into climate education.

This educational storyworld product combined the strengths of visual and experiential learning with entertainment in an urban context in Greece. It was informed by scholarship advising that climate change education be oriented toward the future, helping students "envision their goals and learn about the steps they can take to achieve such goals" (Gulezian et al., 2019, p. 2). As Crookall advocates, "the topic of climate change needs to become the backbone of education around the world" (Crookall, 2013, p. 196).

Flattening Hierarchies Through Games

Each transmedia action research project described previously began with a need identified by sponsors to communicate scientific information. The community-based organizations could not rely solely on formal scientific and policy products "to rapidly deploy the knowledge needed to scale up [climate] adaptation" (Sundin et al., 2018, p. 2). Hence, the need to pursue grassroots communication efforts on climate adaptation. This led to the creation of multilevel, multi-platform climate resilience storyworlds focusing on managing risks, surviving events, and recovering from them. This dimensional approach can be crucial for communities, families, children, and business owners who are most vulnerable to evolving, and worsening, climate-driven realities. Often, local stakeholders lack power or adequate social or financial capital to initiate adaptation measures. Interactive storyworld assets, whether formal or informal, facilitated or passive, analog or digital, together can support the necessity to learn, make different decisions, and take action.

In each of these IQPs, serious, facilitated games emerged as a central feature of each storyworld. Both complex and accessible games communicate hazards associated with climate change by simplifying complex systems and making discussions about realistic solutions understandable (Boycoff & Osnes, 2014). Furthermore, by virtue of being immersive environments, the games helped "flatten hierarchies as players bring their own experiences and worldview into the game system, thus enabling inclusive learning and equal participation of women and men, young people and elders, powerful and marginalized" (Mendler de Suarez et al., 2012). What makes participatory games so compelling is that they:

> position all involved on an even playing field, thus helping dismantle real or perceived hierarchies, in part by supporting the participation of people who have rich life experiences who are often in direct relationship with the environment, who possess knowledge from lived experience, and who hold dear many traditional views and beliefs.
> (Boycoff & Osnes, 2014, p. 5)

Conclusion: Knowledge, Emotion, and Action

One of the primary strengths of transmedia action research is that it invites stakeholders and researchers to address multiple, simultaneous needs that support the development of personal agency while encouraging community action. Transmedia action research is, fundamentally, iterative, experimental, and improvisational in nature. Nevertheless, as the previous cases illustrate, transmedia action research can provide a coherent engagement strategy in which stakeholders and researchers share in the translation, composition, production, and distribution of storyworlds that bolster social change. In its full expression, transmedia action research, with its mandate on participation, storying, and social benefit enables what Biggs (1989) refers to as "collegiate" participation when "researchers and local people work together as colleagues with different skills to offer, in a process of mutual learning where local people have control over the process" (as cited in Cornwall & Jewkes, 1995).

A transmedia action research logic harnesses storyworld tools and techniques to encourage personal responsibility and community action. Responsibility, though, cannot be extricated from an appreciation of how people make decisions under stress, or in anticipation of stress. Those decisions are informed by memories, experiences, emotions, and perceptions, and transmedia action research makes explicit the importance of these influences. By engaging the mind and emotions, storyworlds become more compelling and memorable, thereby increasing the likelihood that information contributes to social change and social benefit. Approaches that prioritize knowledge for action can also help address issues related to inaccessible information, which are often compounded in poor and underserved communities. As Geekiyanage et al. (2020) note, vulnerable populations are often left out of planning and recovery efforts. Furthermore, citizen-generated storyworlds can help assure that cultural norms and values are taken into account and that local solutions are tailored to meet local needs (Vanderlinden et al., 2017). This is congruent with Cornwall and Jewkes' (1995) recognition that local perspectives should inform research and drive change. "Not only can insights of local people improve the quality of research and ensure face validity, their involvement has important implications for the sustainability and appropriateness of interventions" (p. 1674).

In cases where extant media does not address or meet the needs of stakeholders, transmedia action research approaches that generate multiple, and multi-platform, storyworld assets can help bridge stakeholder groups that do not often "meet in the same place" (i.e., meteorologists and marginalized groups; psychologists and local farmers; manufacturers and climate scientists; and first responders and women's organizations) for the common purpose of raising awareness and inspiring a willingness to act.

Stealth Learning and Progressive Pedagogy

Facilitated games combined with additional storyworld elements can generate stealth learning, which can promote better recall and understanding than traditional instructional techniques. Games for young people and students help students see themselves as active participants in their education processes (Winn, 2009). Games for both children and adults support "participants to take a wider and longer view of challenges, to practice complex and critical thinking, to examine problem-solving strategies at multiple levels and from multiple points of view" (Boycoff & Osnes, 2014, p. 5).

While stealth learning through games benefited community members, the progressive transmedia action research pedagogy had a broad impact on WPI students. As they grew into their roles as transmedia action researchers, STEM students became more capable information mediators, or infomediaries, brokering content up and down scale, interpreting, reinterpreting, and rescaling mono-logic scientific and institutional material to help make it accessible and actionable for communities most in need.

Core competencies in STEM made it easy for students to understand climate science, flood dynamics, and mechanical vulnerabilities. Conveying how these engineering concepts intersect with human experience was a more challenging pedagogical task that required students to develop the humility and respect that is at the heart of action research (Kemmis et al., 2014). Students consistently reflected that working closely with people in need led to more profound and durable learning experiences.

"Our project brought us to the crossroads of science and society, proving engineering projects are much more than just the design and its technicalities" (Cuendet et al., 2020, p. 61).

"We could feel ourselves going from teachers to collaborators" (Dickinson et al., 2017, p. 109).

Engineering and technical solutions that do not consider those who need to interact with, or implement, these solutions "is irresponsible and inefficient" (Dickinson et al., 2017, p. 110).

As Cornwall and Jewkes (1995) note, "participatory research is about respecting and understanding the people with and for whom researchers work. It is about developing a realization that local people are knowledgeable and that they, together with researchers, can work towards analyses and solutions" (p. 1674). By extension, transmedia action research blends progressive pedagogy with citizen-inspired storyworlds in an environment of respect, research, and commitment to social change.

References

Ashley, H., Kenton, N., & Milligan, A. (2009). Community-based adaptation to climate change. *Participatory Learning and Action*, 60.

Bachofen, C., Suarez, P., Steenbergen, M., & Grist, N. (2012). *Can games help people manage the climate risks they face? The participatory design of educational games*. Red Cross/Red Crescent Climate Centre.

Boycoff, M., & Osnes, B. (2014). *Collaborative research: Evaluating serious games and participatory learning tools for climate risk management and community-based adaptation* [Grant Proposal: Decision, Risk and Management Sciences]. National Science Foundation.

Clerveaux, V., & Spence, B. (2009). The communication of disaster information and knowledge to children using game technique: The Disaster Awareness Game (DAG). *International Journal of Environmental Research*, 3(2), 209–222.

Climate Centre. (n.d.). Red Cross/Red Crescent Climate Centre. Retrieved February 7, 2020, from www.climatecentre.org

Cordero, E. C., Todd, A. M., & Abellera, D. (2008). Climate change education and the ecological footprint. *Bulletin of the American Meteorological Society*, *89*, 865–872. https://doi.org/10.1175/2007BAMS2432.2

Cornwall, A., & Jewkes, R. (1995). What is participatory research? *Social Science & Medicine*, *41*(12), 1667–1676. https://doi.org/10.1016/0277-9536(95)00127-s

Crookall, D. (2013). Climate change and simulation/gaming: Learning for survival: Editorial. *Simulation & Gaming*, *44*(2–3), 195–228. https://doi.org/10.1177/1046878113497781

Cuendet, J., Hunt, A., Kring, N., & Taurich, N. (2020). *Adapting to rising sea levels in Seaview Gracefield, New Zealand developing the Seaview sea-level "Seanarios" Climate game* [Interactive Qualifying Project]. Worcester Polytechnic Institute.

Deutsche Gesellschaft für Internationale Zusammenarbeit (GIZ). (2015). *Flood risk management plan: Shkodër Region*. Deutsche Gesellschaft für Internationale Zusammenarbeit.

Dickinson, K., Dione, D., St. Pierre, S., & Weiss, T. (2017). *Reducing flood risk in Shkodra through community engagement* [Interactive Qualifying Project]. Worcester Polytechnic Institute.

Fischhoff, B. (2013). The sciences of science communication. *Proceedings of the National Academy of Sciences*, *110*(S3), 14033–14039. https://doi.org/10.1073/pnas.1213273110

Geekiyanage, D., Fernando, T., & Keraminiyage, K. (2020). Assessing the state of the art in community engagement for participatory decision-making in disaster risk-sensitive urban development. *International Journal of Disaster Risk Reduction*, *51*, 1–12. https://doi.org/10.1016/j.ijdrr.2020.101847

Georgakopoulos, T. (2017). *The impact of climate change on the Greek economy*. www.dianeosis.org

Gulezian, O., Puchovsky, A., Tavares, V., & Utheim, K. (2019). *Educating Greek students about climate change through serious games* [Interactive Qualifying Project]. Worcester Polytechnic Institute.

GWRC. (2017). *Whaitua climate change predictions*. Greater Wellington Regional Council. www.gw.govt.nz

Hagmann, J., Almekinders, C. J. M., Bukenya, C., Guevara, F., & Halemichael, A. (2003). Developing 'soft skills' in higher education. *Participatory Learning and Action*, *48*, 21–25.

Hancox, D. (2014). Amplified activism: Transmedia storytelling and social change. *The Writing Platform*. http://thewritingplatform.com

Hancox, D. (2017). From subject to collaborator: Transmedia storytelling and social research. *Convergence: The International Journal of Research into New Media Technologies*, *23*(1), 49–60. https://doi.org/10.1177/1354856516675252

IFRC. (2011). *DREF operation final report*. The International Federation of the Red Cross and the Red Crescent.

Institute of Development Studies (IDS). (n.d.). *Participatory Learning and Action (PLA)*. Participatory Methods. www.participatorymethods.org/glossary/participatory-learning-and-action-pla

INTRAC. (2017). *Participatory Learning and Action (PLA)*. INTRAC.

Jenkins, H. (2003, January 15). Transmedia storytelling. *MIT Technology Review*. www.technologyreview.com/2003/01/15/234540/transmedia-storytelling/

Jenkins, H. (2011, July 31). *Transmedia 202: Further reflections*. http://henryjenkins.org/blog/2011/08/defining_transmedia_further_re.html

Joubert, M., Davis, L., & Metcalfe, J. (2019). Storytelling: The soul of science communication. *Journal of Science Communication, 18*(5), 5. https://doi.org/10.22323/2.18050501

Kemmis, S., McTaggart, R., & Nixon, R. (2014). *The action research planner: Doing critical participatory action research*. Springer.

Koelle, B., & Annecke, W. (n.d.). *Community based climate change adaptation (CBA): Adaptation and beyond*. Indigo Development & Change. https://idl-bnc-idrc.dspacedirect.org/bitstream/handle/10625/46034/132520.pdf

KPE. (n.d.). KPE: Who we are. www.kpe-thess.gr/en/who-we-are/

Mendler de Suarez, J., Suarez, P., & Bachofen, C. (2012). *Games for a new climate: Experiencing the complexity of future risks* (Pardee Center Task Force Report). The Frederick S. Pardee Center for the Study of the Longer-Range Future, Boston University. http://tinyurl.com/BUPardee-G4NC

Reid, H., Alam, M., Berger, R., Cannon, T., Huq, S., & Milligan, A. (2009). Community-based adaptation to climate change (CBA). Special Edition: *Participatory Learning and Action. Special Edition, 60*. www.iied.org/pla-60-community-based-adaptation-climate-change

Suarez, P. (n.d.). *From darkness to illumination: Climate grief and resilience in a sea of warnings*. Climate-KIC. www.climatecentre.org

Sundin, A., Andersson, K., & Watt, R. (2018). Rethinking communication: Integrating storytelling for increased stakeholder engagement in environmental evidence synthesis. *Environmental Evidence, 7*(6), 6. https://doi.org/10.1186/s13750-018-0116-4

Taylor, P., & Fransmann, J. (2003). Learning and teaching participation in institutions of higher learning. *PLA Notes, 48*.

Thomas, S. (2001). *What is Participatory Learning and Action (PLA): An introduction* (p. 7). Centre for International Development and Training, University of Wolverhampton. http://idp-key-resources.org

Vanderlinden, J., Baztan, J., Touili, N., Kane, I., Rulleau, B., Simal, P., & Zagonari, F. (2017). Coastal flooding, uncertainty and climate change: Science as a solution to (mis) perceptions? A qualitative enquiry in three coastal European settings. *Journal of Coastal Research, 77*, 127–133.

Winn, B. (2009). The design, play, and experience framework. In *Handbook of research on effective electronic gaming in education*. IGI Global.

10 Water From Fog
Transmedia Storytelling and Humanitarian Engineering

Jamila Bargach and Leslie L. Dodson

Framing Fog

"Nebulous ideas!" was the standard reaction in 2010 when the staff of Dar Si Hmad for Development, Education and Culture began seeking community engagement to build what was, at the time, a mere experimental site atop Mt. Boutmezguida, in the heart of the Anti-Atlas mountains (*Dar Si Hmad*, n.d.). The practice of fog collection, or fog harvesting, is a mechanism for obtaining potable water from cloud formations that has been in use in many forms for centuries (Gioda et al., 1995; Marzol-Jaén, 2011). While novel innovations in the past few decades have increased the efficiency of some fog nets or fence technologies, there are few fully functioning fog collection systems in the world that provide a reliable and sustained source of water using this method. Past forays into the use of fog collection, while well-intentioned, have not resulted in long-term stable sources of water for the communities they intend to benefit. This is mainly due to a combination of technical, monetary, managerial, political, and community dynamic issues. As with any system, the sustainability of a fog harvesting project for water supply to rural communities is a multivariate problem (Fessehaye et al., 2014; *FogQuest: Sustainable Water Solutions*, n.d.; Klemm et al., 2012).

Shape-shifting fog is an apt metaphor for this transmedia storyworld, as story elements emerge, re-order, and spill into an evolving transmedia logic. From the very moment of its birth in the Atlantic Ocean as a natural phenomenon, this product of the Canary cold current and atmospheric pressure moves through aerial corridors to finally halt at the majestic Anti-Atlas mountains. At this landing station, it then unfolds multiple new storyworlds: local apprehensions when this wet blanket covers the landscape and masks all known visual references; promises that it can be a valid source for the much needed water in an increasingly water-starved environment; assumptions regarding solutions to radically transform beneficiaries' lives with plenty of water to meet all human and livelihood needs; foundations for educative initiatives for children and empowerment programs for the community; and inspirations for a variety of uniquely creative and artistic adventures that open and invite novel connections to the environment that nurtures us as living beings.

DOI: 10.4324/9781003150862-10

The scope of the fog harvesting project in the Anti-Atlas Mountains of Morocco extends across time, distance, and form. It took a decade to build the trust necessary to build the fog system with its nets and nearly 40 kilometers of pipes that carry potable water to rural hamlets. Along the way, the project has absorbed interest and innovation from around the globe to now be a site of water production supporting the Amazigh communities, the indigenous inhabitants of North Africa living under the hegemony of Arabic central power, and a site of creative expression and knowledge production hosting a complex transmedia story-web of water, of music, of engineering, of ecological art, and of scholarship and pedagogy.

In its organic expansion and multidimensionality, the fog harvesting storyworld does not distinguish between education and art—documentation resides in conversation with artistic representation in nonhierarchical planes of learning and sharing. Like the transmogrification of fog, this transmedia galaxy invites and sustains artistic productions, panels, sculpture and interactive music, ecological concerts, and educational curricula. These realms of creativity and knowledge are described in the following in an effort to frame, but not constrain, the fog water storyworld.

We illuminate this storyworld galaxy by chronicling the hydrological and meteorological research at the peak of Mt. Boutzmeguida that informed the development of the fog system, which drew in the expertise of engineers and innovators and a cadre of creatives leading to profound epiphanies of art and music that resonates with the Amazigh Aït Baamrani culture and custom. Concurrently, educators developed water curricula for Amazigh children coupled with humanitarian engineering courses and kits for STEM students in Morocco, France, and the United States.

Fog Collection: Social Context and History of the Initiative

Scarce water, compromised wells, and climate-change-induced droughts have destabilized traditional Amazigh communities and have created added burdens on women. Traditional water management in this region of Southwest Morocco was predicated on parsimonious water use; people used to hand-dig wells and build cisterns for rainwater catchment to meet their needs, wait for rain for their agriculture, and provide water for their animals at troughs in a select number of wells. Modern techniques for finding water using drilling machines to reach deep aquifers cause pollution, and are expensive and unsustainable. Given the increasing cycles of drought, the scarcity of rain, and low aquifer recharge rates, fog is an excellent, reliable, sustainable, and supplemental water resource that relieves pressure on aquifers, wells, and women with water-gathering responsibilities. The communities of the region, like many other geographically similar areas, are suffering from great anxiety concerning the lack of water and the recurrence of droughts. Rural poor families in Aït Baâmrane, the tribal community where the Dar Si Hmad organization works, live in ecologically fragile zones where water is scarce, topsoil is eroded, and drought is on the rise (*Dar Si Hmad*, n.d.).

Vulnerable populations and fragile zones overlap, producing added burdens on the residents. Women, in particular, devote 3.5 hours daily to the chore of fetching water. Given the lack of rainfall, water was a major concern for survival especially during the dry season, not only for humans but also for livestock and for the biotope in general. In response, many households migrated to cities and sold their livestock. Cultural heritage and ancient practices, from agriculture and apiculture to language, are no longer transmitted to the younger generation.

The Dar Si Hmad for Development, Education and Culture nongovernmental organization has made the project *Drinking Fog: Fog Collection in Southwest Morocco* its main mission (*Dar Si Hmad*, n.d.). With its German partners who designed efficient harvesting nets, dubbed *The CloudFishers*, along with additional partners, Dar Si Hmad has built this unique initiative and is running what is, effectively, the largest functioning fog project in the world (*Dar Si Hmad*, n.d.). The fog-collecting nets were built atop Mount Boutmezguida in the Aït Baamrane territory of Southwest Morocco. This area, on the edge of the Sahara Desert, approximately 35 km from the Atlantic Ocean, is classified as pre-Saharan, with an arid climate and low rainfall (annual average of 112 mm). Although drought is endemic, its frequency and intensity have increased since the 1980s (Taheripour et al., 2020). A hot Saharan wind called the *Chergui* sometimes blows over the region and dries it even further. However, while Southwest Morocco is water-poor, abundant fog drapes the area of six months of the year, for a total of 143 days, and it is this harvested fog that Dar Si Hmad delivers as drinking water to the community. With 1,700 m^2 of nets, 59 km of pipes, and an efficient system of distribution, Dar Si Hmad succeeded in the challenge of connecting the mountain-dwelling population with safe drinking water. As of December 2019, 16 villages and 1,000 individuals, including returning laborers, have access to a sustainable water source. There is now a notable decrease in the level of anxiety, improved hygiene, and young girls and boys are going to school instead of helping with the water chore. Fog had always been considered a nuisance, now it is considered a viable source for water, further supporting the work of the fog research scientific community that launched its experimental testing in the 1960s (Eugster, 2008; Klemm et al., 2012; Marzol, 2010).

This fog collection initiative has given birth to many separate yet connected worlds, woven together in a galaxy-shaped storyworld that embraces university-based explorations of weather data, women's traditional games and dances to chase away fog and call the sun, along with the sum of beliefs about dead and living water. The storyworld resonates with oral histories collected by Dar Si Hmad during fieldwork in the villages, and the accounts of water dowsers of incorporeal possessions. These exist in a kind of precarious harmony with the proofs of geo-hydrologists and meteorologists.

Let us start with the community here, as our first storyworld element.

Disorientation

Harvesting water out of fog seemed as disorienting to the "natural" order of things for these villagers accustomed to water scarcity and to managing this rare resource in optimal ways as their ancestors did. Here, then, emerges our first story that sketches the contours of a world reversed by change. Shifting a set of beliefs firmly rooted in one's deep culture can only evolve through time with tangible proofs, as Dar Si Hmad has experienced with fog and the community's reception of fog water. The transformation of the community required a pedagogy of practice and forbearance, not one of conceptual learning. The nascent sense that another possibility is about to be born to the world was the structuring element of such pedagogy. The idea of drinking and amassing fog attracted idealists and doers, akin to a magnet, each participating to make this strange concept real and sustainable. During the decade of community engagement that was required to get this fog collection initiative off the ground and into the air where the fog lives, there was one solid consistency: *fog fascinates*.

The CloudFishers

The units that harvest and collect fog, designed by German engineer Peter Trautwein, are stories of observation and knowledge (*CloudFisher for Fog Harvesting*, n.d.). Reaching beyond the common practices of engineering, the design has incorporated an understanding of culture, environment, human, and financial capacity to yield a simple yet elegant system that has the power to change the course of people's livelihoods and lives. Fog initiatives were often plagued by the fragility of the collecting structures, but the CloudFisher prototype not only addresses structural limitations of previous designs, notably the collapse of the units due to high winds, but also has dramatically increased the overall potential water yield of the system. Attention to comprehensive sustainability has been, from the onset, the overarching goal. For the project to be a success, not only must the physical components of the system resist the demanding environmental conditions of the high elevation mountain site but also the operation of the fog collection nets and hardware must be understood and maintained by local staff. This philosophy has been considered in nearly every aspect of the system, manifested by the need for only two tools—a ratchet and a wrench—to assemble and repair the system.

But there is yet another story to the CloudFishers than engineering efficacy, on the top of the flat mountain, they are an art installation, like the unfurled sails of a ship navigating the high waters at a steady speed, the CloudFishers dance with the wind, embrace the fog, expand through the heat, and remain immobile through all the elements, hinged to thick steel cables, which, in their turn, are buried in mounds of mortar and cement. This is the land of extremes, howling 120 km/hour gales, scorching heat that can attain 50 degrees Celsius, or plummeting temperatures descending to 0 degrees Celsius, or thick fog soaking one's clothes, rendering one's movement an extraordinary achievement. In this environment, the CloudFishers, like many art installations, call attention to themselves including their small component pieces, to the space where they are implemented, to the sphere of ideas and possibilities in which they move. Each distinct element opens into a world of reflection, building layers upon layers of connections.

Artistic Explorations

Artistic explorations, be it painting, model design, sculpture, or musical conversations, have all been found in fog and the fog collection initiative material to expand and reflect upon.

On the wall of the Boutmezguida Center is a landscape panel called the *Ballad of the Fiancé of Fog* in which one sees oneself as a walker (Lample, n.d.). Drawn by Titouan Lample, a student volunteer from the French Versaille School of Landscape Design, it invites a type of zen-walk through sinewy paths (Lample, 2018). Each of the 30 CloudFisher units bears the name of an endemic and unique plant of this ecosystem. The top of the mountain and surrounding area is designated as a SIBE (Site d'Intérêt Biologique et Écologique) zone of ecological and biological interest, a classification of the Moroccan Agency of Water and Forestry, in that it has unique flora where desert gales intermingle with the cold winds emanating from the Atlantic Ocean cold current. This proto map functions equally as a pedagogical tool in that it indicates the precise spot of the units upon visiting but is also associated with movement and awareness of one's surrounding environment. Walking in this ecosystem, as suggested by the panel, is inviting poetical associations, perhaps of a strange nature, between the steel uprights and the plants underfoot. The organization has used this representation in multiple venues, colloquia, and workshops, and never has it failed to deepen inquiry and discussion. "Why such a choice?" is often the triggering question, and part of the response is about connecting this specific spot, that hosts seasonal thick fog events, to a unique flora that feeds unique fauna and human practices. The use of this panel is a storyworld element that has opened for the organization and the visitors yet another dimension to what could simply and prosaically be a water project. It is this aesthetic dimension of the panel, with its soft, almost surreal colors, that transforms the CloudFishers from a solid structure of steel and nets to a gentle arrangement standing still, strong, yet welcoming fog and conveying water to reservoirs (Figure 10.1).

A sculpture by renowned Moroccan artist Hassan Darsi called *The Boutmezguida* is a minimalist and sober piece (Darsi, 2016). An erect translucent plexiglass rectangle to which is hinged mid-way a painted 2D piece, with the mountain and cubes for villages; the piece is, in so many ways, an

Figure 10.1 Ballad of the Fiancé of Fog

evocative enactment of the project. At this scale, *The Boutmezguida* is a delicate sculpture, with an eerie premonitory air hinting to the project's fragilities. The effects of global warming on fog—frequency, seasonality, and consistency—are becoming less predictable and less known. In this storyworld element, the salience of the artistic dimension is integral to explaining and sharing an engineering project even in formal venues where only exact instruments and proven results dominate.

The Rhizomes Residency and the "Brui-Art: Le son du paysage" Ecological Concert: A Communion of Artists

In 2019, Dar Si Hmad organized an artistic residency called *Rhizomes*, and a concert event called "Brui-Art: Le son du paysage" *(Fog-Art: Landscape Sound)*, which is a play on the French word *bruit* meaning sound noise, and also the first syllable of the French word for fog, *Bouillard* (*Brui-Art: Le Son Du Paysage*, 2019). The slogan for the event was "with art, we inspire awareness surrounding environmental issues and sustainable development." Rhizomes, the knotted roots, each stem sending roots and shoots from its nodes, grow horizontally and upward, permitting new shoots to grow up out of the ground. The beauty and complexity of this image was a potent way to convey the aspirations of the event. Intersections of different artistic creations with fog—a resonating sound box, the *rebab* musical instrument, paintings, a video installation, and a lighting concert—combine the sonorous and visual facets of fog and the mountain ecosystem in an artistic co-creation.

In 2018, Dar Si Hmad welcomed an experimental installation to collect the sound of fog on top of Mt. Boutmezguida that became a seed in the Brui-Art exhibition. The sound box project by Kris Adler, named "Clouds Pace," built on a previous experiment titled *"Listen to the sound of the melting Vernagt Ferner Glacier"* by the German artist Aldis Kaller, who had installed a sound box on top of the CloudFishers (Adler, 2019; Kaller, 2018). This unique "instrument" is composed of a wind-resonating tube which tracks, listens, and records the local atmosphere using wind energy that is then altered into vibratory energy, generating hypnotic variations of wind and fog. Sound art is also united with other art forms.

Since the overall image of the arid areas of Morocco cannot be complete without picturing its landscape, the French landscape architect Christophe de Saint Just enchanted the sound art with paintings and tableaux describing the humidity in the air and soil, with mixtures of satellite, fog, and Argan tree imagery (de Saint Just, 2019). When light beams highlighted de Saint Just's paintings, which danced behind a screen of artificial fog, the stage came alive with images and colors that called one's attention to a rich landscape portrayed in different scales and perspectives. One could not but relate to fog, the trees, the mountains, and the humans as more than a landscape.

From the heart of the mountains and the history of the Amazigh people, the ancient rebab instrument and the artist Raiss Lmouden stood out, reproducing a long tradition of the troubadour chanting about attachment and country (Lmouden, 2019). Young video and light artists, tracing their origins to the Berberophone Guancho ethnic group of the Canary Islands, staged a performance of lights, colors, and fog machines to suggest an atmosphere in which the resonating box and the rebab box entered into the joust of sometimes harmonious, but most times disjointed, sounds of the *Brui-art* event. The dissonant counterpoints between the rebab—a bowed or plucked string instrument related to a lute or lyre—and sounds of the fog recorded in the sound box were described as an ecological concert. For sound artist Kris Adler and musician Raiss Lmouden, the mixing of the two sounds could not be about harmonious melodies only but also about a soundscape that portrays ecological tensions and realities. Recorded fog, emanating deep from the cold current of the Canary Islands, bearing the weight of the atmospheric pressure and dragging itself to Boutmezguida, is a sound of planetary dimension, and for the artist Adler, it was a strident call for change.

The ecological concert offered a comprehensive journey through feelings without need for the verbal language. The goal was not simply to look at ecological changes but to understand how the fog project became an incubator for environmental activism (Figure 10.2).

Figure 10.2 "Brui-Art: Le son du paysage" (*Fog-Art: Landscape Sound*)

The Tea

Exhibitions are forms of ceremony, as are rituals for food and drink. The tea ceremony is of extremely high significance among Amazigh communities. The type of green tea, the type of sugar, and especially the quality of the water are of paramount importance among the tea-loving Amazigh. Unlike in northern regions where mint is added and where the color is light yellow, this southern tea is served almost black like coffee, in tiny glass cups, pouring the tea into the cups, and returning it to the pot, like a circular churning gesture, until the foam fills the small cup and only then is the precious liquid poured to fill in its bottom. This tea ceremony could be repeated in any household up to 20 times a day. The water for tea must be free from minerals which are believed to corrupt the purity of the tea's taste. While water in cisterns historically served this purpose, today the tea drunk among the Aït Baamrane is made with pure fog water; the fog is now used to reaffirm Amazigh identity and take its place in the performance of ritual.

The Cemetery Wall

At the midpoint between Id-Soussan and Id-Aachour—two of the 16 villages drinking fog water—lies a cemetery with a towering Argan tree, bald in its lower branches but bushy on top like a Hermit Ibis bird. In this region, tombs are seldom elevated above ground level, and hence, tend to disappear except for a rock placed at the head and through the memory of those still living. Village elders decided to build a wall to mark the spatial and visual boundaries of the cemetery. Funds were gathered, help hired, and bricks purchased. "But how to mix the mortar?" they asked. "Could fog water be used?" It is "dead" water after all, lacking salts and minerals. Having not been in the entrails of the earth, it has not flowed over rocks or been mixed with soil. "Should such water be used?" some of the elders wondered. At Dar Si Hmad, some technicians found such a question irrelevant, as water is water. But other members insisted on the highly symbolic nature of this query, because not all water is the same. The building of the low wall was halted and much exchange ensued before reaching the decision to bring well water for the mortar and to keep the fog water for the whitewash—the idea is that the virtue of white and clean was enhanced by the purity of fog water.

All of these—tea rituals, sound boxes, cemetery walls, adapted nets, sculptures, ballads, and rebab music—are profound examples of the importance of local contexts and the infinite creativity and meaning that adheres to context. What might appear insignificant or trivial to the "outsider" (who self-identifies as such) is of deep consequence in a culture that incorporates the spirit world into daily life, and where being conversant with the natures of souls and the ephemerality of fog is not unusual. It is only by being awakened to and available to understand internal and external landscapes, sonic and engineered systems, and the whispers of wind and fog that one can fully participate in the consideration of the complexities inherent in imagining (let alone bringing) "solutions" to unfamiliar terrain.

Humanitarian Engineering Education

The transmedia story system that originated in the Amazigh heartland found its way into educational odysseys as curriculum for humanitarian engineering at an American university, as data for Ph.D. and masters students from American, European, and Moroccan universities spanning geographic information systems, physical geography, environmental studies, design, and anthropology.

Dar Si Hmad's novel approach to providing an alternative source of water drew the attention of U.S. educators who imbued engineering curricula with transmedia storyworld content, featuring context-rich STEM and humanities story elements produced in fog communities. After attending the inauguration of the fog water system in Aït Baamrane in 2015, faculty from Worcester Polytechnic Institute (WPI), a STEM university in Massachusetts, developed a deep respect for the social, cultural, spiritual, artistic, and technical intricacies of the project. On campus, faculty perceived the fog water project as an opportunity to explore innovative, transmedia pedagogical approaches that could integrate humanistic and engineering concepts into STEM education. These efforts produced the Humanitarian Engineering: Fog Project curricula, which guides students to heighten their understanding of the complex world.

Conveying the complexities of life in water-scarce rural hamlets in the Anti-Atlas mountains, while also trying to instruct students on the technical features of an alternative water system, is a daunting educational task. That challenge required a collaborative effort by WPI faculty from chemical, civil, mechanical, and biomedical engineering, scholars from Dar Si Hmad, and faculty from the humanities department and the Global Lab who together imagined nontraditional, transmediated humanitarian engineering courses and curricular kits. Each of these transmedia learning endeavors incorporates culturally and geographically relevant STEM and humanities content that addresses complex, open-ended challenges whose solutions require students (and practitioners) to think across disciplinary silos.

Faculty conceived of learning journeys immersed in the fog water storyworld, which expanded to include a range of new analog and digital media, data, and experiential activities. Project-based Humanitarian Engineering courses traveled across disciplines to relate seemingly unrelated notions to authentic, real-world circumstances. Lab-based simulations of the fog water project were united with coursework addressing social contexts such as indigeneity, marginalization, gender inequities, colonial histories, and the intersection of state religion and tribal traditions. The Humanitarian Engineering: Fog Project curriculum was congruent with Dar Si Hmad's ethical, community-centered mission to promote local culture and create "sustainable initiatives through education and the integration and use of scientific ingenuity, within the communities of Southwest Morocco" (Adler, 2019).

The transmedia-intensive pedagogical approach inspired faculty members to open creative pathways for learning and knowledge sharing. Student and faculty media-making teams traveled to the fog project bearing audio recorders, video cameras, and other documentary devices to produce digital storyworld elements. During these media expeditions, teams collaborated with scholars at Dar Si Hmad to interview Amazigh elders who recounted their experiences during Spanish colonial rule in southern Morocco, helping to convey the relatively recent historical and political context of southwest Morocco, supplemented by texts and archival photographs. Storyworld teams also gained the trust of Amazigh women who agreed to mount Go-Pro cameras on their hats while fetching and hauling water from wells. Audio soundscapes of domestic life enlivened class discussions about the burdens of water-hauling for women and girls. Documentation of the mechanical features of the fog project, such as the pipes, reservoirs, and pumping stations, was accompanied by 360-degree photographic images of the fog net installation to present an immersive view of the fog water engineering systems.

Ethnographic inquiry was embedded in coursework and strengthened by storyworld components. Throughout the courses students were immersed in the cultural, social, political, and economic aspects of the fog water project, while simultaneously studying the engineering concepts of fluid flow, climate change, materials selection and strength, and mass and energy conservation.

Bench-scale models and prototypes of fog chambers provided hands-on opportunities to manipulate fog generators, simulate wind conditions (using fans), and test rates of fog water capture on nets designed to promote condensation and coalescence of fog. Additional "storified" STEM content included video vignettes of the fog chamber puffing out fog and producing potable water, echoing material presented in the hydrodynamics labs.

Transmedia-rich curricula also featured 3-D printed topographic tiles of the area around Mt. Boutmezguida showing the physical terrain that contributes to the accumulation of fog at the mountain peak. Accompanying laminated maps provided a more expansive view of the landscape between the Atlantic Ocean and the Sahara Desert—visual information to help students understand the geographic, ecological, and social landscapes that support the fog project. Texts, audio recordings, photography, and video segments helped illuminate the "lived landscapes" of daily life in villages at the tail end of the Anti-Atlas Mountains. The storyworld galaxy allowed American students, from within their classrooms, to be transported to Aït Baamrane, thanks to the varied nature of this curriculum which presented distinct angles of the landscape, endowing it with a complexity almost like the one experienced in situ. If maps give the viewer spatial representation, the 3-D tiles enhance the experience with heights and dips, adding details that make a map almost into a living experience rather than a simple representation. (Titouan Lample also explored this concept of the living and enriched map, reproduced at the site of fog collection itself, but in a different format.)

Imagery remains a vital teaching tool, whether in the walking map at the fog observatory atop Mt. Boutzmeguida or around a team table on campus. Photo documentation of rural life in southwest Morocco provides students with insight into domestic duties, gender roles, and the particulars of place. Visual storyworld assets blend with experiential and embodied learning, where sound and voicescapes recorded in the countryside offer an aural introduction to the local Amazigh dialect (*Tachelhit*), thus linking language and culture to place and history. Audio recordings of community members and local water engineers speaking about the fog project in the local dialect are complemented by interactions with the *Tifinagh* (Berber) alphabet, where students learn to write simple sentences in the glyph-based alphabet. These experiential, transmedia activities deliver students from their sometimes-rigid STEM training to a recognition of the political and historical roots of the language, while also gaining an appreciation of the difficulties low-literate Berber women might face when learning to read or write.

Gastronomy, too, is an important catalyst for cultural understanding, and food and tea became sites for storytelling and cultural transmission (Santich, 2007). Culture and custom were expressed (and consumed) through shared meals and strong tea, with students and faculty dining on couscous and chicken tagine surrounded by a soundscape of local music and a slideshow of life in the *douars* (villages).

Artifacts from the *bled* (countryside) furnished tactile learning opportunities: Students were invited to touch and try on various objects such as traditional cooking vessels, bridal jewelry, and samples of the *melhefa*, the traditional 4-foot-by-16-foot gauzy fabric worn by many Amazigh women in southern Morocco. Artifacts such as these make culture tangible, generating resonance between quantitative and qualitative perspectives.

The transmedia curriculum was further enriched by video exchanges between engineering students in Massachusetts and young Berber professionals in Morocco. These conversations encouraged learning and friendship, and learning through friendship. Online gatherings and social media connections helped dispel the disquiet some students experience when confronted with unfamiliar cultural contexts such as rural, marginalized communities and helped them better understand their Muslim contemporaries.

The Humanitarian Engineering: Fog Project courses integrated ethnographic and empirical work with evidence-based learning. Storyworld assets including quantitative datasets provided new perspectives on water-scarcity and water-related behaviors prior to the delivery of fog water. Utilizing Dar Si Hmad's extensive household survey, students explored a rich dataset on water consumption, socio-economic and educational attainment, and family and community demographic information, helping them better comprehend social and gender marginalization in rural Aït Baamrane, where water and opportunity are scarce, and where culture and tradition prescribe daily life for women. This project-based learning typically encompasses "attributes such as: the impact of social issues on technological systems, the impact of technology on social structures, the questioning of social values and structures, skills development and analysis in the societal, humanistic and technological disciplines" (DiBiasio, 2019).

Data Science and Visualizations

Transmedia pedagogy, with its invitation to create and collaborate, drew new partners from outside of academia who offered novel approaches to understanding the fog project. One partnership involved a crowdsourced data science and visualization competition sponsored by Driven Data and Dar Si Hmad. Driven Data hosted a multi-month online social challenge "where a global community of data scientists competes to come up with the best statistical model for difficult predictive problems that make a difference" (DrivenData, n.d.). In this case, the challenge was to analyze years of information on weather patterns and water yield collected by Dar Si Hmad. Participants competed to develop a model to predict the yield of Dar Si Hmad's fog nets using historical data on meteorological conditions and the fog net installation. The competition enticed more than 500 data scientists from around the world to model the water output and to create rich visualizations for classrooms and fog communities.

Curricular Fog Water Kits

The fog project storyworld courses reached beyond the university to the creation and provision of transmedia curricular kits for middle and high school STEM classes in the United States (Boudreau et al., 2019). The distributable kits highlight the complex, socio-technical concerns that surround the fog water project, coupling it with engaging content that aims to strengthen student engagement with engineering and humanities content. Applying a transmedia pedagogy logic, faculty created a suite of storyworld media-based and experiential assets so young people could appreciate the intricacies of the fog communities and could understand the fog capturing technology on Mt. Boutzmeguida. Storyworld components for the curricular kits include a scale model of a fog-generating machine, a larger one for teacher training and a mini-unit that can be transported to classrooms for hands-on lab experiences. The units contain hands-on lab experiences that supported students to design and build their own fog nets at home, including a fog generator, fans to move fog to various net types, and piping to collect and measure the resulting water flow rate. Curricular kits also include a mini-documentary on water scarcity in Morocco and video interviews of local and global STEM professionals sharing a "Day in the Life" of their work. Because transmedia pedagogy encourages a cycle of instruction, experience, and reflection, students share videos of their own fog net projects on a web-based learning management system and consider reflection questions about how the fog water project might catalyze economic and cultural changes in the region.

Concluding Thoughts

It is not possible to fully collapse the distance between the classroom and the countryside, but applying a transmedia mindset with storyworld tools and techniques made it possible to create an immersive educational experience of the fog project that interweaves human and engineering concepts. The transmedia logic that informs the humanitarian engineering curricula nurtures students through coursework, homework, projects, and experiential assignments that promote humanitarian learning outcomes.

There is compelling evidence that "integrated (STEM + humanities) learning experiences can have profound positive impacts on student motivation, engagement, success, and learning (across a wide array of cognitive and metacognitive outcomes)" (Boudreau et al., 2020). The transmedia-intensive humanitarian engineering curricula and the fog water curricular kits deliberately transgressed disciplinary boundaries to help students understand that both liberal arts and engineering, together, are crucial to any pursuit of just, equitable and sustainable solutions. Humanitarian engineering faculty recognized that a pedagogical approach that centers transmedia storytelling in course design would challenge traditional, often inflexible, methods of teaching STEM material, which normally exclude humanities content or avoid a humanistic approach (DiBiasio, 2019).

Given the increasingly global nature of engineering, curricula that incorporate a transmedia approach that centers and elevates the human and social complexities that accompany engineering interventions allow students to connect with the material on both an intellectual and emotional level, which serves their development as compassionate, empathetic, and technically proficient engineers.

Human-centered pedagogy, transmediated to offer context and content, is designed to help students see how their STEM education can help people and communities in need, consistent with Dar Si Hmad's mission to create opportunity for marginalized groups, both around the world and in southwest Morocco.

Fog water is now sustaining a new generation of learners and leaders in the countryside who are relieved of the water-hauling task. Where once it was hard to know water because there was so little water, Dar Si Hmad launched the Water School for underserved pupils, ages 6–11, who grew up running the slippery sides of their surrounding mountains as fog draped their world. However, little did they know where it originated, how it traveled, how it can be harvested, and the ways it can bring hope to their realities in which they suffer from the effects of increasing drought and climate change. The Water School curriculum, simple and basic in each one of its aspects, breathed interest in learning because studying also meant discovery, fun, and play. The first edition of the Water School developed into a more ambitious program serving all children beneficiaries who drink fog water, plus 100 children from adjacent villages (potential future beneficiaries), who all learned about water, conservation, and fog. They visited, for the first time in their lives, the sea. These hands-on and (figurative and literal) immersive lessons affected the children and their families in ways that formal schooling has not. Parents reported that their daughters and sons were eager to attend the Water School and how they proudly reported what they learned, careful to confirm the water-conservation gestures practiced in class. The children had become the teachers.

For Amazigh residents who expressed initial apprehension—even derision—at the early stages of the fog collection initiative, events, material, and production of this transmedia story have shown no preference for intellectual or artistic hierarchies. This ethos allows engineering to coexist with poetry, sociology with meteorology, and sound art with gastronomy, to name just a few inspired pairings. The limitless storyworld of this one fog collection initiative traveled from fog doubters to fog believers, through a conversion of the community, to abundance, beauty, and purpose.

References

Adler, K. (2019). *Clouds Pace* [Sound art].
Boudreau, K., DiBiasio, D., & Dodson, L. (2019). *PBL To Go: Bringing STEM experiential learning to a classroom near you: Women's Impact Network grant*. Worcester Polytechnic Institute.
Boudreau, K., DiBiasio, D., & Dodson, L. (2020). *PBL To Go: Women's Impact Network grant*. Worcester Polytechnic Institute.
Brui-Art: Le son du paysage. (2019, September 29). [Concert].
CloudFisher for fog harvesting. (n.d.). Aqualonis. www.aqualonis.com
Darsi, H. (2016). *The Boutmezguida* [Sculpture].
Dar Si Hmad. (n.d.). http://darsihmad.org/vision-mission-2/
de Saint Just, C. (2019). *Brui-Art: Le son du paysage* [Painting, tableau].
DiBiasio, D. (2019). *Whiting Foundation proposal* [Unpublished document].
DrivenData. (n.d.). *From fog nets to neural nets*. www.drivendata.org/competitions/9/from-fog-nets-to-neural-nets/
Eugster, W. (2008). Fog research. *Die Erde*, *138*, 1–10.
Fessehaye, M., Abdul-Wahab, S. A., Savage, M. J., Kohler, T., Gherezghiher, T., & Hurni, H. (2014). Fog-water collection for community use. *Renewable and Sustainable Energy Reviews*, *29*, 52–62. https://doi.org/10.1016/j.rser.2013.08.063
FogQuest: Sustainable water solutions. (n.d.). www.fogquest.org/
Gioda, A., Hernandez, Z., Gonzales, E., & Espejo, R. (1995). Fountain trees in the Canary Islands: Legend and reality. *Advances in Horticultural Science*, *9*(3), 112–118.
Kaller, A. (2018). *Listen to the sound of the melting Vernagt Ferner Glacier* [Sonic Art].
Klemm, O., Schemenauer, R. S., Lummerich, A., Cereceda, P., Marzol, V., Corell, D., van Heerden, J., Reinhard, D., Gherezghiher, T., Olivier, J., Osses, P., Sarsour, J., Frost, E., Estrela, M. J., Valiente, J. A., & Fessehaye, G. M. (2012). Fog as a freshwater resource: Overview and perspectives. *AMBIO*, *41*(3), 221–234. https://doi.org/10.1007/s13280-012-0247-8
Lample, T. (n.d.). *Ballad of the fiancé of Fog* (Boutmezguida Center, Aït Baamrane, Morocco) [Panel].
Lample, T. (2018). *Oasis de Brouillard dans les Montagnes des Ait Ba'amrane*. [Presentation]. issuu.com/titouanlampe/docs/lampe_titouan_brouillard_diplome_is
Lmouden, R. (2019). *Brui-Art: Le son du paysage* [Rabab music].
Marzol, V. (2010). Meteorological patterns and fogwater in Morocco and the Canary Islands. *Proceedings of the 5th International Conference on Fog, Fog Collection and Dew*, 56–59.
Marzol-Jaén, M. V. (2011). Historical background of fog water collection studies in the Canary Islands. In *Tropical montane cloud forests: Science for conservation and management*, 352. Cambridge University Press.
Santich, B. (2007). The study of gastronomy: A catalyst for cultural understanding. *International Journal of the Humanities*, *5*(6), 53–58.
Taheripour, F., Tyner, W., Haqiqi, I., & Sajedinia, E. (2020). *Water scarcity in Morocco: Analysis of key water challenges*. https://doi.org/10.1596/33306

11 Encounters
Art, Science, Clouds, and Water

Ana Rewakowicz

Introduction

Since ancient times, the image of the cloud has held profound meaning for the human psyche (Basker, 2006, p. 112). It has been a sign of divine presence. For example, the Ancient Hebrews adapted the image of the cloud for Yahweh, and a symbol of creation, fertility, power, and protection (Basker, 2006, p. 113). From the industrial revolution onward, the meaning of the cloud has expanded to include human control and power, as represented by the factory chimneys' clouds (Evans & Hansen, 2016, p. 34). More recently, clouds have come to symbolize connectivity, as illustrated by the computational cloud of information, becoming an emblem of both real and virtual pollutions at the same time. The cloud "will forever elude our human understanding" (Basker, 2006, p. 111), as it defines limits of our knowledge and the impossibility of seeing clearly. "Symbolically the cloud form is as much a reminder of our loftiest aspirations and dreams as it is of the gathering storm unchecked environmental deterioration has us riding straight into" (Schütze, 2011).

Clouds are essential elements of the hydrological cycle responsible for water circulation from the surface of the earth to the atmosphere and then back again. This cycle is considered the engine of life on Earth. Both the weather and climate depend on it and so do we, with the rest of biota on this planet. We are part of this cycle.

This chapter presents research on the collection of water from fog as an alternative source of freshwater, undertaken in collaboration with scientists, Camille Duprat and Jean-Marc Chomaz, at the Hydrodynamics Laboratory (LadHyx) at École Polytechnique in Paris. One could say that the artistic path that led me to work on the problem of water shortage is a story of encounter with clouds through touch.

This account is written in the first-person narrative voice as a participant meandering through memories, reflections, as well as artworks, the scientific process, and accounts of events.

DOI: 10.4324/9781003150862-11

Artist Trajectory

Similar to clouds, mobility has been the story of my life. I was born in northern Poland and grew up under communism. As survivors of World War II, my parents were deported from their own land and culture, and endured imprisonment and persecution. My body became a living memory of their stories, engaged in the practice of survival. My art took me on explorations of habitat and sustainability, as an undertaking of ethical responsibility to provide the basic needs of shelter, food, and water.

The body is our first house and home simultaneously, defining the boundaries of inside and outside, and navigating in between them in an ongoing and never-ending relationship. The body sends and receives signals, it responds, reacts, does, makes, creates, and changes until it ceases to separate, and dissolves into the nothingness of an inside-out-ness, becoming one without boundaries. But before that, it establishes home "at the heart of the real" says writer Mircea Eliade (as cited in Berger, 2005, p. 55). Art critic and writer John Berger (2005, p. 64) observes home not as a thing or a place but as doing, "a practice or a set of practices," where "everyone has its own." Home is "the untold story of a life being lived."

To dissolve the boundaries of inside and outside, in one of my early works, I took an imprint of a room in my Montreal apartment, covering the ceiling, walls, and floor in many coats of rubber latex to build up a desired thickness. When finished, I peeled off the entire surface and ended up with a transportable "skin" containing original moldings, cracks, and other remains like dirt or hair—memories of lived experiences. I turned it inside out (what used to be a negative impression—a mold, became a reverse impression—cast), and constructed outside layers, and connected them to the skin of the room in order for the whole structure to inflate or deflate as desirable. The *Inside Out* room created a twofold viewing situation allowing the visitor to look at the exterior structure of a room, as well as to enter into it to experience touchable memories of the whimsical and unsettling space inside. I took this room-like skin (my portable body house) on a cross-Canada trip, during which I camped in it at different urban areas (local parks, underground parking structures, private and public backyards, unoccupied buildings, street corners) and rural locations (parks, campsites, abandoned villages), as shown in Figure 11.1.

The trajectory of moving, or being moved by circumstance has instilled in me a sense of impermanence and fluidity that have always been part of my art practice. For many years, I *breathed* air into mobile structures that questioned our relationship with the body and the environment in the context of nomadic architecture.

I was inspired by the visionary ideas of architectural groups from the 1960s, and in particular the British architectural group Archigram, who combined playful design with technological fascination to develop socially responsive forms and create alternative propositions for living. Stimulated

Figure 11.1 Inside Out and Traveling With My Inflatable Room

Note: Sculpture & video stills. Montreal, Canada: Saidye Bronfman Gallery & Musée d'art contemporain.

Source: Copyright (2021) Ana Rewakowicz.

by their concept of "clothing for living in" (Cushicle & Suitaloon, 2016), I harnessed technology (solar panels, batteries, ventilators, sensors) and created a series of dresses titled *Dressware* (playing with the phrase "you never know where/wear" to encompass both humor and poetics) that, through inflation, changed function, enabling survival in different habitats (land, air, water).

In another piece, together with students from the Department of Mechanical Engineering at McGill University in Montreal, I developed a solar bicycle prototype for urban commuting and dwelling.

My costumes and objects were air-filled, mobile, and concerned with the places and people that activated them. Working with inflatable structures, I was drawn to American thinker Buckminster Fuller's interest in lightness and the weight of materials as a means to counteract excessive materialism and waste. In the context of contemporary issues such as environmental degradation, climate change, social displacement, or population growth, we need to think about lightness, and how to live, travel, and transport our goods with reduced impact on the environment.

Striving for integrity of processes, materials, and ideas, and influenced by Fuller's concept of *Synergetics*, which is a system of thinking that encompasses a multifaceted approach toward life and design (as cited, Ben Eli, 2010), I worked through and with different materials. I used rubber latex as a material that resembles skin—the largest organ of the body through which we experience the sense of touch. According to feminist theorist Karen Barad: "So much happens in a touch: an infinity of others—other beings, other spaces, other time—are aroused" (Barad, 2014, p. 153). In my case, it was the texture of goosebumps, the involuntary reaction of the skin capable of both connecting us with the environment and expressing inner sensations of excitement (arousal/attraction) or state of shock (fear/discomfort/cold). Using rubber latex with a goosebumps texture, I created a body-sized mattress, a series of clothing as a second skin, and the *Come Closer* installation in which I covered an entire room in the texture of goosebumps.

The long-term durability of inflatable materials still eludes us, yet their potential for both usefulness and playfulness is paramount. As an artist, I have investigated not only the material potential of inflatables (durability, lightness, portability, thermal and structural properties, fabrication processes, material memory, biodegradability) but also the cultural and aesthetic implications of *lightness* as a possibility, among others, for employing humor.

In my installation *The Conversation Bubble*, at any given moment five participants breathe the same air while sharing the common space of the inflatable bubble. Their bodies are squeezed between two layers of vinyl while their heads are free to move inside a big inflated and transparent balloon. During the performance, no one is able to leave on their own accord, and the duration depends on the five participants' agreement.

By inviting people to enter the wobbly space of the latex room where there is nothing to catch hold of when losing balance, wearing and residing inside dresses, touching the texture of goosebumps, or inviting participants to converse inside an inflated bubble, my objective is to provide various platforms of interaction and create new patterns of engagement through the artworks' space of materiality and meaning (matter and mattering). In these artworks, participation is a responsive relationship, creating a temporal meaning, always to the exclusion of other meanings. Every conversation inside the *Conversation Bubble* is different, just as every touch of the texture of goosebumps creates different reactions and different meanings. The artist is not a creator of meaning, but rather a creator of an invitation for participation through active response.

Cloud Encounter

In 2011, I invited people to use small hand pumps with one-way valves to pump water into a large cloud-shaped object floating in a gallery space. The cloud produced rain when activated this way by participants. In this work, my interest laid in the object's and participants' relationships and co-dependencies. Writer Bernard Schütze comments on the project's "poetically pragmatic rainmaking function" (Schütze, 2011) and says: "Brought so close to view in our big interior this cloud leaves little room to evade the current condition: in this change of atmosphere we are now all weather makers of one sort or another" (Schütze, 2011).

I have moved and lived in many different places, countries, languages, and cultures, and I was surprised to discover that the color of the sky in Toronto was the same as in Rome, as there is only a 1.5-degree difference in latitude between them. In contrast, I was born 10 degrees farther north where the skies were different, with purple, red, and yellow sunsets lasting forever.

Ever since my first airplane flight and seeing clouds from above, I could imagine myself spending my entire life in the clouds. I did not want to land, I just wanted to stay in the sky. For a period of more than ten years, I obsessively recorded clouds from planes, first with a Super 8 camera (I liked the blurriness and grainy black and white feel of the image as it reminded me of old photographs from family albums), then with video cameras, and finally with smartphones. I have accumulated hours upon hours of cloud footage. Still, it was not enough to simply look at them from afar, I needed to zoom in, to get closer, so close that I could touch them.

That happened in 2017, when I was visiting the fog-collecting site on Mount Boutmezguida in Morocco. For the first time in my life, I was able to extend my hand and feel a gentle and intangible presence moving through my fingers, uncatchable, and yet all embracing. Before that moment I was not aware that fog is a cloud and that it is possible to touch clouds from the ground. And there I was, not on a plane looking at them from a distance, but on a mountain, enshrouded in the invisible milkiness inside a cloud.

This intimate sensation gave rise to the feeling of quietude and stillness. I was in the clouds, and at rest, among many small water droplets suspended in the air that were being moved by wind, coming from and going to somewhere else.

By this time, I was immersed in research on collecting water from fog at LadHyx at École Polytechnique in Paris as a Ph.D. researcher, after being an artist-in-residence in 2014. Considering that air and water have been flowing in and out of my art production since the beginning, the invitation to jointly collaborate with scientists on water scarcity presented itself as an exciting opportunity. It strongly resonated with my art practice that addresses basic survival needs such as shelter, food, or water, and my desire to build interdisciplinary bridges.

Mist Collector Project

Thinking Diffractively With Water

The *Mist Collector* project connects two critical aspects of my research: the water shortage (problem) and collecting water from fog (possible solution) with the practice of ethical "response-ability" (the practice of creating an invitation for inclusive participation). Art enmeshed in the practice of ethical response-ability, employs imagination to expand the circle of inclusion, and invites water and wind to become participants in the collaboration. This invitation for participation is also extended to the general public through immersive art installations in which the viewer/participant is invited to experience an encounter with water, wind, and clouds.

Due to the excessive exploitation of water sources through issues and systems like privatization, monopolization, mono-agriculture, population growth, and climate change, we are facing a rising problem of water shortage in the world, especially in arid and semi-arid areas where water sources are already scarce. Under these circumstances, research into alternative freshwater sources that do not require a great amount of energy is crucial and of great consequence. One possible alternative is the collection of atmospheric water (hydrometeors) from rain, dew, and fog. While water harvesting from rain and dew is also substantial, my research has focused on fog (which is a cloud close to the ground), merging my long-term fascinations with clouds and an artistic practice centered on survival.

The *Mist Collector* art and science project started with the scientific question of efficiency involved in the collection of water from fog and evolved into an artistic response through the creation of four artworks. In the section titled *Art: The Response*, I present (I) *Through the Looking Mist . . .*; (II) the *Porous Sail* prototype; (III) *Misty Way*; and (IV) *Nephelograph (Mist Impressions)*. These artworks comprise a response to the scientific investigations of fog water collection efficiency with flexible parallel vertical fibers, which I describe in *Science: The Question*.

Science: The Question

My 2014 artist-in-residency period at LadHyx played a crucial role in the development of our research. It not only specified the study question but also mapped out technical research that had to be done to achieve an adequate experimental setup for the hypothesis of increasing efficiency with flexible parallel vertical fibers. Our scientific research focused on two essential aspects involved in the process of fog water collection: mesh and structural forms. When dealing with the question of efficiency in mesh design, our aim was to address the problems of clogged drainage and re-entrainment impeding fog water collection. The clogged drainage problem happens when water droplets fill entire holes in a grid-like net and gravity cannot overcome surface tension for water droplets to fall into the net's collecting gutter. The problem of re-entrainment occurs when incoming water droplets are blown away by the wind before they are able to reach the critical size to be pulled instead by gravity. Our second aspect took into consideration effects of the wind on the collection of water from fog and proposed two novel propositions for structural forms: a flower (fleur) forest and a porous sail.

The residency provided the foundation of my own scientific understanding of the physics of collecting water from fog. By being exposed to scientific terminology, I learned to comprehend these problems, but not without learning a new language. I could not imagine myself collaborating with scientists without understanding what they were talking about. Thus, my first encounters with LadHyx researchers were a series of lessons in the language of science and the scientific method.

When we encounter someone or something new what do we do? We interact by engaging in an attempt to understand, to get to know better. Language is one of the most common means by which we do that. However, each group or profession tends to use words and expressions that are particular to their practice and are difficult to comprehend from outside. Understanding this specialized language gives access to its members and excludes those who do not understand. We use these specialized languages for many reasons, primarily because they are faster and easier (the path of least resistance) to communicate, and often we do it unconsciously. It takes extra effort to notice, and a willingness to change—one must walk the extra mile to meet the other halfway. Additional difficulty piles up if one comes from a different cultural background. In this case, one must not only overcome comprehension but also linguistic gaps. Communication can become quite a complicated thing, but how else could we know anything at all?

Art: The Response

In *Science: The Question*, our research proposed a new paradigm of flexible parallel vertical fibers, suggesting that through the understanding of physical properties, we could achieve better efficiencies for fog collection at lower costs and without chemical enhancement.

There are different ways of relating. One involves seeing entities we encounter as separate things producing interactions, while the other focuses on actions we perform, recognizing that entities are result of our actions (Barad, 2007). The latter approach discerns the impossibility of the separation between ontology (*what is*) and epistemology (*how it became to be*), or to put it differently, between questions we ask and the answers we get. Thus, interactions become intra-actions (Barad, 2007), connecting us to current, previous, and future actions.

My path of intra-acting with science generated an image of a forest that launched experiments with flexible parallel vertical fibers. Technical research and experimentation fell into three strands: artificial fog production, new fabrication methods of parallel fiber nets (substrate), and novel propositions of fog-collecting structural forms.

Art: The Response presents my artistic response to the scientific investigations that were undertaken. Owing to the fact that three out of four of these artworks rely on spatio-visceral experiences in physical environments, my intent is not to provide a descriptive representation (as if their meaning were independent of this process) but rather to (re)create their meaning in a different way. To do that, I use a diffractive method of narration, in which inside voices carry the reader through vignettes of philosophical reflections, scientific interludes, logs, poetic encounters, recounting of public responses, as well as images. It is a journey that stitches together a new landscape so as to offer a relational experience of creation. To capture the nonlinearity (a lack of continuity) of this process, I employ various formal strategies such as text divisions into columns, boxes, and poems with the goal of engaging the reader to become part of changing relationships with the artworks, and hence part of the creation of meaning.

Artwork I: *Through the Looking Mist . . .* (2014 and 2016)

Seeing a Void

Through the Looking Mist . . . is a large video projection of slow-motion water droplet coalescence on parallel vertical fibers. The video was edited from clips recorded as part of initial experiments, in which we attempted to evaluate our novel proposal of collecting water from fog with flexible parallel vertical fibers. Projected large, visitors are able to see drops slowly appearing, growing, and then falling. This spatiotemporal change of scale invites the spectator to examine their point of view and experience the phenomenon at the scale of each emerging water droplet. Not differently to the heroine in *Alice's Adventures in Wonderland*, whose body proportions depend on different spaces she passes through, the piece brings focus to the world, where significance is not dependent on size, but rather on the interaction of forces.

Through the Looking Mist . . . premiered in an exhibition at Zayed University in Abu Dhabi (UAE) as part of the International Symposium on Electronic Art (ISEA) in 2014. It was also projected 10 meters tall on a large building façade inside the Centre de recherches interdisciplinaires (CRI) as part of Nuit Blanche in Paris in 2018.

It is always a complement when people stay with an artwork longer than 10 seconds—a short attention span—which was the case with the *Through the Looking Mist* . . . video. I was surprised by how much time people spent with the piece.

Lab Log 1

September 29, 2014, at 9:30, Prefab, LadHyx, École Polytechnique, Palaiseau, France.

A fast computer-controlled camera captures consecutive images of water collection from generated mist-like snapshots in time. The high-speed camera is capable of taking up to 10,000 images per second, which is more than I can distinguish with my eyes, meaning my conscious brain. For example, when I look at fog, I cannot perceive individual water droplets but with a fast camera I can see differently sized dots moving around. If seeing depends on slowing downtime, does it mean that if every cell in my body could stop, I could see everything?

Lab Log 2

September 30, 2014, at 14:30, Building 67, LadHyx, École Polytechnique, Palaiseau, France.

Buckminster Fuller said that our bodily senses are tuning apparatuses "within the physical, sensorial range of tunability of the electromagnetic sensing equipment with which we personally have been organically endowed" (Fuller, 1979, Synergy 100.62). Furthermore, Fuller indicates that things that we are not aware of are simply things that we have not tuned into yet, or perhaps touched. Could the camera as an extension of my eye bring me closer to a water droplet?

Lab Log 3

September 30, 2014, at 17:30, Building 67, LadHyx, École Polytechnique, Palaiseau, France.

Watching water drops coalescing on parallel fibers I could not but think of time in water's generative cycle of giving and receiving, living and dying, and the temporal nature of life. I saw in them an *ode* to the cycle of emergence and disappearance, in which time is not linear but cyclical. And if everything is cyclical, there is nothing to progress toward other than the end of the cycle, which is nothing more than a new beginning.

Lab Log 4

October 8, 2014, at 10:30 am, Building 65, LadHyx, École Polytechnique, Palaiseau, France.

Creation is an anti-entropic activity that decreases entropy by bringing order to the chaos of a multitude of unorganized clips. This order is the one envisioned by the maker and offers more possibilities for the viewer to change it and re-order it through intra-action. The viewer's intra-actions will generate distinct sequences and create meaning that produces higher entropy in the process. Thus, creation presents an opportunity for order defining states, which can generate higher potential.

. . .

Cut. Collaborating with the fast camera is enchanting; we can see things appearing out of an invisible void, the void that is never empty. *Final cut.*

Seeing a Void

From nothingness
a drizzle, or a quiet snow, or a misty rain, or a pelting rain, or a
stinging sleet, or at times a hail materializes and unfolds.
It is mesmerizing to see small water droplets becoming visible points in
space,
emerging on thin lines of flexible threads.
They coalesce, slowly grow bigger
and struggle to stay attached in the airflow.
When their mass overcomes surface tension they give into gravity and
fall.
At other times, the water's surface tension brings two adjacent fibers
together creating capillary bridges that then,
turn into long liquid columns.
Different geometries produce different behaviors;
triangulated threads produce a thin film that deforms fibers by
bringing them closer together,
the film elongates, stretches to the maximum capacity and breaks,
yielding a water drop.
A dance, a cycle between a rise and fall.
Could this be a more efficient way of collecting water from fog?
We measure, we weigh, we observe, we repeat and we wait.

Artwork II: Porous Sail Prototype (2015)

Going With the Wind

The *Porous Sail* prototype comes from research on new aerodynamic structural forms for fog water collection. Since wind is an essential factor in

Figure 11.2 Through the Looking Mist . . .

Note: Video projection. Abu Dhabi, United Arab Emirates: University of Abu Dhabi (right) Rewakowicz, A., & Duprat, C. (2014). Rewakowicz, A. (2015). *Porous Sail* prototype (left). Récollets, Paris, France.

Source: Copyright (2021) Ana Rewakowicz.

harvesting water from fog, as it causes tiny water droplets in fog to coalesce into bigger water droplets upon impact with a substrate, we thought of the idea of "going with the wind," like a sail (Figure 11.2).

As three-dimensional shapes can be geometrically constructed through a series of lines in space (following the logic of the mathematical concept of ruled surfaces), the *Porous Sail* prototype is a structure resembling a double sail with a thread twisting around a central mast, leading downward to patterns of reversed curves cut into plexiglass panels that are positioned perpendicular to the lower end of the mast (Figure 11.2).

Artwork III: Misty Way (2015–2016)

Water Encounter

While the intent of *Through the Looking Mist . . .* centered on the observation of water droplet behavior on flexible parallel vertical fibers, *Misty Way* incorporated a second strand of scientific investigations involving a new net fabrication method and focused on creation of the environment in which fog water collection takes place.

To do that we developed a fabrication technique for parallel fiber nets, which we used as screens for water droplet video footage projection. In this process, we discovered a curious visual effect, in which part of the water droplet footage was visible on the parallel fiber screen and the rest, bypassed the screen and spread on the floor, creating a double projection, and a tunneling guise where water droplets appeared to be moving away and disappearing into the darkness.

This captivating optical illusion inspired the creation of an installation titled *Misty Way* that took place at Centre Intermondes in La Rochelle, France in 2016. For this artwork, I collaborated with students from the University of La Rochelle to produce nine parallel fiber panels of 1 × 10 meters that were then combined into three large-scale screens of 3 × 10 meters each, and installed in three areas of the gallery, divided by two columns. Hanging along on a curve (not unlike a hammock), these panels created a large tripartite video projection area.

For video footage, we re-filmed water droplets with an even higher magnification, deliberately experimenting with their various sizes (100 microns to 0.5 mm) and movement trajectories from left to right, diagonally, or up and down in different formations. These different shots are edited together into a movie and split into three computer-controlled projections intended to evoke a feeling of water drops traversing in space.

Misty Way (re)constructs the environment in which mist water is captured with a textile net of parallel fibers. In this installation, viewers are immersed among swirling virtual fog droplets that have been captured in extreme close-up with a high-speed camera. These projected *waterlight* droplets drift on breezes from hidden fans around and through billowing fibers suspended from the ceiling of the room, collecting in the net or passing through to the floor. The *waterlight* drops visually splash on the spectator and on the floor creating an immersive environment, where viewers are submerged in a virtual mist of widely spattered drops of light, shadows, and sound. Daniel Schorno, an electronic music composer, created a musical composition embodying reconstruction of noises recorded during our laboratory experiments (Figure 11.3).

Diffraction 1: On Light

> Light plays a fundamental role in all life processes on Earth and beyond. "Light carries information about our surroundings, from distant stars and galaxies to the cells in our bodies to individual atoms and molecules" (Walmsley, 2015, p. XV).

Figure 11.3 Misty Way

Note: Rewakowicz, A., Duprat, C., & Chomaz, J. M. (2016). La Rochelle. Centre Intermondes, France.

Source: Copyright (2021) Ana Rewakowicz.

Light is knowledge and a metaphor for thinking about the world (Walmsley, 2015, p. 1). In fact, philosopher Jacques Derrida says that the entire Western thought is shaped by the concept of light (Miles, 2009). Through the biblical story of creation, the scientific *seeing* to the philosophical *knowing*, light has embodied enlightenment that illuminates the darkness of ignorance, "where all that falls . . . in[to] indeterminate darkness, [is] waiting to be brought to the light" (Miles, 2009). Ian Walmsley, physics researcher and Provost of Imperial College London, remarks that it is fascinating that we can still discover new things about light, considering that optics is one of the oldest of the sciences having originated in the 4th century BCE (Walmsley, 2015, pp. 4–5).

One Hundred and Twenty Kilometers Walked and Stretched One by One

Not everyone is fit to perform repetitive tasks. It requires both patience and concentration that personally I find soothing and meditative, similar to walking or jogging, when your mind wonders off in an enjoyable and carefree way. A small group of students that keep coming back must share the same feeling. It is an amusing way to spend time together. We play music and talk while taking turns walking between two rods that are 10 meters apart and placing the thread into 666 grooves spaced 1.5 mm apart on each rod. Thus, each screen of 1 × 10 meters uses approximately 13 kilometers of thread (666 × 2 × 10 = 13,320 m), as the thread is wrapped on both sides. Thirteen kilometers multiplied by nine panels give us ***one hundred and twenty kilometers*** of walked thread.

. . .

Surprise

From the beginning, my idea was to give participants the possibility of experiencing the piece in a nontraditional way by lying on the floor and looking up at the screens. To do this, I purchase pillows and spread them around the gallery space in such a way that visitors upon entering would face the direction of descent so the *waterlight* droplets start from above and behind passing them over, and finally moving away and into the distance in front. . . . To my surprise, when, I come

> into the gallery room at the end of the opening evening, after everyone is gone, the first thing I notice that all pillows are moved to the opposite side of the room. Intrigued, I lie down where the pillows are and discover a new world! Instead of moving away, the *waterlight* droplet universe is rushing toward me!

Water Encounter

Imagine entering a dark room.
In the pitch black your eyes hurt.
It feels like they grow bigger, become rounder
and stretch to the maximum.
And it takes a stretch of imagination to see in the dark.
Imagine . . .
. . . being submerged in water
shimmering light passes above and through you,
touching your skin and eyes.
Sound, in and out of sync,
calms and other times pierces through your ears.
In the dark,
water passes through every cell in your body
carrying oxygen and nutrients through the tiniest blood vessels against gravity.
Water
transports electrical charges filling your brain with thoughts
that create a stream of consciousness . . .
a dazzling light . . .
a rain of light drops . . .
Gazing at distant stars, asteroids or perhaps a solar nebula,
is that a beginning of life?
dis/oriented . . .
immersed in a darkness of abundant im/possibilities . . .
I listen, you extend my hand
I touch, you touch.

Diffraction 2: On Touching

So matter comes from nothing and disappears into nothing, yet nothing is not nothing, and is full of intra-activity from which all energy we know comes from and to which it returns, just as life in aboriginal stories that comes from, and returns to water (Strang, 2015).

Anthropologist Veronica Strang describes that in many cultures, water is considered a sentient and sacred being. She recounts an Aboriginal story of how:

> human spirit beings "jump up" from their ancestral waters to materialize or "become visible" in human form. At the end of each individual human life cycle, they return to their watery home to be reunited with their ancestors, "becoming invisible" and so dissolving back into collective formless potential.
>
> (Strang, 2015, p. 38)

Participation

During the time in La Rochelle, I shared the residency at Centre Intermondes with Maori artist George Nuku, who was preparing an exhibition at the Museum of Natural History. I invited him to see *Misty Way*. When he came out from the installation space, he was silent, looked me in the eyes, and then bowed his head in a gesture of appreciation. It was the highest compliment I could imagine, as I felt that the piece was able to touch someone from a different culture and a different language, and move them to participation.

Magic happens when we accept an invitation and open ourselves to be affected by what is brought to us. Perhaps only in the suspense of disbelief, in letting go of a desire to *see* (know) sharply and clearly, that we could be touched and touch back. Perhaps in the surrender to the blurriness of darkness we could come close and encounter *the other*, and perhaps this is the difference between a trickster and a shaman. The former uses power to fool you, while the latter offers you the possibility to become a participant in a phenomenon, without mediation, without distance of externality. Once you step in, there is no knowing, only responding through an act of participation.

Artwork IV: Nephelograph (Mist Impressions) (2017–2018)

Touching Clouds

Nephelograph (Mist Impressions) [in French—*Néphélographe (Impressions de brouillard)*] is a cloud machine designed to scribe different forms of clouds. It deals with the production of larger quantities of artificial fog and consists of multiple, stackable units made from clear plexiglass with submerged ultrasonic misters that produce a current of fog bouncing against an obstacle (a leaning transparent plaque) to create a turbulent mass of mist. *Nephelograph*'s name comes from the Greek word for clouds—*néphos*—and refers to *Nephelai*, cloud nymphs from Greek mythology who are traditionally portrayed as young women, nourishing the earth with rain by pouring water from cloudy pitchers they dipped in *Okeanus*—a sky river encircling the Earth (Theoi, n.d).

Nephelograph (Mist Impressions) was part of the *Nous ne sommes pas le nombre que nous cryons être* exhibition at Cité internationale de arts in Paris. For this exhibition, we collaborated with fifth-grade children from Paul Langevin elementary school and used the machine as a message scriber. To engage children in the project, we gave in-class presentations on the science and art of collecting water from fog, and arranged a visit to the École Polytechnique for the kids to experience the cloud machine in action. Afterward, we asked children to write haiku—short poems with messages to the clouds.

We took these haikus written by the fifth graders and programmed the machine to puff them out letter by letter. These poems, carried away and deformed by the wind, created messages that even though not totally legible, echoed a collective dream of a better future.

Composer Daniel Schorno sonified these poems by mapping the machine's 16-unit grid with pre-coded sounds generated in Max/MSP software. The on/off states of foggers activated these sound bites through electric signals. Between poems, we programmed short interludes comprised of varietal, spatially shaped patterns (e.g., spirals, up and down, diagonals, or left to right), producing unpredictable sound compositions. To further integrate sound with the machine, Schorno incorporated the audio system into the existing design.

For the second presentation of *Nephelograph (Mist Impressions)* for Nuit Blanche in Paris in 2018, we expanded our programming capacity to incorporate fans (in addition to foggers), which allowed us to create more sophisticated cloud variations. Using these different formations as vocabulary, we put together an audiovisual composition based on the structure of a symphony in four movements: sonata (or allegro), a slow movement (or adagio), scherzo (or minuet dance), and finally rondo with coda (finale). The opening sonata introduced the main elements of our visual vocabulary, which we nicknamed as "little cloud," "fog tunnel," "tornado," "big cloud," and "fall." The second slow movement (adagio) created a gentle combination of "puffs," "fall away," "dots," and "bubbles." The third movement (scherzo) was made up of a faster motion of such variations as "swirls," "exploding columns," or "fog tunnel window," and the final part (rondo) presented alternating themes of "falls," "denser mix," and "dots," with a coda of "spirals" at the end.

Figure 11.4 Nephelograph (Mist Impressions)

Note: Installation. Paris, France: Nuit Blanche (top left & right) and Cité internationales des arts (bottom left & right). An example of a haiku written by a fifth grader using the machine's alphabet typography (bottom right). It reads: Cloud, how many days did it take you to go around the Earth? (author's translation). Rewakowicz, A., Duprat, C., & Chomaz, J. M. (2018).

Source: Copyright (2021) Ana Rewakowicz.

For the audio component of the piece, the main objective was to create an auditory dialogue with the generated clouds and to integrate sounds as much as possible with the machine's performance. Considering that clouds are turbulences of humid air in the atmosphere, Daniel Schorno explored the concept of irregular change of airflow in turbulences and a cascading (a series of steps) distribution in data processing algorithms to conceive *sound clouds* that could communicate with fog clouds in various rhythms.

Nephelograph (Mist Impressions) created a multisensory environment, where visitors were able to participate in a dialogue with clouds by touching and interacting with them.

Cloud Encounters

Ultrasonic misters break the surface of water
into small droplets that then bounce against transparent plaques
to come together and create turbulent fog masses—small clouds.

Ventilators at the back push these small clouds through honeycomb filters
and small clouds combine into bigger clouds.
The apparatus is alive;
water percolates as it rushes through tubing and hums pumping tunes.
An animal—a dragon or a serpent perhaps,
breathing clouds—
falling clouds, bubble clouds, swirling clouds, spiraling clouds, tornado clouds, little clouds, big clouds, puffy clouds, exploding clouds, tunneling clouds . . .
clouds . . . breaths . . .
being close enough to touch, to sense, to feel, to intra-act with . . .
breath-sounds—
a polyphony played by an orchestra of different electric signals.
You are invited . . .
to come forward,
to touch,
to respond,
to feel,
to entangle with . . .
yourself . . .
clouds . . .
suspended halfway
between earth and sky.

Dance

A couple moves closer to the machine.
He distances himself; she stays.
She sits on the ground and remains still for a long time.
Then slowly, ever so slightly starts removing her shoes.
Her gestures are slow, fluid, gentle, and yet decisive.
She appears and disappears, in and out of clouds, waving her body to cascading sounds.
She astounds me.
I want to touch her . . . but in the dark I cannot find the right settings on my camera . . .
a silhouette against bright lights at the end of the space.
Watch!
In silence she dances to the sounds of clouds.
Time passes—40 minutes!
She casually gets up, sits on a bench and leaves.
I do not know who she was.
I never asked her for her name.

Conclusion

No entity can exist outside of itself. We cannot take apparatuses out of scientific knowledge production, and we cannot isolate audiences from artistic creation, or concepts from theories, or sociocultural and political factors from institutional practices. There is not one meaning, but an indeterminate possibility of meanings and all of them matter even though not all of them could manifest themselves at the same time.

Mist Collector not only tried to address the scientific quest of fog water collection efficiency but also sought to create an open invitation for the visitor to become a participant in the act of connecting with water, the stranger within us, our bodies, our thoughts, our food, and our wellbeing. And in this process, it aspired to bring forward ethical responsiveness that can move us to action.

The *Mist Collector* project brings forward a phenomenological engagement with water and with *the other* that is never totally separate. It asks participants to re-open themselves to ethical response-ability by accepting the invitation to respond. It is through imagination and poetics that we are able to sense what is hidden, feel the heartless, insensible, and indefinite within every being to be/come, and in so doing perform change and create justice in what it means to live responsibly, together/apart with all human, nonhuman, and non-beings on this planet, in the cosmos, and with water. The *Mist Collector* project, by inviting the public to experience water at the scale of a single droplet and (imaginatively speaking) aboard Spaceship Earth, traveling through fog, calls for the necessity to begin building a collective narrative of "an uncertain shadow of an ever failing ecosophic Future/Present/Past" (Rewakowicz, 2020, p. 346) that may still be envisioned and conceived together.

Acknowledgment

The author would like to thank Dr. Leslie L. Dodson for her assistance in editing this chapter.

References

Barad, K. (2007). *Meeting the universe halfway*. Duke University Press.

Barad, K. (2014). On touching—The inhuman that therefore I am (v 1.1). In S. Witzgall & K. Stakemeier (Eds.), *The politics of materiality* (pp. 153–164). Diaphanes.

Basker, J. (2006). THE CLOUD AS SYMBOL: Destruction or dialogue. *Cross-Currents*, 56(1), 110–115. Retrieved February 8, 2021, from www.jstor.org/stable/24461099.

Ben Eli, M. (2010, June 3). *Architecting the Future* [Video]. Vimeo. Retrieved February 8, 2021, from https://vimeo.com/12808820.

Berger, J. (2005). *And our faces, my heart, brief as photos* (Kindle). Bloomsbury.

Cushicle and Suitaloon. (December 2016). Retrieved June 23, 2021 from https://cushicleandsuitaloone3.wordpress.com/

Evans, H., & Hansen, H. (Eds.). (2016). *Man made clouds*. Editions HYX, Paris.

Fuller, B., & Applewhite, E. J. (1979). *Synergetics* (2nd ed.). Macmillan Publishing.

Miles, M. (2009). *Solid States/Liquid Objects* [Pamphlet]. Monash University Art & Design, Melbourne.

Rewakowicz, A. (2020). Art and science intra-action of collecting water from fog: Ethical response-ability in Karen Barad's mattering. In C. Ross & C. Salter (Eds.), *Why sentience? Proceedings of the 26th International Symposium on Electronic Art* (pp. 341–347). Printemps Numérique, Montréal.

Schütze, B. (2011). Change of atmosphere. In Ana Rewakowicz (Ed.), *Here is not there/Ici n'est pas là-bas* [Exhibition Brochure]. EXPRESSION, Centre d'exposition de Saint-Hyacinthe.

Strang, V. (2015). *Water* (Kindle). Reaktion Books.

Walmsley, I. (2015). *Light* (Kindle). Oxford University Press.

12 Addressing Social Issues Through Immersive Media

Kuo-Ting Huang

Introduction

Immersive media, such as augmented and virtual reality, are applied widely in various settings, and the growth in immersive technology applications has led researchers to examine factors that might contribute to improving the effects of virtual environments on users' attitudes, perceptions, thoughts, and behaviors (Cummings & Bailenson, 2016). The increasing popularity of virtual reality head-mounted displays, such as Oculus Rift, HTC VIVE, and PlayStation VR, has elevated the immersive user experience to another level in various fields, including entertainment (Pallavicini et al., 2019), education (Huang et al., 2019), and cognitive training (Huang, 2020).

Immersive technologies are also used for storytelling purposes, especially to address social issues. For example, immersive journalism, which places users within stories using virtual reality and 360-degree video, has been used to promote empathy toward story characters. These new platforms have also led to a new understanding of storytelling. The goal of this chapter is to present a theoretical framework for analyzing and designing immersive stories that address social issues. The chapter starts by offering a definition of immersive media and introduces several theoretical concepts related to immersive storytelling. After outlining the theoretical framework, the chapter presents recommendations for applying immersive storytelling to social issues.

Defining Immersive Media

Researchers have been investigating technological immersion in the context of virtual reality and mediated environments since the 1990s. Steuer (1992) identified two dimensions of technological immersion: *vividness*, which refers to "the representational richness of a mediated environment as defined by its formal features" (p. 81), such as sensory breadth and sensory depth, and *interactivity*, which refers to "the extent to which users can participate in modifying the form and context of a mediated environment in real time" (p. 84) and relates to aspects such as speed, range, and mapping.

DOI: 10.4324/9781003150862-12

The level of immersion is generally determined by the technological quality of the media, and many media scholars have examined the effects of different technological features of media.

As these technologies developed, more system features were added, making mediated experiences more immersive. A meta-analysis of more than 100 experiments on the technological aspects of immersive media found that immersive system features have a medium effect size on a user's feeling of presence, which refers to the psychological experience of being in a mediated environment (Cummings & Bailenson, 2016). More specifically, immersive system features, such as control mapping, stereoscopy, user perspective, and field of view, can impact how users process digitalized environments as actual and physical spaces and can elicit stronger emotional responses from users.

Augmented reality (AR) and virtual reality (VR) are considered the future of immersive media and have begun to be applied to teaching, learning, and instructional design. By definition, AR is a technology that blends digital information with information from physical world environments, enabling users to interact with virtual objects and view the physical environment simultaneously, whereas VR involves real-time immersive simulations in environments rendered entirely through digital graphics. In other words, AR integrates virtual objects into a physical space, whereas VR blocks out information from the physical environment and transports users to a fully virtual world. Thus, VR provides users with the feeling of being psychologically immersed in a virtual environment, and AR allows users to interact with both virtual items and objects in the real world. To improve the design of user experiences, it is necessary to develop a theoretical framework to guide immersive media design.

Building a Theoretical Framework for Immersive Storytelling

This section introduces several theoretical concepts that are frequently used to discuss the potential effects of immersive media and storytelling on users' perceptions during media experiences. It begins with the concept of presence, which explains how the technological features of media generate experiences that are more immersive. It then considers the aspect of storytelling, which is equally as important as technological features, and narrative persuasion, which relates to how storytelling engages an audience. Finally, it examines how social cognitive theory and the Proteus effect explain the psychological impact of media characters on audiences.

Spatial Presence Experience

The concept of presence is difficult to define, which can lead to theoretical and methodical problems (Riecke & Schulte-Pelkum, 2015). Such problems can be traced back to early discussions on how to define presence. The original concept of presence has been developed, and different dimensions have been defined to account for the virtual experience of immersive technologies. These dimensions include social presence, physical presence, and self-presence (Lee, 2004). Wirth et al. (2007) focus on the presence as a metaphor and on the idea of "being there." They conceptualize spatial presence as a two-dimensional construct that includes perceived self-location and perceived action possibilities. The former describes a subjective feeling of being physically situated in the virtual or mediated environment, and the latter refers to the action possibilities of a media user relative to the virtual environment instead of the real world.

The experience of spatial presence has also been conceptualized as a two-step process (Schubert, 2009; Wirth et al., 2007). For media users to experience spatial presence, they must first allocate attentional resources, both media-induced (involuntary) and user-directed (controlled), to construct a spatial situational model, which is a mental representation of a mediated environment. Once they construct the spatial situational model based on the cues from the media environment, the second step is to move from the spatial situational model to spatial presence. Media users decide whether they want to take the spatial situational model as their primary ego-reference frame based on media-related factors (e.g., realism) and user-related factors (e.g., involvement), which influence the transition process. Spatial presence emerges once users accept the spatial situational model created in the first step as their primary frame of reference.

Immersive virtual environments, such as AR and VR, have been found to engender the feeling of presence (e.g., Seibert & Shafer, 2018). According to the two-step model of spatial presence (Wirth et al., 2007), both AR and VR provide rich sensory information, such as spatial cues and stereoscopic dimensions, and therefore allow media users to allocate more attentional resources and enable individuals to construct better spatial situation models. Empirical evidence also shows that media users invest more attentional resources in response to experiences that are more visually immersive (Havranek et al., 2012; Kober et al., 2012) and that immersive technologies contribute to the construction of mental models of virtual environments (Coxon et al., 2016). In other words, immersive technologies allow users to immerse themselves in stories as if they are physically located in the virtual environments in which the stories take place.

Narrative Engagement, Transportation, and Identification

Immersive technologies can also immerse media users in the narratives of the stories, which can contribute to increased empathy and prosocial behaviors. For example, 360-degree journalism films have been found to increase audiences' perceived realism and source credibility, leading to stronger story-sharing intention and feelings of empathy toward the media characters (Sundar et al., 2017). As well as journalism applications, immersive technologies have also been used to promote clinical empathy (Yu et al., 2021). Immersive storytelling is considered a powerful tool to promote empathy and address social issues (Barbot & Kaufman, 2020).

Immersive storytelling can help develop users' empathy by making them walk in someone else's shoes, and several theories have been proposed to explain the effects of narrative engagement on empathy and other prosocial behaviors, including perspective-taking, transportation, and identification. Perspective-taking refers to how media users perceive media character(s) in a narrative. Specifically, perspective-taking enables users to experience different roles. It has been found that individuals tend to be influenced by the character whose perspective they take on (De Graaf et al., 2012; Hoeken et al., 2016). Transportation refers to an experience that engages and absorbs media users and audiences in narrative worlds (Green et al., 2004). Specifically, when stories include imaginable plots and verisimilitude, media users are more likely to be transported into the narrative. Once transportation occurs, they experience enjoyment, which leads to acceptance of the beliefs and attitudes presented in the narrative. Both perspective-taking and transportation immerse users in a narrative world, causing them to develop attitudes consistent with the narrative.

Immersive technologies not only help immerse viewers in the narrative and enable them to understand the perspective of the media characters but also help viewers to build relationships with the characters. As the narrative develops, viewers may adopt a media character's perspective as their own perspective and assume the affective and cognitive responses of the media characters as their own, which is what defines identification (Cohen, 2001). During the process of identification, the audience forms a relationship with the media characters and develops affective and cognitive empathy toward those characters (Igartua, 2010). This identification with the media characters affects the emotions, attitudes, and behaviors of audiences, making them less resistant to persuasive messages presented in the narrative.

Social Cognitive Theory and the Proteus Effect

As previously mentioned, identification leads to greater empathy toward media characters and can even lead to imitation. According to Bandura (1977, 1994, 2004), people learn how to complete a task by directly performing the behavior themselves, which is enactive experience, and by observing and modeling others, which is vicarious experience. In other words, direct experiences are not the only way to learn a task. People can also learn by observing others, including actual people around them, celebrities on TV, and fictional characters portrayed in the media.

Media characters are often regarded as vicarious social models from whom audiences can learn through a process of social learning (Bandura, 2004). The occurrence of vicarious learning depends on several factors, including the modeled behavior, the model, and the observer. When a media character (the model) performs a task (the modeled behavior), the audience (the observer) may imitate the task either intentionally or unintentionally (Pajares et al., 2009; Peng, 2008). During this process, factors such as the complexity of the modeled behavior, the attractiveness of the model, the similarity between the model and the observer, and the learning abilities of the observer all impact the learning process. The intention to learn is also affected by users' motivations to perform the modeled behaviors and reinforcement of the learning process.

Immersive technologies allow media users to be distant witnesses and to participate in vicarious experiences (Gregory, 2015). For example, observing media characters perform prosocial behaviors may encourage audiences to model those behaviors (Carlo et al., 2018), and immersive storytelling can further enhance the effects of the immersive experience by engendering co-presence with the media characters (Cummings et al., 2021). The strength of such vicarious relationships is affected by the attractiveness of the model to the observer and the model's similarity to the observer (Bandura, 1994; Benight & Bandura, 2004). In short, vicarious experiences provided by immersive stories can serve as action templates for observers who can see and learn from media characters.

In a gaming context, media users (i.e., players) can customize the appearance of their avatars. Players may create an avatar much taller or better looking than they actually are in the real world. They can also experience different roles in a game, such as superheroes and doctors. The Proteus effect suggests that players may develop the attitudes and behaviors that confirm the characteristics of their avatars and specific traits and stereotypes associated with the avatars, and immersive technologies make the Proteus effect more salient (Yee et al., 2009). For example, people who were asked to create a taller avatar were more confident in a subsequent negotiation task in the real world than those who created a shorter avatar (Yee & Bailenson, 2007). For another example, using an avatar with superpowers also led to prosocial behaviors (Rosenberg et al., 2013). These findings showed that avatars might impact how their users think and act in the real world. Thus, players may express attitudes and behaviors consistent with their understanding of the avatars they use in a game.

Strategies for Immersive Storytelling

Immersive stories that focus on social issues typically include three main elements: virtual space, media characters, and narratives. When consuming an immersive story, the viewers will form a mental model of the mediated environments, feel connected to the media characters, and be transported into the narrative. Based on the theoretical frameworks discussed in this chapter, several strategies for using immersive technologies to address social issues can be identified. The theory applied depends on the purposes and goals of the immersive storytelling in question, which could be empathy education, health communication, and environmental protection. The choice of a framework to guide the design should be based on the three main elements of storytelling.

First, if the goal is to create immersive experiences that inform audiences about the space in which the story takes place, the formation of spatial presence experiences may be a useful framework to guide the design of the story. For example, when we address issues related to environmental protection, we may consider engendering in audiences a sense of physically being there and of the possibility of action in the virtual space. This helps the audience to form a mental model of the virtual environment and to feel that they can interact with or react to the environment and that they know what happens and what they can do in the space.

We may also want the audience to be immersed in the world of the story and the narrative plots, not just the virtual space. In this case, a theoretical framework based on transportation and narrative engagement should be applied when designing the immersive experience because we want to create an immersive experience that invites viewers to enter into the narrative as if they were a part of the story. As a result, users develop empathy toward and identify with the media characters and are mentally transported into the narrative world. When they are engrossed in the story, their attitudes change to reflect the characters, plots, or values of the story.

If we want audiences to feel even more connected to media characters so they can empathize and identify with them, we may consider incorporating the concepts of perspective-taking and identification when designing immersive stories that focus on the media characters. Finally, if the goal of the story is to have media users imitate the behaviors presented in the immersive story, then social cognitive theory can guide the design. For example, we may present media characters as role models to have audiences imitate prosocial behaviors, such as helping minority populations, eliminating social injustice, and encouraging environmental protection. The Proteus effect can be used to shape player's attitudes and behaviors consistent with the traits and characteristics of the avatars in a gaming context.

Conclusion

Immersive storytelling could be used to promote audiences' empathy and prosocial behaviors. However, immersive storytelling is not just the use of AR or VR. Several elements must be considered, such as the virtual space, the narrative, and the media characters. The theories discussed in this chapter provide some insights into how social issues can be addressed through immersive media. Depending on the purposes and goals of the storytellers, spatial presence, narrative engagement, or social cognitive theory can be used to emphasize different elements of immersive storytelling.

References

Bandura, A. (1977). Self-efficacy: Toward a unifying theory of behavioral change. *Psychological Review*, 84(2).

Bandura, A. (1994). Self-efficacy. In V. S. Ramachaudran (Ed.), *Encyclopedia of human behavior* (Vol. 4, pp. 71–81). Academic Press.

Bandura, A. (2004). Social cognitive theory for personal and social change by enabling media. In *Entertainment-education and social change: History, research, and practice* (pp. 75–96). Lawrence Erlbaum.

Barbot, B., & Kaufman, J. C. (2020). What makes immersive virtual reality the ultimate empathy machine? Discerning the underlying mechanisms of change. *Computers in Human Behavior*, 111, 106431.

Benight, C. C., & Bandura, A. (2004). Social cognitive theory of posttraumatic recovery: The role of perceived self-efficacy. *Behaviour Research and Therapy*, 42(10), 1129–1148. https://doi.org/10.1016/j.brat.2003.08.008

Carlo, G., Streit, C., & Crockett, L. (2018). Generalizability of a traditional social cognitive model of prosocial behaviors to US Latino/a youth. *Cultural Diversity and Ethnic Minority Psychology*, 24(4), 596.

Cohen, J. (2001). Defining identification: A theoretical look at the identification of audiences with media characters. *Mass communication & Society*, 4(3), 245–264.

Coxon, M., Kelly, N., & Page, S. (2016). Individual differences in virtual reality: Are spatial presence and spatial ability linked? *Virtual Reality*, 20(4), 203–212.

Cummings, J. J., & Bailenson, J. N. (2016). How immersive is enough? A meta-analysis of the effect of immersive technology on user presence. *Media Psychology*, 19(2), 272–309.

Cummings, J. J., Tsay-Vogel, M., Cahill, T. J., & Zhang, L. (2021). Effects of immersive storytelling on affective, cognitive, and associative empathy: The mediating role of presence. *New Media & Society*, 1, 24.

De Graaf, A., Hoeken, H., Sanders, J., & Beentjes, J. W. (2012). Identification as a mechanism of narrative persuasion. *Communication Research*, 39(6), 802–823.

Green, M. C., Brock, T. C., & Kaufman, G. F. (2004). Understanding media enjoyment: The role of transportation into narrative worlds. *Communication Theory*, 14(4), 311–327.

Gregory, S. (2015). Ubiquitous witnesses: Who creates the evidence and the live (d) experience of human rights violations? *Information, Communication & Society*, 18(11), 1378–1392.

Havranek, M., Langer, N., Cheetham, M., & Jäncke, L. (2012). Perspective and agency during video gaming influences spatial presence experience and brain activation patterns. *Behavioral and Brain Functions*, 8(1), 34.

Hoeken, H., Kolthoff, M., & Sanders, J. (2016). Story perspective and character similarity as drivers of identification and narrative persuasion. *Human Communication Research*, 42(2), 292–311.

Huang, K.-T. (2020). Exergaming executive functions: An immersive virtual reality-based cognitive training for adults aged 50 and older. *Cyberpsychology, Behavior, and Social Networking*, 23(3), 143–149.

Huang, K.-T., Ball, C., Francis, J., Ratan, R., Boumis, J., & Fordham, J. (2019). Augmented versus virtual reality in education: An exploratory study examining science knowledge retention when using augmented reality/virtual reality mobile applications. *Cyberpsychology, Behavior, and Social Networking, 22*(2), 105–110.

Igartua, J.-J. (2010). Identification with characters and narrative persuasion through fictional feature films. *Communications, 35*(4), 347–373.

Kober, S. E., Kurzmann, J., & Neuper, C. (2012). Cortical correlate of spatial presence in 2D and 3D interactive virtual reality: An EEG study. *International Journal of Psychophysiology, 83*(3), 365–374.

Lee, K. M. (2004). Presence, explicated. *Communication Theory, 14*(1), 27–50.

Pajares, F., Prestin, A., Chen, J., & Nabi, R. (2009). Social cognitive theory and mass media effects. In *The SAGE handbook of media processes and effects*. SAGE.

Pallavicini, F., Pepe, A., & Minissi, M. E. (2019). Gaming in virtual reality: What changes in terms of usability, emotional response and sense of presence compared to non-immersive video games? *Simulation & Gaming, 50*(2), 136–159.

Peng, W. (2008). The mediational role of identification in the relationship between experience mode and self-efficacy: Enactive role-playing versus passive observation. *CyberPsychology & Behavior, 11*(6), 649–652. https://doi.org/10.1089/cpb.2007.0229

Riecke, B. E., & Schulte-Pelkum, J. (2015). An integrative approach to presence and self-motion perception research. In *Immersed in media* (pp. 187–235). Springer.

Rosenberg, R. S., Baughman, S. L., & Bailenson, J. N. (2013). Virtual superheroes: Using superpowers in virtual reality to encourage prosocial behavior. *PLoS One, 8*(1), e55003.

Schubert, T. W. (2009). A new conception of spatial presence: Once again, with feeling. *Communication Theory, 19*(2), 161–187.

Seibert, J., & Shafer, D. M. (2018). Control mapping in virtual reality: Effects on spatial presence and controller naturalness. *Virtual Reality, 22*(1), 79–88.

Steuer, J. (1992). Defining virtual reality: Dimensions determining telepresence. *Journal of Communication, 42*(4), 73–93.

Sundar, S. S., Kang, J., & Oprean, D. (2017). Being there in the midst of the story: How immersive journalism affects our perceptions and cognitions. *Cyberpsychology, Behavior, and Social Networking, 20*(11), 672–682.

Wirth, W., Hartmann, T., Böcking, S., Vorderer, P., Klimmt, C., Schramm, H., Saari, T., Laarni, J., Ravaja, N., & Gouveia, F. R. (2007). A process model of the formation of spatial presence experiences. *Media Psychology, 9*(3), 493–525.

Yee, N., & Bailenson, J. (2007). The Proteus effect: The effect of transformed self-representation on behavior. *Human Communication Research, 33*(3), 271–290.

Yee, N., Bailenson, J. N., & Duchenaut, N. (2009). The Proteus effect: Implications of transformed digital self-representation on online and offline behavior. *Communication Research, 36*(2), 285–312.

Yu, J., Parsons, G. S., Lancastle, D., Tonkin, E. T., & Ganesh, S. (2021). "Walking in Their Shoes": The effects of an immersive digital story intervention on empathy in nursing students. *Nursing Open, 2021*(8), 2813–2823.

13 Immersive Storytelling Case Studies
Eva: A-7063, Lesson Learned From That Dragon Cancer and Coming Home Virtually

Kuo-Ting Huang

Introduction

Storytelling has been used to raise awareness of important social issues, such as social justice education, health communication, and environmental protection; immersive media, such as games and augmented or virtual reality, can enhance the effectiveness of storytelling. This chapter introduces three case studies that harness the power of immersive storytelling to address social issues in different contexts. The first case, an educational program called *Eva: A-7603*, shows how immersive technologies can be used to teach empathy in an instructional setting. The second case, *Lesson Learned from That Dragon, Cancer*, is a role-playing video game that has been used to promote compassion among future healthcare professionals. In the last case, *Coming Home Virtually*, immersive storytelling was used to bring older adults to their hometown virtually, which directly improved their quality of life during the COVID-19 pandemic. Each case study is presented in three parts: a case description, a theoretical framework, and takeaway messages.

Eva: A-7063 Case Study

Case Description

In many U.S. states, public schools are mandated to dedicate a portion of their curriculum to Holocaust education (e.g., Dobrick, 2008; Tall, 2019), the aim of which is to provide education on the importance of respecting the dignity and value of others, regardless of their differences. Holocaust education can cover multiple topics, including history, literature, moral issues, and forgiveness (Hung, 2020). However, teachers have struggled with ways to teach Holocaust-related topics in the classroom (Rich, 2019), despite an abundance of easily accessible primary sources.

Prior research on Holocaust education has demonstrated that using primary sources, such as artifacts, documents, diaries, manuscripts, autobiographies, and recordings, is an effective way of teaching students about the genocide (Polgar, 2018). Primary sources produced by people who experienced that past can provide a direct perspective on events, issues, people, and places, which can help students practice historical thinking skills (Endacott & Brooks, 2018). While primary sources can generate high levels of engagement, the materials were also presented in several different formats, ranging from the written word to documentaries (Riello, 2017).

Immersive technologies, such as virtual reality (VR) and augmented reality, have been found to be effective media formats for teaching empathy in both the short term (van Loon et al., 2018) and the long term (Herrera et al., 2018). To improve Holocaust education in the United States, WFYI Public Media, a public broadcasting service television station in Indiana, collaborated with Ted Green Films to create an education program called *Eva: A-7063* in 2018. This program targets students in grades 5–12 and is aimed at conveying several important concepts, such as empathy, forgiveness, and acceptance, and building positive values, including hope, healing, and humanity.

The main focus of this educational program is to teach students what Eva Mozes Kor, a survivor of Nazi medical experiments at Auschwitz, experienced. The materials include a one-hour documentary introducing Kor's life and a 15-minute immersive video filmed at one of the four Auschwitz locations mentioned in Eva's documentary. Kor was an advocate of human rights, hope, healing, and forgiveness, and these are the messages that this program aims to convey. Kor passed away in 2019, at the age of 85, and the program continues Kor's twin missions to combat racism and educate younger generations.

A series of VR tours were launched in elementary schools in Indiana, and teachers and schools were invited to sign up for the program. Students attending this program were asked to watch the documentary the day before the Eva Project team visited the classroom to show them the VR tour. On the day of the virtual tour, students watched a 15-minute 360-degree video using Oculus Quest and virtually visited one of the four Auschwitz concentration locations with Kor. During the virtual tour, Kor introduced these locations and then announced her forgiveness for the genocidal actions taken there by the Nazi regime. After finishing the immersive video experience, students were asked to share their thoughts on Eva's story and discuss what they learned. The sessions conducted by WFYI showed that the program successfully promoted empathy, perspective-taking, forgiveness, gratitude, and helping attitudes among students. The Eva Project team has reported that teachers have been impressed with the program and that students have also had positive responses and provided positive feedback. Thus, it can be said that immersive stories positively influenced students' attitudes and empathy.

Theoretical Framework

Why do immersive stories promote prosocial attitudes? Immersive technologies allow users to vividly experience situations from a first-person perspective as if the events were happening to them (Herrera et al., 2018).

The vivid images in the virtual environment can elicit a feeling of presence among users, which uniquely positions VR as a powerful perspective-taking medium. Users have a lower extraneous cognitive load when interacting with a virtual environment due to the affordances of VR environments (Andersen et al., 2016), which makes VR a more effective medium for teaching perspective-taking than traditional media.

The psychological mechanisms underlying the effects of immersive storytelling on viewers' attitudes can be explained by the theoretical frameworks of spatial presence experiences, perspective-taking, and identification. According to the two-step model of spatial presence experiences (Wirth et al., 2007), media users first create a mental representation of the mediated environment as a precondition before they can perceive if they are virtually present in the environment. This model suggests that media that provide rich sensory information, such as spatial cues and stereoscopic dimensions, allow users to allocate more attentional resources to the mediated environment. These affordances result in a better spatial situation model and a stronger feeling of spatial presence. Accordingly, watching the documentary on Eva Kor provides audiences with a basic understanding of the mediated environment and enables them to develop a mental model of the Auschwitz concentration camp. Subsequently, watching the immersive video further immerses users in the virtual space as if they were physically located in the concentration camp.

The use of immersive technologies also facilitates virtual interactions between Eva Kor and audiences. As Eva describes her experience in the documentary and the immersive video, viewers can experience her affective and cognitive responses as their own, which is defined as identification (Cohen, 2001). As a result, viewers tend to accept the messages presented in the narrative and the values of forgiveness, healing, and hope emphasized by Eva Kor.

Takeaway Message

This case demonstrates that immersive technologies can immerse users in a virtual environment, enabling them to build a mental model of the space described in the story. When users feel as if they are inside the virtual environment, they are more likely to accept the perspective of the narrator (in this case, Eva Kor). The outcomes of the experiences of spatial presence and perspective-taking were that the audiences accepted the attitudes and values presented by the narrator in the story.

That Dragon, Cancer Case Study

Case Description

Compassion is an important element of high-quality health care (Hofmeyer et al., 2016; Lown et al., 2011). Like the concept of empathy, compassion is a virtuous response to another's pain and suffering and involves a desire to help relieve distress (Roberts et al., 2019; Sinclair et al., 2016). In healthcare settings, compassion among healthcare professionals has been linked to positive clinical outcomes (Lown et al., 2011). However, there is not enough compassionate care in the U.S. healthcare system (Lown et al., 2011). Therefore, training in compassionate care is critical.

Research has suggested that the most effective interventions in undergraduate nursing education are immersive and experiential simulations (Levett-Jones et al., 2019), such as role-playing and scenario-based simulations. However, traditional role-playing activities in classroom settings are costly and therefore rarely used in actual nursing education (Foster et al., 2016). Digital games, which enable players to immerse themselves in different scenarios, have become a useful tool for teaching empathy and compassion in educational settings (Lok & Foster, 2019; Louie et al., 2018). A recent study found that a role-playing video game in which the user assumes the role of the parent of a child cancer patient and experiences the journey the family goes through was effective at improving medical students' empathy (Chen et al., 2018). By providing immersive and experiential simulations, video games can serve as a cost-effective and innovative approach to bring empathy and compassion into healthcare education.

The second case study examined in this chapter is an immersive narrative video game, *That Dragon, Cancer* (Numinous Game, 2016), about the journey of a family with a 4-year-old child fighting cancer. The game includes 14 chapters, each of which focuses on different stages of the family's journey, from the cancer diagnosis to chemotherapy treatment and the palliative care process and, finally, to acceptance of the child's death. The seventh chapter of the videogame, "I'm Sorry Guys, It's Not Good," portrays a pivotal moment in the game when the parents are told in the hospital that their child's cancer is terminal.

This videogame was used as part of a project aimed at investigating the feasibility of using a scenario-based immersive video game to teach compassion to nursing students. A total of 69 nursing students enrolled in two Midwest universities in the United States were recruited to participate in the program. When the students signed up for the program, they were invited to a research lab and asked to complete a pre-test questionnaire. Then, they were randomly assigned to play the video game from one of four perspectives: the father, the mother, the doctor, or the nurse. They heard the inner thoughts of the character they chose. Specifically, participants would be the narrator of the game and experience the story from their own point of view. The player agency was limited as all the conversations were predetermined. After playing the game, participants completed a post-test questionnaire about compassion and experiences of the gameplay. A comparison of the pre-test and post-test questionnaires showed that playing from the perspective of a healthcare provider and hearing their inner thoughts elicited greater compassion for the patient than playing from the perspective of a family member. This finding shows the feasibility of using a VR perspective-taking game for nursing education.

Theoretical Framework

Multiple theoretical frameworks were used to guide the design of this training program, including spatial presence experience, perspective-taking, and social cognitive theory. First, as in the first case study, the mechanism underlying the impact of immersive experience on compassion can be explained by a feeling of presence (Ahn et al., 2016; Schutte & Stilinović, 2017; Stavroulia et al., 2018). When the students started playing the immersive role-playing game, they were immersed in the imagined world of the hospital. This enabled them to build a mental model of the virtual environment and prepared them to participate in the narrative.

Perspective is another crucial element of this training program in which viewers were able to take on the perspective of different characters in the game. Researchers have also suggested that interventions for incorporating empathy and compassion into medical education are effective when they involve role-playing and perspective-taking (Levett-Jones et al., 2019). In this training program, taking on the perspective of the doctor or the nurse allowed students to share in the experience of others. This role-playing and perspective-taking helped the players learn how to show compassion when sharing bad news with a patient's family.

Furthermore, playing the game from the healthcare providers' perspective, which can be described as a vicarious learning process, was found to elicit greater compassion than playing the perspective of the patient's mother or father (Soutter & Hitchens, 2016). According to social cognitive theory, learning from role models is an important way for people to acquire knowledge and skills (Bandura, 2001). Furthermore, people are more likely to learn from someone with whom they share some similarities, such as race, gender, or occupation. This may explain why participants who vicariously experienced how to compassionately deliver bad news to cancer patients by assuming the healthcare provider's role showed greater compassion than those who assumed the perspective of one of the patient's family members.

Takeaway Message

This case shows the feasibility and effectiveness of using immersive stories in the form of a video game in nursing education. Besides the experience of spatial presence experience, the concepts of perspective-taking and social cognitive theory explain how the participants were able to experience both the virtual environment and the character's emotions described in the story. The results of the students' feeling of spatial presence, perspective-taking, and vicarious experience enhanced their compassion for patients.

Coming Home Virtually Case Study

Case Description

In the first two case studies presented here, immersive stories are used to increase audiences' awareness of certain topics and change their attitude toward specific issues. However, immersive storytelling can also directly improve people's lives. Virtual reality hardware has shown potential to improve users' mental health and mitigate a range of mental health conditions. In the final case, immersive stories are used to improve older adults' quality of life. In 2020, seniors had to isolate and avoid gatherings for more than eight months. This physical isolation increased seniors' risk of anxiety, depression, and worsening dementia. The project *Coming Home Virtually* used VR to create tour experiences for older adults to reconnect with the world during the pandemic.

In a VR program, I ran in Muncie, Indiana, from October to December 2020, visitors to the Muncie Delaware County Senior Center—none of whom had any experience of VR—were invited to participate in various VR tours using 360-degree videos. Participants, who were asked where they would like to visit at the beginning of the VR tour, requested two types of places. The first type included famous tourist cities and sites, such as the Eiffel Tower, Venice, and the Grand Canyon. When the participants visited these places virtually, they were also thinking about their family members and imagining they were with them on the virtual tour. The second place they wanted to go was their hometown, such as a small town in Michigan or Kentucky. One participant said that he just wanted to see the street view of downtown Flint, Michigan, because that was the place he grew up. He was not sure if he could ever go back to his hometown given the travel restrictions during the COVID-19 pandemic. Almost half of the participants wanted to visit places in which they had grown up or of which they had fond memories.

After the participants finished the virtual tours, they were interviewed by the researchers and asked about their feelings resulting from the experience. We then analyzed their emotional responses based on the field notes and audio recordings. The findings showed that not only did they feel satisfied but also connected with something or someone even though they had no actual social interaction during the tours. The VR tours succeeded in significantly helping the senior participants feel connected even though they could not physically visit physical places like these. The results suggest that older adults can benefit from immersive storytelling in a VR tour format.

Theoretical Framework

Immersive technologies enable users to temporarily forget where they are and feel as if they are physically in another location and space. As in the previous two cases, the experience of spatial presence best describes why older adults enjoyed the virtual tour experiences and felt reconnected with the world afterward. Regarding the psychological mechanisms underlying this effect, older adults were more likely to allocate their attention to the mediated environment because the experiences were new to them. Moreover, they already had prior knowledge of the places they wanted to visit, so they were more likely to recognize spatial cues with which they were familiar. This meant that they had to expend less mental effort to build a mental model. When the older adults virtually traveled to other places, the experiences and memories associated with the places, such as what they had done there and who they knew in those places, also unfolded.

The use of immersive technologies made older adults feel as if they were physically in the location, and this feeling of presence resulted in enjoyment. The enjoyment that VR tours generate can also be explained by self-determination theory, according to which there are three basic human needs: relatedness, autonomy, and competence (Deci & Ryan, 2012). The virtual tour experiences satisfied the basic needs of older adults by making them feel connected and related to certain places and persons, giving them the autonomy to decide where they wanted to visit, and enabling them to travel without physical and financial constraints. Because their basic needs were fulfilled, they enjoyed the activities and their psychological wellbeing improved.

Takeaway Message

In summary, isolation and resulting loneliness during pandemic situations can result in a multitude of both mental and physical health problems for older adults. Virtual reality tours are a promising technology that could help to ease these problems by fulfilling older adults' basic needs. By applying the theories of spatial presence and self-determination, we can design immersive experiences to improve older adults' quality of life. Enabling older adults, who may be physically or financially constrained, to visit places they want to visit virtually can have a positive impact on their quality of life.

Concluding Remarks

When addressing social issues through storytelling, it is important to enable audiences to see, feel, and experience the characters and narrative worlds. Immersive storytelling can improve society, both indirectly and directly. On the one hand, we can design immersive stories to change people's behaviors and attitudes and teach them how to show more empathy and compassion for others. On the other hand, we can create immersive experiences that fulfill people's need to feel related, autonomous, and competent. The three case studies discussed in this chapter serve as examples of how we can harness the power of immersive technologies to emphasize specific elements of stories and make the world a better place.

References

Ahn, S. J., Bostick, J., Ogle, E., Nowak, K. L., McGillicuddy, K. T., & Bailenson, J. N. (2016). Experiencing nature: Embodying animals in immersive virtual environments increases inclusion of nature in self and involvement with nature. *Journal of Computer-Mediated Communication*, 21(6), 399–419. https://doi.org/10.1111/jcc4.12173

Andersen, S. A. W., Mikkelsen, P. T., Konge, L., Cayé-Thomasen, P., & Sørensen, M. S. (2016). Cognitive load in mastoidectomy skills training: Virtual reality simulation and traditional dissection compared. *Journal of Surgical Education*, 73(1), 45–50.

Bandura, A. (2001). Social cognitive theory: An agentic perspective. *Annual Review of Psychology*, 52(1), 1–26.

Chen, A., Hanna, J. J., Manohar, A., & Tobia, A. (2018). Teaching empathy: The implementation of a video game into a psychiatry clerkship curriculum. *Academic Psychiatry*, 42(3), 362–365.

Cohen, J. (2001). Defining identification: A theoretical look at the identification of audiences with media characters. *Mass Communication & Society*, 4(3), 245–264.

Deci, E. L., & Ryan, R. M. (2012). Self-determination theory. In P. A. M. Van Lange, A. W. Kruglanski, & E. T. Higgins (Eds.), *Handbook of theories of social psychology* (pp. 416–436). Sage Publications Ltd. https://doi.org/10.4135/9781446249215.n21

Dobrick, A. (2008). *History at the gates: How teacher and school characteristics relate to implementation of a state mandate on Holocaust education*. Florida Atlantic University.

Endacott, J. L., & Brooks, S. (2018). Historical empathy: Perspectives and responding to the past. *The Wiley International Handbook of History Teaching and Learning*, 203–225.

Foster, A., Chaudhary, N., Kim, T., Waller, J. L., Wong, J., Borish, M., Cordar, A., Lok, B., & Buckley, P. F. (2016). Using virtual patients to teach empathy: A randomized controlled study to enhance medical students' empathic communication. *Simulation in Healthcare*, 11(3), 181–189.

Herrera, F., Bailenson, J., Weisz, E., Ogle, E., & Zaki, J. (2018). Building long-term empathy: A large-scale comparison of traditional and virtual reality perspective-taking. *PLoS One*, 13(10), e0204494.

Hofmeyer, A., Toffoli, L., Vernon, R., Taylor, R., Fontaine, D., Klopper, H. C., & Coetzee, S. K. (2016). Teaching the practice of compassion to nursing students within an online learning environment: A qualitative study protocol. *Contemporary Issues in Education Research (CIER)*, 9(4), 201–222.

Hung, R. (2020). Ethics of memory: Forgetfulness and forgiveness in the traumatic place. *Educational Philosophy and Theory*, 52(13), 1364–1374.

Levett-Jones, T., Cant, R., & Lapkin, S. (2019). A systematic review of the effectiveness of empathy education for undergraduate nursing students. *Nurse Education Today*, 75, 80–94. https://doi.org/10.1016/j.nedt.2019.01.006

Lok, B., & Foster, A. E. (2019). Can virtual humans teach empathy? In *Teaching empathy in healthcare* (pp. 143–163). Springer.

Louie, A. K., Coverdale, J. H., Balon, R., Beresin, E. V., Brenner, A. M., Guerrero, A. P., & Roberts, L. W. (2018). Enhancing empathy: A role for virtual reality? *Academic Psychiatry*, 42, 747–752.

Lown, B. A., Rosen, J., & Marttila, J. (2011). An agenda for improving compassionate care: A survey shows about half of patients say such care is missing. *Health Affairs, 30*(9), 1772–1778.

Numinous Games. (2016). *That Dragon, Cancer* (Version 1.0.1). [Video game]. Numinous Games, De Moines, IA.

Polgar, M. (2018). How we teach holocaust education. In *Holocaust and human rights education*. Emerald Publishing Limited.

Rich, J. (2019). "It led to great advances in science": What teacher candidates know about the Holocaust. *The Social Studies, 110*(2), 51–66.

Riello, G. (2017). Things that shape history: Material culture and historical narratives. In *History and material culture* (pp. 27–50). Routledge.

Roberts, B. W., Roberts, M. B., Yao, J., Bosire, J., Mazzarelli, A., & Trzeciak, S. (2019). Development and validation of a tool to measure patient assessment of clinical compassion. *JAMA Network Open, 2*(5), e193976–e193976.

Schutte, N. S., & Stilinović, E. J. (2017). Facilitating empathy through virtual reality. *Motivation and Emotion, 41*(6), 708–712.

Sinclair, S., Norris, J. M., McConnell, S. J., Chochinov, H. M., Hack, T. F., Hagen, N. A., McClement, S., & Bouchal, S. R. (2016). Compassion: A scoping review of the healthcare literature. *BMC Palliative Care, 15*(1), 6.

Soutter, A. R. B., & Hitchens, M. (2016). The relationship between character identification and flow state within video games. *Computers in Human Behavior, 55*, 1030–1038.

Stavroulia, K. E., Baka, E., Lanitis, A., & Magnenat-Thalmann, N. (2018). Designing a virtual environment for teacher training: Enhancing presence and empathy. *Proceedings of Computer Graphics International 2018*, 273–282. Association for Computing Machinery. https://doi.org/10.1145/3208159.3208177

Tall, S. (2019). *Holocaust Education in Connecticut: The Passing and Implementation of Senate Bill No. 452* [Honors thesis, University of Connecticut]. https://opencommons.uconn.edu/srhonors_theses/643

van Loon, A., Bailenson, J., Zaki, J., Bostick, J., & Willer, R. (2018). Virtual reality perspective-taking increases cognitive empathy for specific others. *PLoS One, 13*(8), e0202442.

Wirth, W., Hartmann, T., Böcking, S., Vorderer, P., Klimmt, C., Schramm, H., Saari, T., Laarni, J., Ravaja, N., & Gouveia, F. R. (2007). A process model of the formation of spatial presence experiences. *Media Psychology, 9*(3), 493–525.

14 Design Thinking as a Tool for Ethical Audience Targeting

Kevin Moloney

Introduction

Two high-level advantages are provided by transmedia design: richer stories and targeted publics. Scholars, students, and producers of transmedia stories are uniformly familiar with the first. Since its earliest description by Kinder (1991) and Jenkins (2003, 2006), we have embraced the complexity, multimodality, interactivity, and user-contributed richness of transmedia stories produced in any industry. They can be nonlinear and gameful; they jump off of the page or cinema screen and inhabit the corners of our real-world lives; they inspire us to action in the physical world, whether to improve this world or to bring a fiction to this reality. This richness is not only exemplified in major Hollywood transmedia franchises like the Marvel Cinematic Universe or Star Wars but also in socially-concerned storytelling genres from those described in this volume's chapters, to the Pulitzer-Prize-winning 1619 Project by the *New York Times* (Hannah-Jones, 2019; Moloney, 2020), and *FRONTLINE's* transmedia documentary Un(re)solved (PBS, 2021).

The second advantage, however, is very often overlooked by any industry other than advertising and marketing. Thoroughly steeped in the 20th-century publication paradigm—in which to publish content typically required one's own press or broadcast transmitter and income originates with advertising on the media channels those technologies create—journalists, documentary producers, and many activists look foremost to the media channels they produce and control as the publication channels for their projects. Journalists typically write, edit, and produce content for that company's own digital and print, or broadcast editions; documentary producers create works on behalf of a grant partner, a funding client, or a commissioning broadcast channel; and activists launch organizational websites, Facebook pages, and Instagram feeds with little thought about whether that content is reaching the publics it really needs to reach. Although this thinking has changed over the previous decade at larger national organizations like the New York Times Company, *FRONTLINE*, or Black Lives Matter, smaller or more localized efforts still fail to take this second advantage of transmedia storytelling. In order to make meaningful change of opinions

DOI: 10.4324/9781003150862-14

or actions, to counter biases, or to inspire new behaviors and awareness, socially-concerned communicators need to reach beyond their fans and core audiences and put their stories in front of publics who are unlikely to seek them out. Instead, they often simply "spray and pray" (Sangaralingam, 2014) with easy-to-access media or publish on their proprietary channels in a "build it and they will come" wish for a *Field of Dreams* (Robinson, 1989).

The reasons for this are not limited to archaic thinking or lack of insight, however. For producers who understand the many advantages of audience targeting and the need to distribute socially-valuable messages on carefully chosen media channels, access to the data required is either financially out of reach, inaccessible, or not specific enough to the problem being addressed to be useful. Additionally, many media-use metrics are generated through ethically uncomfortable online tracking systems wherein if consumers are notified their behaviors are being tracked, it is only through wordy and too-often-ignored terms of use agreements or privacy disclosures.

Financially Out of Reach

The high-resolution data on media use generated for the advertising and marketing industries are highly valuable. Access to these data will make or break an ad campaign or a product launch, and as a result it is locked down, pricey, and complex enough that it often requires an expensive media analytics service to parse. These data and services would likely cost a socially-concerned storytelling campaign tens of thousands of dollars in professional consulting fees. It would otherwise require trained and experienced personnel on the project and the very expensive subscription fees for access to the relevant databases. Although some of these databases can be freely accessed through some university library systems, the data provided on a lower-cost academic license—as in the case of the high-quality SRDS database (AdWanted Group, n.d.)—are three or more years old. Although it is possible to access low- or no-cost data, the research required is time consuming. When combined with the other limitations that follow, high-fidelity targeting remains a fraught task for socially-concerned communicators.

Inaccessible

Digital media provides unprecedented engagement data, but generally only to the registered owners of a URL, an app, or a feed. Services like Google Analytics or Quantcast for websites, data gathered from use of a custom mobile app, or social media analytics for social channels like Facebook, Instagram, Twitter, and YouTube are cheap and easily accessible only if you manage those channels. Because of that managerial control, proprietary channels like these are often core pieces of a complex, multifaceted transmedia communication strategy. However, reliance *only* on a project's own proprietary channels and feeds usually makes reaching new publics, piercing filter bubbles,

180 Kevin Moloney

or overcoming confirmation biases a matter of dumb luck. We can't build it and hope they will come. We can't spray content to a mythical mass audience and pray it will engage the right people. To reach new publics will almost certainly require getting pieces of your story onto different channels within different filter bubbles and crafting stories that resonate with those often different-minded publics. Transmedia storytelling is not a form of mass-audience broadcasting. It is better described as *bundled narrowcasting*—a collection of related and tightly targeted channels aimed at narrow publics (Moloney, 2015, pp. 36–37). In order to know on which external channels to reach new publics quickly and efficiently, producers need data.

Unspecific

Despite the increasing granularity of contemporary engagement data, large or easily accessible database systems provide information that still models the era of the mass audience and the needs of commercial product advertisers. Demographic and psychographic datasets focus on consumer behaviors. Sociological and political research that investigates attitudes about areas of social concern are oriented most to creating generalizable data for research or policy purposes. A well-planned transmedia campaign needs to not only plan which channels but also define down to the page, feed, wall, or segment how they will reach new target publics (Moloney, 2019). Although almost any accessible data can provide insights on the target publics for a socially-concerned transmedia project, parsing multiple database results well is a hard-earned, time-consuming skill. Rather than only working in this way, time spent also in direct empathy research with members of the target public is more insightful and yields much better understanding of the public you need to reach.

Ethically Uncomfortable

Any reader of this chapter has likely clicked "agree" on hundreds of privacy disclosures, terms of service agreements, EU and California web cookie policy notifications, and more. To read all of them would occupy many hours per week. If you read them and decide their use of your actions and personal data are uncomfortable, invasive, or simply obfuscated behind complicated legal language, your only real option might be to not use the service. Some of these services are now so fundamental to daily life, even in the developing world, that refusal to use them is a severely limiting option. As a result, we are tracked, modeled, and profiled in exchange for our use of most digital services (Peacock, 2014; Tandoc & Thomas, 2015). As socially-concerned communicators, many of us are uncomfortable using data generated in this way, even if it is ostensibly anonymous. If socially-concerned transmedia storytelling aspires to deeply respect its subjects, communicate the value of one human to another, change environmental perspectives, and inform the positive evolution of societies, using data gathered through opaque and extorted means defies the ethos of a socially-concerned project.

The advertising industry is expected to reach a global valuation of $630 billion in 2021 (Guttmann, 2021). As a result of this scale, the access to tools and methods of audience targeting evolve quickly. Competition to traditional data providers can at any time encourage a newly accessible, affordable, specific, and ethical system for targeting data. While big data can describe with extraordinary reliability what large regions or populations might think, how they might act, what stories engage them, and with what media they interact, secondary research like this only forms the base of design thinking processes. By directly empathizing with the individual human members of a target public using tools such as design thinking (see Chapters 3 and 4), socially-concerned transmedia communicators can gain a more nuanced and human understanding of how to solve meaningful problems. Producers can answer questions they didn't know they had.

The following sections describe how design thinking techniques can be used for reliable audience targeting and illustrates them through a project undertaken at Ball State University's Center for Emerging Media Design & Development (EMDD).

Targeting Through Design Thinking

As described elsewhere in this volume, design thinking is an iterative empathy research process developed to understand, engage, and co-create with the users of a product, service, or story. It is a bottom-up process of design that works to mitigate assumptions and examine the problem before jumping to solutions (Brown, 2008, 2009; IDEO, 2015; Kelley, 2001; Lockwood, 2010). Although it is typically deployed to inform the design of content, whether that is a product, an experience, or a story (Moloney, 2018; Serrano Tellería, 2017), it will be described here specifically as a technique for audience targeting. If design thinking is a method being used to design story content, it is an easy addition to add information-gathering and co-creation tasks to plan detailed publication strategy for a project.

Design thinking is commonly described as having five stages: empathize, define, ideate, prototype, and test. As an iterative process, designers often face the need to reevaluate at a dead end and circle back to an earlier phase. Each of these phases will be described in context of the *Water Quality Indiana* (WQI) project at Ball State University (Kuban & Florea, 2016) to illustrate how these phases have been used. Despite the linear description here, expect any real deployment of these techniques to bump into failures or dead ends requiring at least a brief iterative recycle.

WQI is an ongoing experiential-learning documentary project at Ball State University on clean drinking water issues. WQI partnered with EMDD during the 2018–19 academic year to define a target audience in Indiana and understand where and how documentary stories and connected social media could reach publics who are unaware of regional and global water issues. We hoped to inspire the public to act on the information reported by WQI. At the start of the project, the EMDD research team led with the question: *How might we reach specific, open-to-change publics rather than a media-saturated mass audience for WQI stories?*

Phase One: Empathize

The first iterative phase of design thinking seeks to understand the needs of the users of a product or service and to bring them in as stakeholders in the design process. The goal for this phase was to develop a more complete picture of what Hoosiers—as natives of the state colloquially call themselves—know about regional water issues, whether and how they act to mitigate those issues, with what media channels they engage for news and factual information, and which media forms they find most immersive or inspiring. For the WQI project, graduate student researchers 1) studied contexts and similar cases in which stories about humanitarian issues have been successfully communicated, 2) interviewed subject matter experts on communication of water and environmental issues, 3) pored over Indiana state demographic data, and 4) implemented an initial survey of potential audience members.

As a first step, researchers on the project worked to become as familiar as possible with water issues in the state as they could in the time available. Considering the goal of developing a targeted publication strategy, the team also researched the publication patterns of Indiana-based nonprofit Timmy Global Health (2012, n.d.) and the Bill and Melinda Gates Foundation (n.d.). Next, the team conducted ten informal exploratory interviews with members of the WQI project's perceived target audience to initially identify the media they use, the frequency with which they use it, and the causes they support and act upon. The team then conducted expert interviews with two water quality experts, two humanitarian organization leaders, and four professional storytellers to triangulate the commonalities and differences between the audience and the experts. These steps often simply verified assumptions about how a mostly college-aged audience interacts with media and the differences between the information scientists find important and that which storytellers find salient. However, as the old journalism bromide states, "If your mother says she loves you, check it out." A key verified and actionable assumption was that information on water quality, issues, and mitigating actions was dispersed, complex, and not available to the regional public in an easily understood form. Being a water-rich region, Hoosiers give the origin, quality, and threat to water here too little thought.

The team continued with a preliminary survey designed to test questions on media engagement habits, water issue knowledge, and motivations for action on environmental issues. The survey was completed by a convenience sample of 47 respondents, and the results were examined for both baseline knowledge of the audience and the validity and reliability of the questions asked. This convenience sample included limited demographics, however. Respondents were primarily from the millennial age group, left-leaning, and highly educated, making them an amen-shouting choir likely already engaged and active on at least a few environmental issues. Though they would likely prove easily receptive to WQI reporting, systemic change on regional water issues would be limited. Our goal was to reach and activate new publics, not exclusively to reinvigorate current ones.

An intensive statewide survey of Indiana residents would certainly generate an empirical picture of Hoosier media habits and opinions. For university researchers, that scale and set of techniques are within reach, but we intended to develop a toolset for documentary communicators for whom these resources would usually be out of reach. Few documentary producers or journalists have the available time, human resources, or statistical analysis knowledge to conduct research at that scale or the budget to hire consultants for it. We iterated a new question to answer at this stage of empathy research: *How might we use Ball State University as a representative sample of statewide Indiana residents?* The university draws students and employees from virtually every county in the state. Could we first group like counties together as a means of extrapolating media engagement habits and water issue knowledge from surveys and interviews conducted conveniently at the university?

To explore this idea, the team pored over demographic data freely available from STATS Indiana (n.d.), a public service provided by the State of Indiana that collects and publishes data on more than 30 statewide topics. We hunted for demographic similarities by region. While also exploring patterns in available data visualizations, we identified four regions of similarity that form a donut-shaped pattern we dubbed the *Indiana Donut* (Figure 14.1).

This pattern includes the central donut hole of metropolitan Indianapolis and surrounding bedroom communities, the donut-shaped ring of rural and exurban counties that surround that, and distinct border regions in north and south that reflect the influence of urban areas in nearby Illinois, Michigan, Ohio, and Kentucky. Though the counties in each region of the donut are individually distinct, dividing the map using these approximate regions allowed us to more quickly seek comparable counties in the state. Through purposive sampling from among the Ball State University students and employees, we would be able to extrapolate information applicable across each region. While the resolution of the data would be less than that provided by more systematic and empirical methods, it would be both adequate to inform the production and distribution of the WQI project content and would use methods that are approachable and scalable for independent content producers with limited time, personnel, and budget. When producing documentary and journalistic content, higher fidelities of targeting data produce diminishing returns—no matter how detailed and accurate,

184 Kevin Moloney

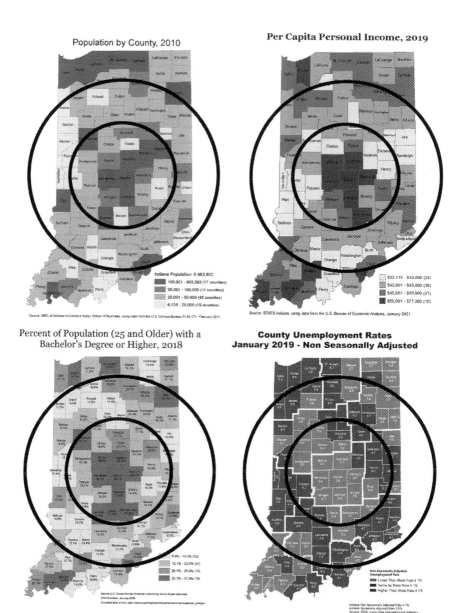

Figure 14.1 The Indiana Donut

Note: Distribution by county of demographic data (clockwise from top left) on population, income, unemployment, and education reveal a regional pattern evident in most demographic data from Indiana.

Source: STATS Indiana.

statistically precise targeting data cannot ensure that members of the public will read, watch, listen, or engage with that content. In developing this prototype method, we sought efficiency in quick, scalable, transferable, and adequately insightful data gathering.

Phase Two: Define

In the define phase of design thinking, information gathered in the empathize stage is sorted, themed, and analyzed to identify specific problems to be solved. Through primary and secondary research, the EMDD team exploring WQI targeting plans identified a psychographic profile for a public of highest value. The team defined them as the *almost care* audience. This subset of the wider public—from a variety of demographic backgrounds throughout the state—is at least somewhat aware of regional water issues, expresses some concern about water quality and reliability (albeit for varying political, commercial, or environmental reasons), and is most likely to be moved to new action to protect Indiana water supplies. By contrast, the publics that express little interest or concern, or outright resistance, would be extraordinarily difficult to move to action. Their already active counterparts who are engaged with water issues and the environment form the choir for this sermon. Like any choir, their engagement is valuable; they make exemplary ambassadors for a message. This congregation needed to grow new membership, however. The team developed hypothetical user personas for members of the *almost care* public across demographics and regions of the state, defining the area of water quality that might concern each persona most.

Each persona connected to one of the five regions of Indiana is identified for distinct targeting. These five regions are those defined by the *Indiana Donut* map created to simplify the economic, social, and educational complexity of Indiana to a level that would be actionable for WQI targeting purposes. This subdivision of the state would also provide a structure for analysis of data from a new, more widely distributed survey of Ball State students, employees, and their social connections. This survey not only focused on social and political demographics and media consumption habits of the respondents but also inquired about how they perceive these habits and perspectives among extended family and social networks in their home counties. The survey was completed by 352 respondents representing 55 of the 92 counties in the state, with a satisfactory number of respondents from each of the five regions. Through this survey, the team was able to build an actionable statewide model of media consumption and social media engagement. An important element of the defined stage of design thinking is the definition of a problem statement. Sometimes complex, and often times quite simple or obvious, the problem statement serves as the core definition of work for the ideation, prototyping, and testing phases. The team defined this one as:

> The contemporary mediascape has complicated the task of delivering important journalistic content to publics that might best put that information to use. Stories about issues of water quality . . . are best targeted to specific, open-to-change publics rather than a media-saturated mass audience.
>
> (Kiesel et al., 2019)

From here, the team would proceed to ideating guidelines for the WQI project designed to inform their producers' decisions on content, media form, and potential publication channels.

Phase Three: Ideate

In the ideation phase, designers put analyzed data and information to use on the defined problem statement and generate voluminous ideas for how to proceed in solving the problem. Often, the stakeholders themselves are brought in to co-create solutions with a design team. At this phase, a socially-concerned storytelling team would begin ideating the content, media forms, and network structure for the storytelling as well as the channels that would put these stories in the path of publics who might act on them. In the project described here, the EMDD team was responsible for proposing the transmedia structure of the WQI documentary project with a particular focus on the audience targeting strategy. We defined the demographics and psychographics of a target audience. The members of this public would be most likely to engage with the documentary content, associate it with the extensive content available across the mediascape in the feral transmedia storyworld (see Chapter 4) of global water quality issues, and act on that information. This *almost care* profile changes somewhat depending on the demographics of a region and the water issues faced there. For example, publics in Indiana's urban donut hole expressed concerns related to environmental justice, and sustainability at a global scale, whereas in suburban regions concerns over water quality related most to family. In rural regions of the state—the donut itself—respondents and interviewees expressed concern over adequate water supplies, downstream fertilizer and pesticide pollution, and access to agricultural water resources.

The first audience is from Millennial and Generation-Z age groups, left leaning, and educated. They live mostly in Indiana's urban and suburban donut hole and predominantly engage in social media for information gathering, sharing, and status building. Social media presents a unique challenge in reach, as the distribution of content there is dependent on ever-changing and difficult-to-influence algorithms. Simply posting content and hoping it both reaches the target public and that they share it to their own diverse networks rarely results in success. Content must be designed for spreadability (Jenkins et al., 2013) and offer the hope of status elevation for the person sharing. This requires not only detailed and thorough documentary film production but quick-hit additive content that leads back to the core story of a project. We recommended hashtags for social content that connected this issue with related issues that had a high follow rate with the target audience in order to connect Indiana water quality issues to other social media conversations.

A second audience identified politically split, Generation-X and Baby-Boom-aged Hoosiers living in the suburbs and exurbs of the donut hole and the two state border zones beyond the rural donut. Here, strategy focused heavily on Facebook, in particular, and encouraged television delivery of the documentary film on public and local-access television channels. Content with this group could cross the spectrum from global environmental issues to rural water supply, but emphasis on drinking water quality and recreation water use would be encouraged.

The third audience identifies young populations in the rural Indiana donut ring as an avenue to engage older family decision-makers in conversation about water issues. While the younger members of regional social groups engage heavily in social media information gathering, their older family members—Baby Boomers and remaining members of the Silent Generation—continue to rely on traditional print and broadcast media. Here, we approach the audience from two directions: social media to reach younger influencers and traditional media to reach their older family members. Personal connection provides the most trusted information source for any population, and this media strategy is designed to support and corroborate it. Traditional media outlets in this region are often hungry for content; publication in local newspapers and on local radio is well within reach of WQI producers so long as the content appeals to the audience of the media channel. The population of this region is heavily conservative, and content approaches would be most effective if they reported on issues that affect the agricultural economy and its sustainability as well as outdoor recreation. Urban and traditionally left-leaning issues like environmental justice or climate change would need to be presented through their direct impacts on rural life and economy, and not with a preachy or accusatory tone.

Due to a division of roles between parallel project teams, content creation was not a task undertaken by EMDD. If it were, the team would proceed to building prototypes of stories and content to test among these target audiences for both reception and learning. For the WQI project, we instead ideated a framework through which the content producers could report, produce, and publish content that reaches these audiences on their terms, and through the media with which they most frequently engage.

Phase Four: Prototype

In this phase of design thinking, designers build rapid prototypes cascading from low- to high-fidelity, iterating changes and testing both internally and with stakeholders. Ultimately, high-fidelity prototypes are tested with the users or beneficiaries of a design to determine whether the problem has been solved, and if not, how might it change to do so. In this stage, the EMDD team began building prototypes of a toolkit for content development that offered suggestions of salient content and story tone, but also the media channels that would reach the publics we defined. The toolkit included PDF documentation as well as an interactive web interface designed using results from empathy research with the reporting team members. The final content for the project would be driven primarily by reporting rather than audience research, but this toolkit would offer perspective on the knowledge, interests, and media habits of their publics.

The Transmedia Communication Strategy (TCS) developed by the graduate student team loosely followed the socially-concerned transmedia production bible template used in transmedia storytelling courses at EMDD. Using concise language and compelling graphic design, the core document of the toolkit described the problem spaces of both water quality communication and the need for thoughtful audience targeting to make the project most effective. It described the empathy research outlined here, and the definition of the target audiences, their demographics and affinities, the media channels that matter to them, and presented personas and user media engagement journeys for each. The TCS also presented suggestions for ways to encourage user contribution to the story itself in order to build ownership of the subject for key audience members. Starting-point story subjects were suggested for each target audience and illustrated with prototype examples that repurposed existing stories. The TCS would be available to inform the storytelling produced by WQI reporters, with enough flexibility to accommodate change and adjustment based on what that reporting uncovered in the field. The toolkit included suggested methods to test the effectiveness of the stories produced by the reporting team.

Phase Five: Test

In this last-listed phase of design thinking, prototypes face repeated and iterative testing with typical users, extreme users, subject matter experts, and design peers. Though this phase appears last on the list, it is as often a new beginning as testing might reveal new issues that require iteratively returning to other phases and cycling through a rinse-and-repeat process. For the WQI project, the EMDD team tested story examples with members of the target audiences who had opted into further interviews. These tests were used to evaluate how receptive these audiences would be to certain types of content, whether they would share them with their social networks (online and offline) and if they would raise their interest level or inspire behavior change even briefly. The TCS documentation itself was tested with the student members of the WQI reporting team to close information gaps and iron out bumps in presentation.

Although the resulting toolkit would ultimately need reevaluation after deployment in real-world storytelling production, the EMDD phase of the project ended before filming began on the documentary and its social media extensions. At this writing, we are now at good timing to revisit the toolkit, the real-world process the WQI reporting team undertook, and what of their decisions were influenced both positively and negatively by the EMDD team's audience targeting design work. This process continues to develop at the Center for Emerging Media Design & Development with a goal of it being applicable across many types of socially-concerned storytelling projects, from traditional documentary and journalism work, to activism, archive presentation, education, and community development and placemaking.

Iteration and Adaptation

We anticipated many of the findings of the empathy research conducted on behalf of audience targeting for the WQI project. However, breaking the paradigm of "build it and they will come" production for a singular website promoted with fingers-crossed social media posts was an important task. Too often, socially-concerned storytellers focus singularly on the rich story forms and structures available through transmedia storytelling and not on how those valuable stories can reach publics that matter. Whether a process like this of working to define, find, and reach needed publics produces anticipated results or a huge surprise, the process itself is an effective means to keep a producer's eye on the task of reaching action-taking publics. I described here a developmental case using techniques that can be adapted to many resource-challenged projects. By using the core phases and basic principles of design thinking, independent producers can easily determine who their target audience should be, how to enter into conversation with them, and on what media channels to do that.

As with all technology now, the tools and techniques of audience targeting change rapidly. This process must iterate to include new industrial audience targeting tools as they are developed or discovered. The first phase of design thinking typically includes study of similar cases, available tools, and other contexts. Any project benefits from a review of that landscape first and adapting them to current needs. The greatest advantage to design thinking is not its embrace of tools, however. The direct, empathetic connection it makes to the users—in this case target publics—will not only provide unexpected insights but also humanize that public far more effectively than the use of big data alone. The process is transparent to the participants, grants them agency in what a producer creates, embraces their input and expertise, and can only work if they knowingly agree to participate.

The design thinking process can easily be adapted to other audience targeting needs. Contextual research and personal insight can direct producers to a tentative idea of what the target public might be. Then through facilitated interviews and insight sessions—with lots of sticky notes on whiteboards—a much more nuanced understanding of the right target public emerges. As the process progresses to the define phase, producers need to avoid letting preconceptions about the public, the form of content to be created, and its outcome from clouding definitions. We unconsciously want data to prove our assumptions right, but outcomes are better if we use it to consciously try to prove our assumptions wrong. Ideation requires a similar awareness of preconceptions and prejudices. As a long-time photojournalist I know that I am predisposed to think visual documentaries are the answer to the world's woes. "If only they could see what I see . . ." we photojournalists tell ourselves. It's easiest to produce what we know how to produce, but if we listen to our publics, we might find that isn't the most effective choice. Prototyping and testing require a fail-early-fail-often approach, and a thick-skinned tolerance for change. These very iterative steps rarely end up where they started, but the outcomes are always better.

At EMDD we will continue to iterate this process and test its outcomes to increase the reliability and validity of the process. As stated earlier, those two qualities are only a couple of the complex influences that determine whether socially-concerned stories will be opened, read, understood, accepted, or embraced. Ease, speed, and accessibility of the process are the more important factors. We also aspire to develop an adaptable database of results for Indiana that can be regularly updated for use on many projects. A plan like this could be highly effective for independent journalists and documentarians working on specific topics or beats. For example, a collective of environmental journalists focusing on a particular region of the world, global topic, or policy-making body could use these techniques to first create, then regularly update, a dataset specific to their needs and across their topics. As a journalist I would also anticipate that a stack of story ideas would emerge from the process as well.

Building transmedia stories requires an astonishing amount of work. The rich, multimodal, and immersive stories that result tug us along the often-stressful path to production. Afterward, we sit and revel in the powerful stories we've gathered, their clever, distributed story arcs, and the breadcrumb trail of intrigue we design to move the public through the storytelling experience. Unfortunately, that's where the planning often stops. We have conditioned ourselves to make the story, feed it on channels we already have or that we build ourselves, and assume that the public will click on our hashtags and follow our feeds. When that happens, it is usually with a public that already embraces the ideas in our stories; we feed the confirmation biases rather than opening compelling doors to new publics. Instead, socially-concerned transmedia producers need to put the second important advantage of transmedia stories to better use. The complex networks of storytelling are a perfect means to design pieces of that network to open doors to new key publics. To continue with the old-time religion analogy, it's always easiest to preach to the choir than to the sinners on the street, but that is not how a new congregation is converted. By finding and reaching those more complicated publics, we can change the world.

Acknowledgment

The graduate student team of Alexis Kiesel, Lindsey Werking, Christina Valdez, and Atilla Akyüz implemented the process described here and produced a comprehensive case study of their work that informs this chapter. It is available at centerforemdd.com.

References

AdWanted Group. (n.d.). *SRDS media planning platform.* https://next.srds.com/home

Bill & Melinda Gates Foundation. (n.d.). https://gatesfoundation.org/

Brown, T. (2008). Design thinking. *Harvard Business Review, 86*(6), 84–92.

Brown, T. (2009). *Change by design: How design thinking transforms organizations and inspires innovation.* Harper Collins.

Guttmann, A. (2021, January 15). Advertising market worldwide–Statistics & facts. *Statista.* www.statista.com/topics/990/global-advertising-market/

Hannah-Jones, N. (2019, August 14). The 1619 Project. *The New York Times.* www.nytimes.com/interactive/2019/08/14/magazine/1619-america-slavery.html

IDEO. (2015). *The field guide to human-centered design.* IDEO.org. www.designkit.org/resources/1

Jenkins, H. (2003, January 15). Transmedia storytelling. *Technology Review.* www.technologyreview.com/s/401760/transmedia-storytelling/

Jenkins, H. (2006). *Convergence culture: Where old and new media collide.* New York University Press.

Jenkins, H., Ford, S., & Green, J. (2013). *Spreadable media: Creating value and meaning in a networked culture.* New York University Press.

Kelley, T. (2001). *The art of innovation: Lessons in creativity from Ideo, America's leading design firm.* Currency/Doubleday.

Kiesel, A., Werking, L., Valdez, C., & Akyüz, A. (2019). *Water quality Indiana design brief* [Design Brief]. Center for Emerging Media Design & Development. www.centerforemdd.com/index.php/projects/water-quality-indiana/

Kinder, M. (1991). *Playing with power in movies, television, and video games: From Muppet babies to teenage Mutant Ninja turtles.* University of California Press.

Kuban, A., & Florea, L. (2016). *Water quality Indiana.* Water Quality Indiana. http://waterqualityin.com/

Lockwood, T. (Ed.). (2010). *Design thinking: Integrating innovation, customer experience, and brand value.* Skyhorse Publishing, Inc.

Moloney, K. (2015). *Future of story: Transmedia journalism and National Geographic's future of food project* [Doctoral dissertation, University of Colorado]. https://scholar.colorado.edu/downloads/2227mp94w

Moloney, K. (2018). Designing transmedia journalism projects. In R. R. Gambarato & G. C. Alzamora (Eds.), *Exploring transmedia journalism in the digital age* (pp. 83–103). IGI Global. www.igi-global.com/chapter/designing-transmedia-journalism-projects/198024

Moloney, K. (2019). Proposing a practical media taxonomy for complex media production. *International Journal of Communication, 13*(2019), 3545–3568.

Moloney, K. (2020). All the news that's fit to push: The New York Times Company and Transmedia Daily News. *International Journal of Communication, 14*(2020), 4683–4702.

PBS. (2021, May 4). FRONTLINE announces un(re)solved, an unprecedented multi-platform investigation of civil rights era cold case murders. *FRONTLINE*. www.pbs.org/wgbh/frontline/announcement/frontline-announces-unresolved-unprecedented-multi-platform-investigation-civil-rights-era-cold-case-murders-till-act/

Peacock, S. E. (2014). How web tracking changes user agency in the age of Big Data: The used user. *Big Data & Society, 1*(2), 2053951714564228. https://doi.org/10.1177/2053951714564228

Robinson, P. A. (1989, May 5). *Field of Dreams*. Universal Pictures. www.imdb.com/title/tt0097351/

Sangaralingam, K. (2014). IAB based classification approach for mobile app audience measurement. *ICSOFT 2014 Doctoral Consortium*, 11.

Serrano Tellería, A. (2017). Journalism, transmedia and design thinking. *Estudos de Jornalismo, 6*(2), 68–87.

STATS Indiana. (n.d.). Retrieved June 9, 2021, from www.stats.indiana.edu/index.asp

Tandoc, E. C. Jr., & Thomas, R. J. (2015). The ethics of web analytics. *Digital Journalism, 3*(2), 243–258. https://doi.org/10.1080/21670811.2014.909122

Timmy Global Health. (n.d.). www.timmyglobalhealth.org

Timmy Global Health. (2012). [YouTube Channel]. www.youtube.com/channel/UCPeX71_ih3tYbdAV-NtF4zQ

15 *The Revolutionist: Eugene V. Debs*

A Transmedia Experience for Public Media Audiences

Kyle Travers

The popularity of "tune-in" television is waning. On-demand options and internet-based content have fractured the audience of broadcast's former heyday when three or four channels dominated the airwaves. The Corporation for Public Broadcasting (CPB) was created in 1969 as a way for the United States government to support a nonprofit educational alternative to the commercial television landscape that in 1961 former Federal Communications Commission chairman Newton Minow called "a vast wasteland" (Minow & Cate, 2003). From the CPB, the Public Broadcasting Service (PBS) was created in 1972 as a network of local public television stations, sharing content and resources across a national system. However, as the media landscape grows in complexity, PBS's broadcast impact has diminished. With hundreds of channels serving fragmented audiences and huge streaming companies creating thousands of hours of original content, the competition is fierce (Chan-Olmsted & Kim, 2002).

Yet public broadcasting has a unique opportunity. Many member stations are dual-license, meaning they carry both PBS television channels and National Public Radio (NPR) radio channels and therefore reach two very different groups. The typical PBS audience skews older, male, white, and conservative, while NPR audiences are younger and more liberal (Sefton, 2017). Also, because each public media station is independently operated and supported directly by local viewers and listeners through donations, they have a community tie to audience and content. In February 2019, PBS President Paula Kerger said:

> Netflix is not in every community around this country. Amazon isn't. But our stations are. . . . The more that we can continue to focus on that unique aspect of the fact that we are a media service that lives and breathes on the community level and that there's stuff there that they can't find on Netflix that's going to be of great value.
>
> (Nguyen, 2019, para. 7)

This relationship with the public and a nonprofit funding model has built the perception that PBS is a trustworthy and high-quality brand. Researchers

DOI: 10.4324/9781003150862-15

argue that it is imperative that PBS, in spite of increased commercial competition, retain its non-commercial identity as this differentiation is crucial to its future success (Chan-Olmsted & Kim, 2002).

Public broadcasting stations may be able to leverage these strengths through the use of transmedia storytelling in their local content creation. Transmedia storytelling does not simply reuse the same content across channels but emerges and intersects on various media with interlocking pieces to a complete storyworld. It is intentionally designed to expand audiences and increase engagement (Jenkins, 2006). Some PBS programs *have* successfully used transmedia. *Half The Sky*, an experience highlighting women's inequality issues, included a four-hour documentary airing on PBS, live social media engagement, web videos, music downloads, online games, and more. The creators designed the project to find audiences that would normally not watch PBS in places where they usually consume media, such as Facebook (Astle, 2012).

But good design does not just come from a clever idea. It also involves executing that idea to create an immersive experience (Brown & Katz, 2009). Furthermore, it is crucial that the design be human-centered and meet the needs and wants of the user (Norman, 2013). That's where design thinking comes in. Content creators must conduct empathy research, lead brainstorming sessions, and prototype various iterations of a product if they wish to develop something satisfying and innovative for their users (Brown & Katz, 2009). KQED-PBS in San Francisco is implementing these central tenets of design thinking. The station is focusing on experimentation and a user-centered approach, undergoing a culture shift from assuming the station knew what audiences wanted to using data and audience feedback (Burg, 2016).

I am a television producer at WFYI, the PBS and NPR station in Indianapolis. The majority of WFYI's past attempts at creating "cross-platform" media have focused on broadcasting the same content on television, radio, web, and social media, but have failed to use a transmedia approach. In addition, WFYI seldom works with users to find out exactly what audiences want. The typical strategy is to produce, broadcast, and hope someone watches. How might WFYI engage radio, television, and digital audiences through one locally produced transmedia project? WFYI produced a historical documentary about socialist leader Eugene Debs for broadcast on WFYI's television channel on October 3, 2019. Debs led national labor strikes in the late 19th century, ran for president on the socialist ticket five times, was sentenced to ten years in prison for speaking out against World War I (Salvatore, 1982), and was a native of nearby Terre Haute, Indiana. However, most people I talked to about Debs had only a vague recollection of learning about him in school, if they knew of him at all.

Because of this lack of familiarity, it was essential to present information about Debs where users already consume media in a style they prefer. Two principles of the user experience theory of multimedia instruction demonstrate this importance of learning about a subject early and often. First, the *pre-training principle* asserts that presenting terms and key ideas before a narrative sequence better prepares people to learn and retain the information. This learning not only focuses the attention of the learner on what will be important but will strengthen associations and limit distraction later (Hall & Stahl, 2012). Furthermore, the *personalization principle* of multimedia learning indicates that by using conversational language, in both narration and text, a viewer is more likely to learn the information; when they feel involved with the subject, they will want to understand it (Mayer, 2003). By using these ideas to create a transmedia production that not only could inform people about the upcoming documentary but also might teach them about the subject matter, users would be better equipped to learn about Debs. Executing this involved telling different parts of the story across multiple media to reach potentially interested publics who do not already watch WFYI.

In addition, by using design thinking to engage the audiences, WFYI determined what users wanted and the best way to present each of these individual story threads so they might draw audiences across the storyworld. Through design thinking, stakeholders were asked to ideate and prototype potential transmedia vehicles for the Eugene Debs story. These users came from two groups. The first group was a "transmedia committee" of seven WFYI employees who work in television, radio, social media, community engagement, events, and marketing. The second group included four members of WFYI's young professional group called the WFYI Nerds. I led these groups through design thinking sessions in order to co-create transmedia ideas. WFYI then implemented those ideas across several channels, including broadcast television, radio, websites, social media, and physical spaces, to create the transmedia storyworld of Eugene Debs.

In the future, WFYI will be able to replicate this user co-created process for future documentaries. Though each project will need to go through its own design thinking process and transmedia design, WFYI may be able to think differently about media delivery and audience engagement. This could represent a sea change for the organization and an example for other PBS affiliate stations. With increased engagement across social platforms and between PBS and NPR channels, public broadcasting stations have the potential to expand their reach to larger, more diverse audiences through ever more popular digital channels. This increased breadth and depth of usership could translate to added financial support for public broadcasting stations, thus ensuring present and future success in the digital age (Knight Foundation, 2017).

Tools and Contexts

For the Eugene Debs project, design thinking served as a crucial tool in developing a transmedia storyworld for audiences. A rich experience is what now drives consumers to buy a product or continue using a service. Users no longer want to passively consume media; they want to participate in creating it. Yet it is more effective to ask users to adapt behaviors they already know rather than create new ones. In order to find out what behaviors exist and how to adapt them, it is important to first observe people, and then determine how to streamline or improve those interactions (Brown, 2009).

These tenets of design thinking are useful for media design. Experiences can be physical, digital, or both, and transmedia storytelling relies on a fluid combination of the two. First, the idea that people want to go beyond passive consumption to an active experience may seem obvious; but in the world of public television, stations rarely give them that opportunity. Therefore, engagement could increase if WFYI offered a more participatory way to learn about Eugene Debs. Second, the idea of using established behaviors is attractive. If people read wfyi.org for news, it may be interesting to include a news story from 1918 about Debs' arrest and insert it in its original format next to current headlines. Finally, allowing design thinking at all levels could be an interesting way to garner ideas for producing the documentary from colleagues and stakeholders. Also, the users themselves could contribute through design thinking *before* production so that WFYI knows what experiences are desirable.

Heather Chaplin (2016) describes how design thinking can be used to improve journalism by applying a more user-centered approach. Yet she warns that following design thinking structure to the letter may be limiting for journalism, and that the industry must instead follow eight general tenets of design thinking.

1. Journalists must understand how their stories fit into the larger world.
2. Remove the focus from technology and place it on people, resisting the need to use the latest and greatest technology just for the sake of using it.
3. Clarify what the problem is before trying to solve it.
4. Use empathy research to truly learn about users' lives in order to report on what matters.
5. Generate ideas through ideation.
6. After ideation, construct and clarify coherent ideas.
7. Integrate prototyping in order to move from ideas to real solutions.
8. Test the prototype and observe the possible solution being used by actual users.

These steps follow design thinking and allow resources to be invested in actual problems, enabling the media company to interact with the audience and move toward community-led journalism. Chaplin outlines a company-wide approach that would be helpful for WFYI and clearly articulates how design thinking could improve not only internal functions but also external relationships with the audience. This report could serve as a useful tool for educating staff as to why design thinking is beneficial.

Like design thinking, transmedia storytelling is still a somewhat foreign concept at public broadcasting stations, which typically produce news and documentary-style media. It may seem impossible to "create" a nonfiction storyworld equivalent, as the parameters cannot be changed when telling a story journalistically. However, there are valuable lessons to be learned from the way imaginary storyworlds are constructed. WFYI could try to think outside of the usual public media boxes, and borrow from fiction in order to draw out the life and times of Eugene Debs. Reality can be just as intriguing as fantasy, and documentarians can create intersections between influential people, places, and events in order to give the story context, structure, and interest. These threads can present competing points of view that engage the viewer and encourage submitting their own opinions and experiences (Jenkins, 2016).

Yet nonfiction transmedia in public broadcasting isn't entirely new. *Half the Sky* was a transmedia experience highlighting women's inequality issues, centered around a book that expanded into a four-hour documentary airing on PBS (Astle, 2012). It included live social media engagement during the broadcast, web videos, music downloads, online games, and more. One unique aspect of this project was its ability to serve both an audience interested in helping at-risk women, and the at-risk women themselves, as different components served different groups. The structure of this project allowed users to focus on a specific issue, such as education, or expand into all the issues presented. This design enabled it to reach a variety of audiences at different levels of engagement. The creators also stressed the importance of finding audiences that would normally not watch PBS in places where they usually consume media, like Facebook (Astle, 2012). This is a fascinating approach, and it was transferable to the Eugene Debs project. For example, stakeholders in Debs' hometown of Terre Haute might have different interests in the story than a wider, regional audience. Parts of the storyworld could be designed to reach this specific group.

Project Design

This project was driven by a single guiding question: How might WFYI design its own audience-engagement strategy around the video documentary *The Revolutionist: Eugene V. Debs*? To address this question, this project used design thinking and transmedia storytelling to tell the story of Eugene Debs and aimed to explore the different media forms, storytelling techniques, and channels with which they already engage. By allowing users to generate ideas for transmedia elements *themselves* using design thinking, the station can tap into the desires of an audience of devoted viewers, listeners, and members. The station can then use the innovative ideas generated with design thinking and expand to new audiences who are not familiar with WFYI as well. Design thinking allows media consumers to participate in the design process and enables "high-impact solutions to bubble up from below rather than being imposed from the top" (Brown & Wyatt, 2010).

Participant Recruitment

Using this philosophy to create the transmedia story elements for *The Revolutionist*, I recruited two groups to participate in design thinking sessions: a committee of employees who are also avid WFYI consumers and a group of young professional public media enthusiasts called The WFYI Nerds. The first group consisted of seven WFYI employees from departments outside of video production, including marketing, social media, radio, community engagement, events, and development. These individuals are typically responsible for creating content and promoting WFYI's mission. They are highly engaged users of public media but previously have not had a major role associated with a video documentary. These seven employees were invited via email to join a transmedia committee and attended five one-hour-long meetings where design thinking sessions helped create and refine transmedia story elements about Eugene Debs.

A second group consisting of four members of "WFYI Nerds," a group of young professionals interested in public media, also participated in design thinking sessions. This group is highly engaged and is seen as ambassadors of the brand. Members of this group were recruited through a direct message to the WFYI Nerds email list inviting them to join a brainstorming session in order to design an event about Eugene Debs for young professionals. Ten participants responded saying they would attend. On the day of the meeting, four participants actually attended.

Design Thinking and Other Methods

In order to explore what audiences WFYI was trying to reach with the Eugene Debs transmedia experience, committee members created audience persona profiles. These sketches are derived from research and give content creators a way to visualize the audience they are serving for each medium (Luma Institute, 2012). Using recent PBS audience research and each employee's experience with local audiences, we created personas for television, radio, website, and social media audiences. Each persona included age, education, political affiliation, and needs and wants. Using these profiles, the group brainstormed ways to engage those specific audiences with the important issues of Eugene Debs' life as identified in the first activity. The group discussed and voted on their favorite ideas.

Participants then chose an idea their department could focus on and created storyboards. They visualized their concept and also helped the rest of the group understand the idea (Luma Institute, 2012). The group imagined how these ideas could be implemented within WFYI's structure and associated with other existing projects. Other low-fidelity prototypes in the form of scripts and grant proposals allowed participants to describe their ideas in detailed language. We continued to develop these ideas and imagined how they could fit together in a transmedia storyworld.

Finally, we tested the low-fidelity prototypes. For example, we created various elements for a social media campaign, and then committee members voiced their concerns about the concept. The critique followed a recommended design thinking structure so feedback was constructive. This allowed us to move forward with a social media campaign better suited for Facebook, Twitter, and Instagram (Luma Institute, 2012).

We also implemented design thinking into a single session with the WFYI Nerds group. Using the following "statement starters," participants were asked to brainstorm about the following questions:

1   How might we improve the Nerds experience?
2   How might Nerds engage with local content?
3   Why should we care about Eugene Debs?
4   How might the Nerds design an event around Eugene Debs?

Using the saturate and group method, ideas were discussed and grouped for similarities. At the end of the session, participants voted for their favorite ideas using the "Visualize the Vote" method (Luma Institute, 2012).

Analysis and Creation

The WFYI design thinking sessions produced a lot of information. From dozens of ideas, WFYI committee members voted for the transmedia pieces they thought would work best in the current WFYI environment and with the constraints of time and budget. These ideas were then compiled into a list of nine transmedia story elements that were created by the committee. The ideas that WFYI Nerds voted as their favorites were then presented to the WFYI committee to determine their feasibility. The committee selected an idea for an event, but ultimately, it was not produced.

Project Deployment

Using the ideas generated by design thinking, the internal committee of WFYI employees and the participants from WFYI Nerds created a series of transmedia elements to build the storyworld of Eugene Debs and educate people about his life. However, the *Notable Hoosiers* series and the documentary itself were created because WFYI partnered with outside organizations which provided funding. This combination of design thinking and traditional methods resulted in nine unique plans for events and media campaigns that informed and entertained users across media.

Element 1: Wine Fest Booth

WFYI's event coordinator, a committee member, presented the idea of a booth at the WFYI Wine Fest fundraiser for *The Revolutionist* early in the

Figure 15.1 Elements of The Revolutionist booth at Wine Fest

Note: Elements include Eugene beer samples, campaign buttons, postcards, tote bags, monitor playing film trailer, and cutout of Eugene Debs.
Source: Courtesy of Kyle Travers.

design thinking process. Wine Fest is an annual event that attracts public media fans but also wine enthusiasts who know little about WFYI. The event coordinator had been looking for ways to engage guests with WFYI content. The event was held from 6 to 9 p.m., March 1, 2019, at the Biltwell Event Center near downtown Indianapolis and drew 1,104 attendees (Personal communication, August 11, 2021). To prepare for the event, it was necessary to finalize a title for the documentary and design a graphic look and logo. WFYI's graphic designer created a large poster to catch guests' attention and also designed a postcard to hand out to guests. The poster displayed a photograph of Eugene Debs along with one of his most recognizable quotes: "While there is a lower class, I am in it, while there is a criminal element, I am of it, and while there is a soul in prison, I am not free."

The postcard had information about Eugene Debs life. Additionally, the graphic designer created a life-size cutout of Eugene Debs so people could interact with the display. The booth had a small monitor that played a trailer of the documentary with captions so people could get the information in the loud space. On the table of the booth, there were replica buttons from Eugene Debs presidential campaign for guests to take with them. There were also a limited number of tote bags participants could win if they answered a trivia question about Eugene Debs. Finally, to attract participants to the booth, we poured *Eugene*, a porter beer from Revolution Brewing in Chicago with an image of Eugene Debs on the can.

Element 2: Side Effects Event During Spirit and Place

Side Effects Public Media is a health reporting collaborative of several Midwestern public radio stations. Side Effects' community outreach coordinator

The Revolutionist: Eugene V. Debs   201

was part of the Eugene Debs committee and wanted to address current healthcare issues by comparing them to issues during Eugene Debs life 100 years ago. She thought it would be helpful to create a program as part of *Spirit and Place*, an annual festival in Indianapolis that combines events around the city under a common theme. The theme for 2019 was "R/Evolution" and the website asks the questions: "What do history, geography, art, science, astronomy, sociology, religion, political science, and culture teach us about revolution and evolution? What contemporary issues, in our backyard and elsewhere, are calling out for revolution?" (spiritandplace.org). *The Revolutionist* fit the 2019 theme perfectly and *Spirit and Place* also has an enthusiastic, loyal audience. She thought it would provide a unique

Figure 15.2 The Medical History Museum in Indianapolis
Note: This room was used as an operating theater for medical students from 1896 to 1969.
Source: Courtesy of Kyle Travers.

opportunity to talk about the Eugene Debs, the struggle of the working class, and access to health care.

To unite the past and present, we met with the Medical History Museum in Indianapolis to form a partnership for the event. The organization was seeking to "humanize" its collection of medical artifacts and was excited about the idea of partnering for the event. They offered up their operating theater, used by medical students in the early 20th century. The space embodied the perfect era and atmosphere for a discussion about the evolution of health care since the time of Eugene Debs (Figure 15.2).

During this meeting, we designed the program for the Spirit and Place Festival. Participants would watch a short video about health care during the time of Eugene Debs, and then a panel of experts would lead a discussion about health care then and now.

The Spirit and Place event was called "Stagnation and Agitation" and used the life and times of Eugene Debs as a catalyst for discussion about today's health care and workplace inequities. It took place at the Medical History Museum on November 7, 2019, at 6 p.m. The moderator was one of the producers of *The Revolutionist*, Kim Jacobs, and the panel consisted of Carl Ellison, CEO of Indiana Minority Health Coalition, Sarah Halter, executive director of the Indiana Medical History Museum, Dr. Dawn Haut, CEO of Eskenazi Health Center, and Wesley Bishop, assistant professor of history at Marian College. Forty-one attendees participated, and when asked what follow-up action they would take after the discussion, some listed "Read more about Eugene Debs," "Vote for change," and "be more aware of political activities as relates to job & job equalities."

Figure 15.3 Website banner showing Terri Jett promoting "Simple Civics" episodes related to Eugene Debs

Source: Courtesy of WFYI Public Media.

Element 3: Simple Civics Web Series

Another committee member, WFYI's social media manager, suggested creating a web series of two-minute videos about politics and government to be distributed through social media called *Simple Civics* (Figure 15.3). For *The Revolutionist* project, we launched with three episodes devoted to Eugene Debs topics: "Can you run for president from prison?" "Freedom of Speech During Times of War" and "How does the draft work?" The series was hosted by Butler University Political Science Professor, Terri Jett. The first three episodes were released in the weeks following the broadcast premiere of *The Revolutionist* on October 3, 2019, and were featured on the webpage.

Element 4: Notable Hoosiers Television Series

Another committee member, WFYI's director of development, proposed re-broadcasting past WFYI documentaries about prominent figures from Indiana in the weeks leading up to the on-air premiere of *The Revolutionist*. This series, marketed as *Notable Hoosiers*, includes five programs created by WFYI over the past decade and documentaries about Senator Richard Lugar, author Kurt Vonnegut, Governor Edgar Whitcomb, President Benjamin Harrison, Indianapolis Mayor Bill Hudnut, and Holocaust survivor Eva Kor. Sponsorship for this series is sold to generate additional money for WFYI. The programs aired every Thursday in September in order to promote the last installment of the series, which was the premiere of *The Revolutionist: Eugene V. Debs*, on Thursday, October 3, 2019.

Element 5: Cultural Manifesto Radio Program

WFYI's Radio Station Manager, a committee member, introduced the idea of dedicating an episode of *Cultural Manifesto*, a popular WFYI radio program about music history, to Eugene Debs. The host and producer of this program, Kyle Long, loved the concept. Being a fan of Eugene Debs, he suggested many ideas of how to devote an episode to labor music. On the day of the premiere, October 3, 2019, he aired a special about protest music in honor of the Eugene Debs documentary.

Element 6: Video Extras for the Website

WFYI's radio station manager also thought it would be possible to include short radio news packages about Eugene Debs in the morning and evening drive time blocks of programming during the week of the broadcast premiere. She put me in contact with the host of the evening block of radio programming. However, he started a new position and therefore, I instead created three short supporting videos for the website. These videos cover the premiere of the documentary in Terre Haute, a discussion with the Eugene Debs museum curator, and an interview with the film's musical composer.

Element 7: The Revolutionist *Web Page*

In committee meetings, WFYI's web content producer suggested that there be a digital space for the various transmedia elements and suggested a web page on wfyi.org. This webpage contains all videos related to *The Revolutionist* including trailers, extra content, and the documentary itself as YouTube embedded players. The website has links to the episode of *Cultural Manifesto*, *Simple Civics* series, and news about upcoming events including the *Spirit and Place* event, and screening opportunities.

Element 8: *#DoYouKnowDebs Social Media Campaign*

Social media carried the theme and hashtag *#DoYouKnowDebs*. During the design thinking process, various presentations, and informal interviews, the majority of people I talked to did not know Eugene Debs. We created this campaign to demonstrate that while today he has low name recognition, in his era, he was both famous and infamous. Social media posts presented contradictory opinions about Eugene Debs from sources such as Theodore

Figure 15.4 Prototype social media post
Note: The animated GIF post rotates through the views that appear in the figure.
Source: Courtesy of WFYI Public Media.

Roosevelt, Helen Keller, Woodrow Wilson, and Clarence Darrow. This juxtaposition not only informed people about the importance of this figure and a general sense of his place in history but also piqued the interest of those who know nothing about him.

Element 9: The Revolutionist Documentary Video

The core piece of this transmedia project is an hour-long documentary that aired locally on WFYI on October 3, 2019, called *The Revolutionist: Eugene V. Debs*. It illustrates the life of Eugene V. Debs, born on November 5, 1855, in Terre Haute, Indiana. He started work on the railroads at the age of 14 and went on to lead the American Railroad Union in a transformative nationwide strike against the Pullman Company in 1894. This conflict involved more than a quarter-million railroad workers, stopped the U.S. mail and passenger service, and ended in violence when President Cleveland called in the national guard. Debs became famous and, while jailed for the strike, began to see socialism as the way to fair treatment of workers. He helped found the Socialist Party and ran for president on its ticket five times. He was a renowned orator and toured the U.S. delivering his message of equality and workers' rights to huge crowds. In 1918, while speaking out against U.S. involvement in World War One, he was arrested for violating the Espionage Act and was sentenced to ten years in a federal penitentiary. From there, he ran for president a final time and won almost one million votes from his cell. This documentary's goal is to inform and educate people about this influential American and encourage them to think about historic issues in their current iterations. As this is the most in-depth piece of the transmedia storyworld, it serves as the centerpiece and other threads of the story reference and promote it. This program was also streamed on the project's webpage, WFYI's YouTube channel, and in 2020, was distributed nationally through American Public Television.

Discussion

The WFYI committee and the WFYI Nerds group generated dozens of ideas through design thinking. From those exercises, we narrowed the ideas down to eleven executable pieces of the transmedia storyworld to be carried out by members of the committee. Eight pieces were completed as planned, one was eliminated, and one was altered significantly. These elements were released during the months of August through November 2019.

At the beginning of the project, most people with whom I'd spoken did not know who Eugene Debs was. At the Wine Fest event, I was able to interact with dozens of people and talked to them about his life. Even more surprisingly, many guests seemed surprised that WFYI was producing the documentary, and some did not seem to know the organization created local content. This person-to-person interaction increased knowledge of WFYI's mission and hopefully made a lasting impression, as this event took place in March, nine months before the release of the documentary. This was also true for the WFYI Nerds brainstorming session. The women who participated did not seem to know much about Eugene Debs, but by the end of the evening, had a broader understanding of his influence and how it could be applied to current issues.

Internally, the creation of the transmedia committee for the Eugene Debs project and our monthly meetings increased awareness within the organization. Most members of the committee had no idea who Eugene Debs was when they started, but as we create transmedia story elements, their knowledge increased and so had their capacity to share their knowledge with others. Also, because committee members came from almost all departments within WFYI, they were able to act as ambassadors for the project and spread the word to other employees.

Design thinking allowed committee members to create transmedia with a sense of ownership, and they were not assigned pieces of the transmedia story. In their day-to-day jobs, many employees are handed a task, and can only be creative in *how* they handle the problem. This project offered more freedom. Instead, they brainstormed, discussed, and tailored their ideas to match their department's resources and expertise. I do not have the knowledge of marketing, events, community engagement, and radio production that my committee members do. As experts in their fields, they were able to take the story of the documentary and craft it to the channel through which their piece of transmedia is told. This also allowed for a division of labor that was helpful as I finished production of the television documentary. As I worked in my area of expertise, I could be assured that transmedia elements were being created and executed by the experts of each channel.

Design thinking also led to increased engagement with WFYI Nerds. By beginning the session with broad questions about what they would like out of the Nerds experience, participants really shed light on what is working and also how Nerds could expand. They expressed a desire to see a more diverse group participate at Nerds events and even said that more men should get involved. They also said that they would like more volunteer opportunities to do good in the community and also opportunities to volunteer with WFYI. The Nerds responses also showed that they were not familiar with WFYI local productions, especially from the television department. Yet when asked how they would like to get involved with the organization, they said they were very curious about seeing how local productions are put together and even suggested that the Nerds take a "field trip" on an upcoming shoot.

This project also came at a very beneficial time for WFYI. PBS stations around the country are being encouraged to emphasize audience engagement and digital content through a program called the "Digital Immersion Project." At WFYI, this has led to a committee known as "Wires and Waves," a group of employees from all departments who are charged with implementing a digital culture by "aligning content to our audience at the right time, on the right platform, in a way that matches our station goals," through a "solid multi-platform strategy to create meaningful content, distribute it intentionally, and effectively engage desired audiences" (Personal communication, 2018). I am on this committee, and so far, it has largely addressed the issue based on past experience and broad, general looks at future projects. *The Revolutionist* has provided a tangible project that acted as an experiment for these ideas. Many of the members of Wires and Waves also belong to the transmedia committee and have been able to put into practice the ideas of brainstorming, audience segmentation, strategic release of multi-platform media, and measuring success through audience data. *The Revolutionist* afforded WFYI the opportunity to try new things. The idea for the web series, *Simple Civics*, had been on our social media coordinator's mind for some time, yet he didn't know how to get started. By using *The Revolutionist* project as a catalyst, we created episodes related to Eugene Debs in the weeks leading up to the broadcast premiere and used this momentum to continue the series with episodes on other subjects. This project gave us the excuse to try something that will last beyond *The Revolutionist*.

Most of these elements seemed to have had a measurable impact on viewership of the broadcast documentary or total engagement with the subject of Eugene Debs. In Indianapolis, viewership for the night of the premiere, October 3, 2019, was 5,199 households, and Indianapolis area viewership for multiple airings including WTIU (Bloomington) and WIPB (Muncie), totaled 27,317 households. Additional national viewership distributed by American Public Television through the end of 2020 led to a total audience of 108,712 households. The national impact didn't stop there. The documentary was narrated by Danny Glover, a famous actor and advocate for workers' rights. He was an active supporter of Bernie Sanders during the 2020 presidential election and told Sanders about his involvement in the project. Bernie, a big fan of Eugene Debs and his principles, then held a Facebook Live event on June 22, featuring the documentary and a panel discussion. During the event, there were approximately 7,100 viewers at any time, and over 200,000 total views by the following morning.

It is my hope that *The Revolutionist* transmedia project will stand as an example of what PBS stations can do. Other stations will see that with a little planning and investment, a documentary project can live beyond the broadcast and reach audiences who would have never tuned in. In the future, I would focus more on how the transmedia pieces fit together and lead users from one to another. This may be easier on a fictional piece or a broader subject, but hopefully covering different aspects of Eugene Debs' life in different ways will translate into a variety of experiences for those who do follow every piece of the transmedia story. It would have also been beneficial to engage with other local media outlets, like newspapers, and with audiences who do not already engage with WFYI in order to get some fresh perspectives and have an even wider reach. But with the obstacle of Eugene Debs' obscurity, educating people about WFYI, Eugene Debs, and the other pieces of transmedia seemed daunting. I determined that internal, organizational buy-in was just as important, if not more so, in what seems to be our station's maiden voyage into design thinking and transmedia storytelling.

References

Astle, R. (2012, October 1). Half the sky & social documentary transmedia. *Filmmaker Magazine*. Retrieved June 21, 2018, from https://filmmakermagazine.com/52826-half-the-sky-social-documentary-transmedia/

Brown, T., & Katz, B. (2009). Returning to the surface. In *Change by design: How design thinking transforms organizations and inspires innovation* (pp. 109–128). Harper-Collins.

Brown, T., & Wyatt, J. (2010). Design thinking for social innovation (SSIR) [Weblog]. *Stanford Social Innovation Review*. ssir.org/articles/entry/design_thinking_for_social_innovation

Burg, S. (2016, April 5). Investing in innovation. Retrieved June 21, 2018, from https://medium.com/disrupting-public-media/investing-in-innovation-e3fd42ce2835

Chan-Olmsted, S. M., & Kim, Y. (2002, June). The PBS brand versus cable brands: Assessing the brand image of public television in a multichannel environment. *Journal of Broadcasting & Electronic Media*, 46(2), 300+. Retrieved from http://link.galegroup.com.proxy.bsu.edu/apps/doc/A89583554/BIC?u=munc80314&sid=BIC&xid=9808082b

Chaplin, H. (2016, July 13). A guide to journalism and design. Retrieved June 21, 2018, from https://towcenter.org/a-guide-to-journalism-and-design/

Hall, M., & Stahl, K. A. D. (2012). Devillainizing video in support of comprehension and vocabulary instruction. *The Reading Teacher*, 65(6), 403–406.

Jenkins, H. (2006). Searching for the origami unicorn. In *Convergence culture: Where old and new media collide* (pp. 95–134). New York University Press.

Jenkins, H. (2016, November 15). *Transmedia what? By Henry Jenkins*. Retrieved June 21, 2018, from https://immerse.news/transmedia-what-15edf6b61daa

Knight Foundation. (2017, November 14). Understanding public media's most engaged podcast users. Retrieved July 15, 2018, from https://medium.com/informed-and-engaged/understanding-public-medias-most-engaged-podcast-users-bb592cd7e03e

LUMA Institute. (2012). *Innovating for people handbook of human-centered design methods* (1st edition). LUMA Institute.

Mayer, R. E. (2003). The promise of multimedia learning: Using the same instructional design methods across different media. *Learning and Instruction*, 13(2), 125–139. https://doi.org/10.1016/S0959-4752(02)00016-6

Minow, N. N., & Cate, F. H. (2003). Revisiting the Vast Wasteland. *Federal Communications Law Journal*, 55(3), 407–434.

Nguyen, H. (2019). PBS doesn't see Netflix as competition; still open to making American dramas. *IndieWire*. www.indiewire.com/2019/02/pbs-netflix-amazon-mercy-street-paula-kerger-tca-1202040764/

Norman, D. (2013). Design thinking. In *The design of everyday things* (Revised and expanded ed., pp. 217–257). Basic Books.

Salvatore, N. (1982). *Eugene V. Debs: Citizen and socialist.* University of Illinois Press.

Sefton, D., & Editor, S. (2017, April 7). Beyond politics, public media audiences and Trump supporters have some things in common. Retrieved July 15, 2018, from https://current.org/2017/04/beyond-politics-public-media-audiences-and-trump-supporters-have-some-things-in-common/

16 User Experience Design and Testing for Socially-Concerned Storytelling

Jennifer Palilonis

User experience design (UXD) is a well-established discipline that encompasses a number of subcategories, all focused on ensuring that audiences find value in content and experiences you create for them. Designing an effective user experience requires that its designers have a deep understanding of audiences—what motivates them to engage, what they value, their usability needs, abilities and limitations, and more (User experience basics, 2014). Generally speaking, meaningful and valuable experiences are useful, usable, desirable, findable, accessible, and credible. Together, these principles serve as a framework for building many types of user experiences, from websites to apps, cross-platform storytelling, and more. Thus, user experience design is increasingly relevant to a wide range of pursuits and careers, including project management, user research, usability evaluation, information architecture, user-interface design, interaction design, visual design, content strategy, accessibility, and web analytics, to name a few.

Traditionally, the term "user experience" has been used to describe end users' self-reported interpretations of their interactions with a digital system—usually a website or app. Included in user experience are considerations of whether users can accomplish their goals with the system (usability), how easy it is for users to find and start using a system or a device (adaptability), whether the system is fun, engaging, and/or better than others like it (desirability), and whether the system is valuable to users (value) (User experience basics, 2014). As such, user experience designers should understand and anticipate users' needs and expectations when developing new systems.

Of course, usability and user experience can be applied to many different domains. For example, there is an abundance of ways that media professionals can leverage the rich storytelling potential of different digital platforms to engage audiences. Likewise, the emergence of transmedia storytelling in the 1990s has contributed to the ongoing evolution of how narratives are constructed and the ways in which audiences interact with them. Henry Jenkins defines a transmedia story as one that "unfolds across multiple media platforms" (2006, p. 95), including digital media and print products and even live events. Sometimes referred to as cross-platform storytelling or distributed narrative, transmedia storytelling is fundamentally defined by its

DOI: 10.4324/9781003150862-16

use of multiple media platforms to tell a single story. Moreover, one of the primary goals of transmedia storytelling is to immerse and engage people in storytelling in ways that transform them from passive consumers to active audiences. Thus, to effectively convey a single, cohesive story across several platforms, the individual parts of a transmedia story must contribute to a stronger, more satisfying whole.

In the Center for Emerging Media Design & Development (EMDD) at Ball State University, students from interdisciplinary backgrounds collaborate in a master's degree program that joins usability and user experience research and design with transmedia storytelling to design, develop, and deploy large-scale projects. EMDD pairs a traditional graduate curriculum with hands-on lab experiences in which students work with public and private partners, many of which are nonprofit organizations, education foundations, and other socially-concerned groups. EMDD students and faculty believe in the power of human-centered design and storytelling to solve big problems. To do so, the program brings together students who have a wide range of undergraduate backgrounds and career experience, including journalists, computer scientists, artists, writers, designers, historians, social scientists, programmers, and more to tackle real-world problems using technology and digital media. As part of their first-year experience, graduate students take a course in usability and user experience research methods, as well as a course in transmedia storytelling and publishing.

The multi-platform nature of transmedia storytelling makes it an obvious target for user experience evaluation. However, where most user experiences are developed and examined one at a time, a transmedia narrative is simultaneously designed as both the whole story and the individual sum of its parts. This presents interesting challenges for user experience designers. For example, the user experiences fostered by different media platforms—i.e., websites vs. apps, mobile devices vs. desktop computers, etc.—are inherently different and, thus, require individualized approaches to storytelling and design. The story must unfold in a way that plays to the strengths of each platform. Likewise, each part of a transmedia story must be developed to stand alone so that if someone only sees one part, they still have a complete experience. Yet it must also exist as part of a cohesive whole so that together, the parts contribute to a larger, more robust narrative. Finally, because transmedia stories are distributed across a variety of audiences, the individual parts must be findable, distributable, and extendable. One of the hallmarks of an effective transmedia story is that it provides opportunities for deep audience engagement, and sometimes even allows the audience to contribute to the story.

However, transmedia creators face the possibility that some segments of the audience may not engage with the story across all platforms, which may exclude those who are older or less tech-savvy (Neptune, 2020). Likewise, although multiple entry points into a single storyworld may entice a larger, more diverse audience, it is also possible that some individual entry points may be less appealing and push consumers away. In essence, a transmedia story is only as good as its weakest part. And effectively distributing a single story across diverse platforms—each with potentially different inherent strengths and weaknesses—is a tricky business. Additionally, the more content producers and platforms contained in a transmedia campaign, the more difficult it is to manage. Ultimately, a single inconsistency, redundancy, or noticeable hole in the story can kill a whole transmedia campaign. However, there are a number of strategies transmedia designer can employ at the early, middle, and end stages of project development that can help mitigate these types of problems.

Although user experience design and testing can take many forms and can happen at any point in a project, it can be helpful to approach the process as a series of systematic activities that occur at the beginning, middle, and end of a project. At the beginning of a project, empathy research methods—like interviews, observations, social media analytics, surveys, etc.—can help a designer develop a clearer understanding of who the audience is, the media platforms they gravitate toward, and where they get their news and information. Then, during the story-building and design phases, designers can engage in a series of iterative prototyping and incremental testing strategies through the most intense story-building and design phases. After a project has been designed at a relatively high level of fidelity, summative user testing can provide an assessment of the user experience across the entire transmedia storyworld.

Core Usability and User Experience Principles

User experience is generally subjective; user experience principles can be applied to a wide variety of disciplines related to transmedia storytelling. For example, interaction designers responsible for creating websites, games, apps, and other digital experiences apply UI/UX principles to the creation of prototypes at various levels of fidelity and to create full design solutions for cross-platform projects. Content creators can refer to UI/UX principles as they consider how story, platform, and experience effectively converge to engage and immerse audiences. Prior to an exploration of methods to understand and define audiences, to identify and leverage transmedia platforms, and to engage in iterative testing and development processes, it is useful to define the core UI/UX principles commonly used in product design and digital design.

User Experience (UX)

Both usability and user experience are critical considerations for building transmedia experiences, but they are often confused. User experience (UX) design and testing focuses on gaining a deep understanding of users. UX is concerned with all aspects of a user's engagement when interacting with a product, service, environment, or facility. Thus, user experience is the parent of usability. User experience author and pioneer Peter Morville identifies seven factors to explain each facet of user experience (The Interaction Design Foundation, "The 7 Factors," 2021). He notes that for experiences to be valuable and meaningful, they must also be useful, usable, desirable, findable, accessible, and credible. In the following, we explore these factors through the lens of socially-concerned transmedia storytelling.

Useful: Content should be original and fulfill a need for your audience. James Baldwin—one of the most significant American novelists, playwrights, essayists, poets, and activists of the 20th Century—once said:

> You write in order to change the world, knowing perfectly well that you probably can't, but also knowing that literature is indispensable to the world. . . . The world changes according to the way people see it, and if you alter, even by a millimeter, the way . . . people look at reality, then you can change it.
>
> (Romano, 1979, p. 1)

Baldwin's writing explored racial, sexual, and class distinctions in the United States, and he was both lauded and vilified for his work. Today, his writing on America and race still resonates as powerfully as it did in the heat of the Civil Rights Movement of the 1960s. Although Baldwin's work was not necessarily indicative of modern transmedia storytelling, the usefulness of his work is undeniable. Baldwin made his audiences think; he leveraged the power of language and story to spark emotion; and through storytelling, he provided incisive analysis of racism and the pain, frustration, and despair of the Black and gay communities at the time. Like Baldwin's work, socially-concerned storytelling intends to be—first and foremost—useful to those who consume it.

Usable: Digital products, such as websites, apps, and games, as well as physical exhibitions like those experienced in museums or other public spaces, must also be easy to use. The distributed nature of transmedia storytelling makes the role of usability critical to success. Not only must individual platform experiences be easy to use, but so too must the cross-platform experience. In other words, it must be easy for your audience to transition and migrate from one transmedia element to another. Therefore, careful attention must be given to interaction design strategies, visual design, and how users of one platform are alerted that the story extends into other spaces. Usability is explored further in the following section.

Desirable: An audience experience ensures that the content and its transmedia design evokes emotion and appreciation. Like any other story, cross-platform storytelling projects must be compelling. Likewise, because transmedia stories often engage users in digital platforms, the visual design, interactive experience, and platform choices must also be desirable, engaging, interesting, and satisfying.

Findable: *Findability* refers to how easy it is for consumers to find content on a website. In other words, web content needs to be navigable and locatable both on the website and off. When applied to transmedia storytelling, the concept of findability is more complex and, arguably, more crucial. Expertly designed transmedia stories seamlessly move audiences from one platform and one experience to another; so much so, that audiences may not even realize they are engaged in a distributed experience. On the other hand, poorly designed transmedia experiences may leave important parts of the story underdeveloped, simply because users cannot find them, or worse, don't know they exist at all. To avoid this, storyworld creators are advised to develop detailed user journey maps that diagram the range of routes through a cross-platform story users may take and the contextual cues that will guide them there.

Accessible: Content in digital spaces must be accessible to people with disabilities that might impair their ability to see, hear, or interact with content.

> Accessible sites present information through multiple sensory channels, such as sound and sight, and they allow for additional means of site navigation and interactivity beyond the typical point-and-click-interface: keyboard-based control and voice-based navigation. The combination of a multisensory approach and a multi-interactivity approach allows disabled users to access the same information as nondisabled users.
> (Accessibility Basics, 2015, para. 2)

Credible: In the entertainment arena, transmedia credibility often refers to whether a story exhibits continuity across platforms. "In this case, some transmedia franchises encourage consistencies to achieve maximum credibility among all extensions" (Byun & Kwon, 2016, p. 1). Certainly, in the context of socially-concerned storytelling, credibility also refers to the necessity for users to trust and believe in the veracity of the content. For example, something as simple as providing a list of sources for information included in a storyworld is an important step toward ensuring that your audience views the work as trustworthy and credible.

Usability (UI)

At its core, usability is about how well the design of your experience matches users' behavior.

> Usability is a measure of how well a specific user in a specific context can use a product/design to achieve a defined goal effectively, efficiently and

satisfactorily. Designers usually measure a design's usability throughout the development process—from wireframes to the final deliverable—to ensure maximum usability.

(The Interaction Design Foundation, "What is Usability," 2021, para. 1)

According to Usability.gov for experiences to be usable, they must also be learnable, efficient to use, memorable, error free, and satisfying, as defined in the following (Nielsen, 2012, para. 2):

- **Learnability:** How easy is it for users to accomplish basic tasks the first time they encounter the design?
- **Efficiency:** Once users have learned the design, how quickly can they perform tasks?
- **Memorability:** When users return to the design after a period of not using it, how easily can they reestablish proficiency?
- **Errors:** How many errors do users make, how severe are these errors, and how easily can they recover from the errors?
- **Satisfaction:** How pleasant is it to use the design?

It is worth noting that these usability principles can be applied to both digital and physical experiences. From websites to apps, to exhibits and interactive live events, design flaws and confusing interaction patterns can frustrate and alienate your audience. Both formative and summative usability testing can help ensure your transmedia experience is easy to use.

Transmedia and User Experience

The successful development of a transmedia storyworld is dependent upon a well-developed user experience strategy. This strategy will guide you to effectively transform ideas into compelling and cohesive narratives, identify and understand different audiences, evaluate which technologies and platforms best serve your story, create cohesive user experiences across different platforms, and engage audiences to participate in the storyworld.

Understanding and Defining Audience

Unlike many traditional story forms for which audiences are considered passive consumers, there are many ways in which transmedia audiences are integral to the story itself. Transmedia storytelling often invites audience participation; some transmedia experiences provide opportunities for the audience to contribute to the story. As described in Chapter 3, a team of EMDD graduate students at Ball State developed in 2017 a global transmedia campaign in collaboration with Circle of Blue, a nonprofit organization focused on covering the water and energy crisis around the world. Circle of

Blue comprises an international network of leading journalists and climate scientists and is a nonprofit affiliate of the Pacific Institute, a water, climate, and policy think tank. The Circle of Blue staff—globally recognized as leaders in reporting on the world's freshwater crisis—challenged the EMDD team to engage young people in the story of the value of water. To meet this challenge, the students launched the Blue Roots Project #MyWaterStory social media challenge, which gathered more than 800 stories from users in 27 countries about their relationships with water. The campaign was designed to foster a global conversation about the value of water around the world leading up to and during the 2017 Watershed conference in Rome, Italy.

Prior to landing on the Blue Roots Project idea, the EMDD project team conducted dozens of interviews, deployed surveys among students on the Ball State campus, and engaged in design thinking sessions with focus groups of 18- to 24-year-olds to better understand four central user-centered themes: 1) the audience's knowledge of global water issues, 2) the types of water stories that would most likely resonate with them, 3) what generally motivates them to engage with news and information, and 4) what platforms and activities were most likely to garner their attention. The decision to develop a social media campaign was not made by chance; it was part of a deliberate effort to establish a clear list of requirements for their project. Through this work, the team decided to give 18- to 24-year-olds an opportunity to share their ideas, brainstorm solutions, and engage in a dialogue with others interested in the topic of water. They also determined that the best way to reach this audience was to engage them where they regularly spend time: online and on social media. Central to their transmedia campaign were two websites. The first, http://worldwatervalues.org/, was developed in collaboration with Circle of Blue in preparation for World Water Day 2017. At this event, Pope Francis and 400 thought leaders from around the world came together to discuss the water crisis and possible solutions. The site prompted audiences from around the world to share their water stories through Facebook, Instagram, and Twitter using #MyWaterStory based on six core themes: climate, energy, food, management, politics, and quality (http://worldwatervalues.org/waterthemes/). The second website, http://bluerootsproject.org/, promotes additional content distributed across other platforms, including a World Water Day teacher curriculum and a podcast. The Blue Roots Project recognized that transmedia stories are carefully distributed across space and time to bring the audience closer to the storyworld. Each part of the transmedia story—the podcast, the websites, the social media campaign, and the three-day conference in Rome—engaged audiences in different ways and also merged into a single distributed story.

User Personas and Experience Journeys

User-centered transmedia design begins with a clear understanding of the users of the multi-platform story you are building. In fact, one of the best things you can do for your story is to know your audience so well that you can envision how they will engage with the story, interact with the platforms on which it is distributed, and what will motivate them to stay with the story. One way to form this understanding is to develop audience personas and experience journeys that map the paths users may take through your storyworld. Personas are semi-fictional descriptions of members of your intended audience. Empathy research, including interviews with members of your intended audience, will help form personas that can be extremely useful as you develop a broad plan for your transmedia story.

In 2019, a team of EMDD and journalism students built personas to crystallize their understanding of the audience for an original documentary and transmedia storytelling campaign that explores opportunities for minority and underserved communities within volleyball, the fastest growing boys' and men's sport in the United States. *Match Point: The Rise of Boys' and Men's Volleyball* follows the U.S. Men's National Volleyball Team head coach John Speraw and several other youths and collegiate coaches and players on a quest to showcase the sport in the United States, as well as the challenges associated with attracting new athletes to the sport. The Ball State team partnered with First Point Volleyball Foundation, a nonprofit organization founded by Speraw to raise participation in and awareness of the sport. In addition to the documentary, which served as the tentpole for the project, the transmedia campaign included a website (matchpoint-mvb.com), a podcast called *Match Point: Aces Only*, and a competitive app called *Match Point, The Game*. After interviewing volleyball coaches, players, fans, influencers in the volleyball community, and even youth in other sports like basketball, the Ball State team identified three primary user personas to build their storyworld around: 1) 11- to 15-year-old boys, 2) parents of athletes, and 3) sports influencers and athletic directors. For each of these groups, they developed simple personas that described these groups by age, motivations, goals, interests, and social media presence. Not only did the *Match Point* personas help inform a storyworld that would appeal to three very different—but equally important—audiences, they also helped determine that content on each major social media platform—Facebook, Instagram, and Twitter—should cater to a distinct audience based on their preferred platforms. Approximately 72% of the *Match Point* Instagram audience is younger than 24, while only 15% of the Facebook audience is younger than 24. As a result, *Match Point's* Facebook content targets middle-aged fans, coaches, and parents, while Instagram content targets middle- and high-school-aged athletes. Ultimately, developing personas at the start of the project allowed the team to leverage diverse approaches to storytelling and create different points of entry into the *Match Point* storyworld to meet audiences where they are and speak to them on their terms.

Testing Stories Across Digital and Physical Spaces

There are myriad ways that a transmedia storyworld can take shape. Like any good story, the presentation, distribution, and narrative strategy of a

218 *Jennifer Palilonis*

transmedia package should be defined by the nature and needs of the story at hand. In other words, a good transmedia story leverages the strengths of each platform it employs to reveal each part of the narrative. Multi-platform projects also rely heavily on the form and structure that each platform provides. Thus, the choices you make about the platforms to include in a transmedia storyworld are directly related to audience/user experience. Following is an analysis of some of the most common platforms and content formats used in socially-concerned transmedia storytelling, as well as some insights about the benefits and potential drawbacks of each.

> **Apps:** The mobile era is upon us, and designers and developers often debate over whether an app or a website is the better route for everything from ecommerce to storytelling. There are a number of ways in which apps might provide a better user experience for socially-concerned transmedia stories. Mobile apps allow for personalized user experiences, including the ability to send users' notifications. Apps can also take full advantage of touch screen interactivity, such as swiping and tapping, making them more suitable for certain types of experiences like interactive games. Research has also shown that users spend more time with apps than websites on their mobile devices, and well-designed mobile apps often perform actions quicker than a mobile website (Deshdeep, 2021).
> **Blog/Vlog:** Weblogs and vlogs are often included in transmedia storyworlds. They can be used to extend a story, as a platform for character development, and as a means for promoting a transmedia story.
> **Documentary film:** Often used as a transmedia tent pole, documentary films are often used in socially-concerned storytelling to generate empathy in audiences, share compelling stories, foster awareness, invite engagement, and support social change.
> **Game:** Socially-concerned transmedia storytelling often includes both analog and digital games that place users into real-world scenarios or simulations. Games can be used to fulfill a range of objectives, including to educate or inform in an entertaining format. Likewise, goal-driven game formats with high production value can be used to extend transmedia narratives.
> **Live event:** Hosting a live event as part of a transmedia campaign or storyworld—such as a speaker series, performance, exhibition, and the like—can bring a story to life and invite audience engagement.
> **Physical installation:** Transmedia projects often cross digital and physical spaces. Physical installations may include fixed physical structures, artifacts, exhibitions, interactive kiosks, or audiovisual installations. Additionally, live events, such as festivals or limited-run exhibitions, are often the catalyst for audience engagement and interaction.
> **Podcast:** Podcasts are an increasingly popular and effective tool of transmedia storytelling. They provide a convenient method for serializing a story through episodic content delivery.

Printed materials: Printed magazines, newspapers, newsletters, flyers, postcards, brochures, and other forms of printed media can also be included in a transmedia storyworld by serving as a tangible representation of content. The tangible nature of print media can provide audiences with a sense of permanence that can immerse readers in ways that often ephemeral digital experiences do not.

Social media: Using a range of existing social network channels—i.e., Facebook, Instagram, Twitter, Snapchat, TikTok, YouTube, and more—to deliver fictional or factual narratives is a popular way to capture a wide audience. Social media can be used both to promote a transmedia story, to extend the narrative, and to invite audience participation.

Website: Websites often serve a tentpole role in socially-concerned transmedia stories. One or more websites within a single storyworld can be used both as part of the central narrative and as a place to promote the transmedia network.

Virtual world: Augmented and virtual reality platforms provide highly immersive experiences for transmedia audiences. Virtual shared spaces can also allow users to socialize and create their own stories around a shared theme.

New platforms will continue to emerge, providing you with limitless possibilities for how to choose and combine platforms for a single transmedia storyworld. Although the terminology may vary across professions, industries, and purposes, it is critical to choose platforms with a deliberate and clear understanding of the individual and collective roles they will serve in telling a specific transmedia story.

Formative User Experience Testing

Applied in the early stages of transmedia design and development, formative user experience testing can help identify usability issues, as well as the user experience pitfalls of a particular approach to storytelling. Formative testing can also help identify solutions to problems identified early in the design phase, before time and resources have been invested in the project. Formative testing can help determine which design elements and content built into individual platform experiences are effectively resonating with audiences. It can also help identify where the combination of platforms and distribution of content is working well and where it is not. There are a number of formative UI/UX testing methods that can be conducted internally by the storytelling team, as well as some that can be conducted with a small group of potential users.

Formative testing is a discovery-based, iterative process that allows testers to answer the following types of questions: What usability issues exist in our interfaces? Do users understand our navigation? Do audiences understand how the narrative arc is distributed across platforms? Are audiences able to easily navigate from one platform to the next? Formative methods include concept testing, A/B testing, iterative usability testing, heuristics inspections, and cognitive walkthroughs, to name a few. The following sections provide a few more details on some formative methods that can be useful to socially-concerned transmedia storytelling projects.

Concept Testing and A/B Prototype Testing

It's easy to assume you have a great idea. However, to ensure you get it right, consider testing your ideas with customer segments to collect valuable insights about whether your idea actually makes sense and is appealing to a real audience. Concept testing is the process of soliciting feedback from members of your prospective audience about narrative approaches, platform choices, or transmedia strategy ideas. Concept testing can be simple and quick or iterative and sophisticated.

A concept test can be delivered either as a survey or as a user interview. Either way, the first step is to present the concept to a prospective user. This can take the form of a designed, low-fidelity prototype, story treatment, or a visual map or diagram of your proposed transmedia storyworld. After examining the concept, user participants should first be asked how likely they are to engage with or consume the finished transmedia story as presented. Next, respondents should be asked what they like and dislike about the concept. You can design this as an open-ended question or as a series of close-ended questions about likes and dislikes of specific features of a platform or parts of a story. Then, you can ask questions designed to elicit feedback about users' perceptions of value, uniqueness, interest, quality, and whether respondents would recommend the story to others. Again, both open- and close-ended questions can be effective for gauging your audience's level of interest in your ideas. Concept tests can also be conducted in an iterative cycle that allows you to collect audience feedback about both newly developed and revised ideas at various stages in the development process.

A/B testing follows a similar process but is more comparative in nature. A well-designed A/B test involves showing two variants at the same time—of the same concept, platform design, narrative structure, or another aspect of the transmedia storyworld—and comparing which version receives more positive feedback. For example, you could show two different approaches to website design using wireframe prototypes. Or you could show two different approaches to narrative structure or two different ideas for how a part of the story could be distributed across media platforms. The two approaches to design and/or content could be shown to the same users for the sake of direct comparison or to two different sets of users to provide more objective feedback about each approach. A/B testing can also be delivered via a survey or semi-structured interview that begins with some established questions that characterize what you want to learn about the concepts or prototypes you are testing.

Cognitive Walkthrough

A cognitive walkthrough is a task-based evaluation that requires members of the internal storytelling or design team to walk through a system or experience completing the key tasks as the audience would. Whether you are testing a website, physical exhibition, app, game, transmedia strategy, or any other interactive experience, a cognitive walkthrough is a valuable for testing some of the user experience assumptions you have developed for a project. For example, imagine you are designing an interactive game as part of the transmedia storyworld. You would first identify a few tasks that are required for a user to play the game or achieve a goal within the game. These tasks might be things like: *Sign in and set up your player account within the app*; or *begin playing level one of the game*. Then, you and your collaborators can walk through the app, completing the necessary steps to begin playing the game as a user would. A cognitive walkthrough answers four main questions:

1. Will users understand the subtasks that are required to start playing the game or to achieve a specific goal within the game?
2. Will users notice that the correct action is available at each step along the way?
3. Will users understand that a task has been achieved by each action?
4. Does the user get appropriate feedback that indicates they have successfully completed a task?

As you and your team walk through each task, consider how successfully a user will be able to complete the task, as well as any missteps or roadblocks they might encounter along the way. Make note of those problems, and then take steps to remedy them in the next round of prototyping. Again, cognitive walkthrough can be conducted iteratively at various stages of development.

Summative User Experience Testing

Applied at the end of the development of transmedia design and development, summative user experience testing can be employed to assess individual parts of a particular story or a transmedia project as a whole. Summative tests are typically done after the transmedia project has been launched in the market. Conducted by a group of more than 20 users (typically members of your target audience), the results of a summative test can be used to explore how successful your project has been at reaching and engaging its intended audience.

The Role of Analytics

A number of analytics tools can be applied to digital products, such as websites, social media platforms, and apps, to measure, collect, and analyze data related to the number of people who have engaged with your content, how long they engaged, and what paths they took through a transmedia experience. As such, analytics data can provide a robust, quantitative picture of your audience and their activity. For example, Google Analytics can easily be applied to web-based experiences to examine user activities. Likewise, most apps and social media platforms have built-in analytics tools to help measure user/audience engagement. Analytics can also provide a pretty clear indication of which parts of a transmedia storyworld received more attention, as well as which parts received little to no attention from the audience. This information could be used to assess whether parts of the story are less interesting and/or more difficult for your audience to find. Finally, analytics can set the stage for additional types of testing. For example, if your analytics show that a portion of your project is receiving less attention from your audience, you may want to develop a follow-up survey to understand why.

Summative Surveying

Surveying audience segments about the overall quality of a user experience can also be an effective way to test the efficacy of a socially-concerned transmedia project. For example, surveys can explore your audience's opinions about the quality of the transmedia storyworld, individual story platforms, project design, narrative arc, and individual storylines. Surveys may include open-ended questions designed to allow your audience to reflect on their feelings about, understanding of, or experiences with your storyworld. For example, you could include questions like *What did you think about the game portion of this story?* Or *Describe your experience navigating from one part of the storyworld to another.* Or, it may include close-ended questions designed to provide your audience with a quick and efficient way to provide feedback about specific aspects of your transmedia experience. For example, you could include items that ask respondents to rate their level of agreement on a Likert scale of one (strongly disagree) to five (strongly agree) on questions like *I was easily able to move from one platform to another.* Or *The website was easy to use.*

Task-Based UI and UX Testing

Similar to a cognitive walkthrough, a task-based usability/user experience test presents participants with a series of tasks that they must complete. However, in this case, participants should be composed of members of your intended audience as opposed to members of your internal design team. For example, you could develop a task that asks users to explore your project's website, looking for references to all of the other platforms in your storyworld. Then, you can observe and record whether they are easily able to identify all of the parts of your storyworld. Or, you could design a task that asks participants to articulate the main goals of a gaming app designed for your storyworld. Task-based usability and user experience testing are best applied when you want to determine whether your audience is able to identify, understand, interact, and/or engage in the ways you intended. This type of testing can also identify ways your audience might engage with the system that were unintended by the design team, which can be just as, if not more, enlightening.

Conclusion

When carefully and thoughtfully executed, a transmedia experience can cater to fragmented audiences, provide myriad ways to engage with consumers, expand the potential market and reach, and present stories in richly innovative ways. This is especially true when we consider transmedia in the context of socially-concerned storytelling. Broadly speaking, the functions of socially-concerned storytelling are to foster learning, organization, education, and advocacy, thereby affecting potential "change in public attitude, behavior, culture, and policy" (VanDeCarr, 2015). Not only is this an ambitious goal, but it is also the epitome of what it means to be user-centered. Creators of socially-concerned storytelling can use a variety of investigative methods to develop an understanding of user motivations, needs, expectations, and preferences. From early audience research and analysis to summative task-based usability inspections, user-centered strategies can be used at every phase of design and development to ensure that what you're creating is actually resonating with the audience for which it is intended.

References

Accessibility Basics. (2015, February 26). Department of Health and Human Services. Retrieved March 5, 2021, from www.usability.gov/what-and-why/accessibility.html

Byun, H., & Kwon, Y. S. (2016). A systematization of the concept of transmedia: Update, reinterpretation and redefinition of the concept. *International Journal of Journalism & Mass Communication, 120.*

Deshdeep, N. (2021). Why apps are better. *VWO Blog.* Retrieved August 3, 2020, from https://vwo.com/blog/10-reasons-mobile-apps-are-better/

The Interaction Design Foundation. (2021). *The 7 factors that influence user experience.* Retrieved March 5, 2021, from www.interaction-design.org/literature/article/the-7-factors-that-influence-user-experience

The Interaction Design Foundation. (2021). *What is usability?* Retrieved March 5, 2021, from www.interaction-design.org/literature/topics/usability

Jenkins, H. (2006). *Convergence culture: Where old and new media collide.* New York University Press.

Neptune, A. (2020). *Audience engagement in transmedia storytelling—Literature review.* Retrieved March 5, 2021, from https://neptunemade.neocities.org/library/essays/transmediaessay.html

Nielsen, J. (2012). Usability 101: Introduction to usability. Retrieved March 5, 2021, www.nngroup.com/articles/usability-101-introduction-to-usability/.
Romano, J. (1979). James Baldwin writing and talking. *The New York Times*, 23.
User Experience Basics. (2014, February 19). Department of Health and Human Services. User-experience.html.
VanDeCarr, P. (2015). Storytelling and social change. Retrieved March 5, 2021, from https://workingnarratives.org/wp-content/uploads/2016/02/story-guide-second-edition.pdf

17 User Experience Case Study
Professor Garfield's 21st-Century Literacy Project

Jennifer Palilonis

In the Center for Emerging Media Design & Development (EMDD) at Ball State University, students in a 2-year master's degree program use design thinking to define problem and opportunity spaces that can be addressed through strategic communication and transmedia storytelling. In the second year of their studies, small, interdisciplinary student teams earn 12 credit hours—on third of their required coursework—focused entirely on one project in collaboration with an external partner. In the EMDD Creative Development and Applied Research labs, students are given a practical and real-world opportunity to apply what they have learned about storytelling, user-centered experience design, and audience engagement.

In 2017, EMDD began a partnership with the Professor Garfield Foundation, which at the time was the nonprofit arm of Paws, Inc. Before being sold to Viacom in 2019, Paws was, for decades, the international headquarters for Garfield, the cat. Created by Ball State alumnus Jim Davis, Garfield is one of the most famous and beloved cartoon characters in the world. In 2004, Davis launched the Professor Garfield online learning portal and the Professor Garfield Foundation (PGF), a nonprofit educational collaboration between Paws, Inc. and Ball State. This collaboration led to the development of a website that provided interactive digital learning content with a primary emphasis on children's literacy and creative expression. However, a decade after its creation, fast-paced changes in how technology has been integrated into the kindergarten through fifth-grade (K–5) elementary classroom left the PGF website in need of an update. The national dialogue about literacy education had evolved to include the use of digital tools for meaning-making in online and digital environments. As a result, the PGF-EMDD partnership was born.

The project began with a simple problem statement:

> Although K–5 students have more access to technology than ever before, there is a paucity of resources that provide teachers with a clear definition of digital literacy, that helps them understand how to integrate digital literacy instruction in their classrooms, or resources that allow

DOI: 10.4324/9781003150862-17

them to easily and effectively build digital literacy lesson plans for their students.

With these clearly defined challenges in mind, the EMDD team, in collaboration with professors and students from Ball State's nationally recognized Teachers College, executed a clear and focused design challenge: *How might we leverage the rich storytelling potential and celebrity of Garfield to better support K–5 teachers and students in mastering critical digital and media literacy skills for the 21st century?*

To address this question, the team embarked on an ongoing process that includes three phases: empathy research, solutions prototyping, and iterative testing and development. While these phases may seem like linear tasks, one commencing after another. However, it is important to note that as the project has evolved over the past four years (and will continue to evolve after the publication of this book), these phases have been iterative, with each phase revisited and repeated when new transmedia elements are added, new ideas generated, and new user experience feedback gathered. Additionally, a number of EMDD student teams have contributed to the project since its inception in 2017. Those teams have primarily consisted of graphic and interaction designers, computer programmers, writers, videographers, and pre-service teachers, and Ball State Teacher's College faculty. This case study focuses on the user experience aspects of the project and the specific UI/UX activities included in this collaboration, all of which are informed by the early stages of the Professor Garfield project.

Phase One: Research

Digital literacy pedagogy in the United States is still relatively undefined and inconsistently executed. The early research for this project focused on three main efforts: 1) exploring the state of the art in digital and media literacy instructional tools and extant literature related to digital literacy education, 2) a survey of K–5 teachers designed to understand their perceptions of digital literacy and technology use in the classroom, and 3) focus groups with teachers in Indiana and Illinois. This user-centered approach allowed us to better understand teachers' perceptions and knowledge of digital and media literacy, as well as the primary factors that motivate teachers to implement new teaching and learning tools in their classrooms.

Literature Review

A review of extant digital and media literacy literature found that teachers face significant barriers to integrating technology in the classrooms, including their personal comfort and skill with technology (Ertmer et al., 2012), access to professional development associated with technology use (Blackwell et al., 2014), and skepticism about the effectiveness of technology in the classroom (Inan & Lowther, 2010). Although 90% of U.S. teachers recognize the importance of digital literacy instruction, more than half have reported they feel underprepared to use it in the classroom. These findings are consistent with industry analyses, including those from a Samsung executive who states that:

> With the increasing popularity of Chromebooks, tablets, interactive whiteboards and apps in classrooms today, it's evident that technology is a critical tool for today's learners. However, our new research highlights that teachers are not yet receiving full support to harness the power of technology and truly transform classroom learning into a 21st century experience.
>
> (Samsung Newsroom, 2015)

Additionally, existing resources often fail to provide a comprehensive approach to instruction that recognizes the complex path to digital literacy. Instead, they often focus on one or two components of digital literacy, such as using the internet or eSafety. Others fail to address digital literacy at all, assuming instead that the mere act of using the internet is enough to effectively engage today's digital natives. Moreover, most existing web- or app-based tools fail to provide teachers with support to effectively implement them in the K–5 curriculum (Instefjord & Munthe, 2017). As a result, students and teachers alike are often dramatically underserved. The team also found that although today's students have grown up with technology, digital literacy is not innate. Those skills must be taught incrementally over time through age- and grade-level appropriate methods, similar to other subjects. In this context, being digitally literate is the ability to make and share meaning in different modes and formats; to create, collaborate, and communicate effectively in digital environments; and to understand how and when digital technologies can best support these processes (Hague & Payton, 2011).

Teacher Survey

To better understand teachers' perceptions and practices related to digital literacy instruction, Professor Garfield's project also developed and deployed a fully validated survey to 900 K–5 teachers in Indiana and Michigan. A total of 221 teachers responded to the survey. Findings suggested that 1) professional development opportunities are limited for teachers to learn how to teach students to use digital tools; 2) teachers' understanding of digital literacy is relatively shallow; and 3) teachers often focus on tools and software as opposed to underlying principles that govern digital literacy.

Design Thinking Focus Groups

Finally, to form a more comprehensive understanding of teachers' classroom practices related to technology integration and instruction, the research team engaged in 15 collaborative brainstorming sessions with more than

50 K–5 in-service and pre-service teachers over a 6-month period. Teachers were first interviewed about how they integrate technology in their classes. They were also asked what factors contribute to adoption of teaching and learning apps and/or websites. From this work, seven key requirements emerged: 1) teachers must have a clear understanding of digital literacy; 2) instructional materials must be grounded in a framework of digital literacy; 3) resources must provide teachers with support materials, such as video tutorials and lesson plans, and offer clear direction for how to implement them in the classroom; 4) teachers must see a clear connection between what students are learning and established curricular standards; 5) digital and media literacy resources must be age and grade appropriate; 6) teachers must be able to track students' progress toward digital literacy; and 7) teachers must be provided with robust professional development to better prepare them to lead their classrooms in digital literacy instruction.

Phase Two: Solutions Prototyping

Based on these requirements, the EMDD team began prototyping a transmedia learning experience that includes the following components:

- **A new Professor Garfield website** featuring a novel curriculum that provides K–5 teachers with 1) instructional videos and other content designed to advance their conceptual understanding of digital literacy; 2) customizable, standards-based, grade-appropriate digital literacy exercises for young learners; 3) cross-curricular lesson plans and supplemental instructional materials; 4) a learning management system that allows teachers to track students' progress toward digital literacy; 5) a badge-based rewards system that allows students to unlock digital literacy badges and downloadable prizes they can print once a number of digital literacy badges are unlocked; and 6) a dashboard where teachers can create and design their own digital literacy lessons.
- **A virtual professional learning series for teachers titled** Digital Literacy Pathways. This educator's guide to digital literacy includes ten short-term learning modules designed to help them better understand eight core components of digital literacy: 1) effective technology use, 2) finding and selecting information online, 3) effective communication online, 4) collaboration in digital environments, 5) critical thinking with and about technology, 6) creativity in digital spaces, 7) eSafety, and 8) the role of technology in our lives and culture (Hague & Payton, 2011).
- **A virtual, live speaker series** that provides participant teachers with an opportunity to hear from educators and technologists who are experts in digital and media literacy.

In a user-centered approach, designers can provide opportunities for stakeholders to engage in the prototyping process. For the Professor Garfield website, teachers were asked to engage in participatory prototyping as a method for brainstorming interactive exercises that foster digital literacy and reinforce language arts concepts, such as phonemic awareness, reading readiness, and storytelling.

Phase Three: Iterative Testing and Development

Throughout the design and development process, the EMDD team engaged in iterative usability and user experience research with more than 150 K–5 teachers from across the country. Formative UI and UX testing included early-concept testing that presented pre-service and in-service teachers with a variety of ideas about how a digital literacy curriculum might be designed and presented to K–5 students. After receiving feedback on initial concepts, the team developed a series of prototypes at several levels of fidelity to better illuminate the key design and content requirements for an online digital literacy curriculum. Later summative UI and UX testing included remote usability testing with teachers and user experience testing with students to assess website usability, as well as the efficacy of the K–5 digital literacy curriculum and the professional learning series for teachers.

Formative UI and UX Testing

Formative UI and UX testing are often iterative. In the Professor Garfield project, concepts and prototypes were developed and tested with teachers, then revised based on user feedback, and then re-tested. This process was repeated multiple times, with improvements made to design, content, storytelling, and delivery each time based on stakeholder feedback. The user-centered approach to this project design identified key requirements to ensure that the Professor Garfield website and professional learning series meet the functional and practical needs of K–5 teachers.

Concept Testing

Qualitative concept testing was implemented for both the Professor Garfield website and the professional learning series. Concept testing provided the EMDD team with a low-cost, but powerful way to collect teachers' ideas about how best to deliver digital literacy lessons to K–5 students, as well as evaluate their opinions of digital literacy lesson ideas prior to the full development of the curriculum, instructional videos, interactive exercises, and other time-consuming endeavors.

Grounded in an understanding of digital literacy pedagogy, an examination of state-of-the-art technology in digital literacy instruction, and empathy research with K–5 teachers in three school districts, the team developed 20 digital literacy exercises for grades K–5. Teachers from two schools in Chicago, Illinois and Muncie, Indiana were shown prototypes for proposed

230   Jennifer Palilonis

Professor Garfield — The 21st Century Digital Literacy Project
Ball State University EMDD

Taking Pictures
1. Watch the video above to learn about taking photos.
2. Take a photo of an object that rhymes with the provided words.
3. Upload files to the website.
4. Move the photo and frame it within the white lines.

Dog / Bat / Car
Mat / Sock / Pig
Red / Truck / Horn

Badges

Taking Pictures
1. Watch the video above to learn about taking photos.
2. Take a photo of an object that rhymes with the provided words.
3. Upload files to the website.
4. Move the photo and frame it within the white lines.

Bat rhymes with _____

Next

Badges

PHOTO RHYMES

Photo Rhymes requires students recognize sounds and simple rhymes while learning how to shoot photos using a smart device and edit the final images. Students who complete this activity will earn digital literacy badges for functional meaning making, collaboration, and creativity. The badges students collect allow teachers to track student progress. In addition, when students earn enough badges, they will unlock Garfield prizes.

1. Students watch a video tutorial that instructs how to shoot photos using a smart device. The video also teaches students how to edit photos by examing how the image is framed.
2. Students take a photo of an object that rhymes with the words provided.
3. Students upload photos to the Professor Garfield website.
4. Students frame photo to fit within the white box.
5. Students view each others photos and provide comments/feedback.

LEARNING OUTCOMES
STANDARDS

- Identify and produce rhyming words. Tell the order of sounds heard in words with two or three phonemes, and identify the beginning, middle (medial) and final sounds.
- Recognize various types of media.

DIGITAL LITERACY

Functional Meaning Making: Understand and apply knowledge of shooting and editing photos, as well as uploading files.

Collaboration: Comment on peers recordings to provide constructive feedback.

Creativity: Students produce photos to demonstrate expertise in rhyming.

Figure 17.1 Digital literacy exercise sample

Note: Twenty, one-page exercise prototypes were presented to K–5 public school teachers in Chicago and Muncie. Photo Rhymes requires students to use technology to develop creative photo stories associated with rhyming words. This concept was eventually fully developed for the new Professor Garfield website and marries phonemic awareness with two digital literacy components: using technology and creativity in digital environments.

Source: Image provided by Center for Emerging Media Design & Development, Ball State University.

student exercises and asked to provide feedback about the nature of each exercise, as well as the interaction design of the site. In order to evaluate one-page concepts, the team asked the following questions:

- Does the way we have described this exercise make sense to you?
- What do you like about this exercise?
- What do you dislike about this exercise?
- What grade level would something like this be appropriate for?
- Do you have any thoughts on ways to improve this exercise?
- If you were to download a ready-made lesson from a website that you are going to incorporate into your class, how would you want it to be structured/organized?

Teacher feedback was used to transition ideas from the conceptual stage into a more fully realized classroom activity.

During the development of the digital literacy professional learning series—Digital Literacy Pathways—seven K–5 teachers from four school systems in Muncie, Indiana served as consultants to the curriculum development process. First, the EMDD team developed content and design concepts for the professional learning series with input from Kate Shively, an elementary education professor at Ball State. Then, the K–5 teacher consultants were asked to evaluate the concepts, providing input about the content, presentation structure, and overall combination of learning modules. Based on this feedback, the EMDD team was able to collect valuable insights about what information would be most relevant for in-service K–5 teachers, as well as how to design and present the information in a way that would most effectively engage and motivate teachers.

Low- and Medium-Fidelity Prototype Testing

The new Professor Garfield website was prototyped and iteratively tested in two cycles with 15 users each. In each session, a task-based inspection explored usability and user experience with the site at two levels of fidelity. Low-fidelity wireframe prototypes with dummy content and only basic interactivity were designed for the first round of testing. Both in-service and pre-service teachers were asked to walk through wireframes, while a member of the EMDD design team served as facilitator. They were shown wireframe pages one at a time and were asked to provide feedback about the overall site structure, content logic, and interactive elements. Based on their feedback, modifications were made to prototypes, and medium-fidelity prototypes with enhanced graphic design and interactivity were designed for the second round of testing. The first round of low-fidelity prototypes was developed using a wireframing tool called Balsamiq, which allows for rapid wireframing for interactive systems. The second round of prototypes was developed using InVision, an easy-to-use interaction design platform.

Summative UI and UX Testing

Three types of summative usability and user experience testing were conducted for both the Professor Garfield website and the virtual learning series for teachers: remote usability testing with teachers, lesson-level user experience testing with students, and professional learning user experience and efficacy testing with teachers. The following sections detail each of these activities and can serve as a guide for similar projects.

Remote Usability Testing

For the new Professor Garfield website, 100 K–5 teachers from across the United States were recruited at the International Society for Technology Educators Conference to participate in a remote user experience protocol that included a systematic walkthrough of the Professor Garfield website using a remote online testing survey. Participants were contacted via email and asked to complete a task-based survey designed in a remote user testing survey called Loop 11. The survey included nine tasks that required participants to walk through the site and provide feedback about the explanatory content, educational merit, and ease of use. Main tasks focused on the homepage, digital literacy instructional videos, teacher registration process, course creation, exercise summaries, assignment creation, lesson plans, and grading system. A second set of tasks included questions related to the five digital literacy exercises.

The Loop 11 system (and others like it) easily allows usability researchers to create tasks for UI and UX participants to perform. For example, for the Professor Garfield site test, participants were asked to explore specific pages of the website. Then, they were asked to complete survey questions, which included multiple choice, single response, rating and ranking scale questions, open responses, and other standardized usability instruments like the System Usability Scale (SUS) (Brooke, 1996). Loop 11 and similar tools allowed the EMDD team to collect insights about the Professor Garfield website by allowing participants to seamlessly answer UI and UX questions as they interacted with the experience in their natural environments, such as their home, office, or in their classrooms.

Student User Experience in the Classroom

A second UI/UX study explored the efficacy of the "Eight Days of Digital Literacy with Professor Garfield" lesson included on the Professor Garfield website. This lesson includes eight modules that address the core digital literacy competencies: effective technology use, finding and selecting information online, effective communication online, collaboration in digital environments, critical thinking with and about technology, creativity in digital spaces, eSafety, and the role of technology in our lives and culture. The

Figure 17.2 Loop 11 structure

Note: The Loop 11 remote user test included seven key demographic questions and nine tasks that required participants to walk through the site and provide feedback about the content, educational merit, and ease of use for each section and the content management functions of the site. Tasks focused on the homepage, instructional videos, teacher registration process, course creation, exercise summaries, assignment creation, lesson plans, digital literacy exercises, and grading system.

Source: Image provided by Center for Emerging Media Design & Development, Ball State University.

lessons include instructional videos detailing the meaning of each digital competency, along with activities that include options for use with or without technology. Pre- and post-tests, as well as exit tickets for each lesson, assessed students' initial awareness of the eight competencies and measured growth in knowledge over the course of the lessons.

First, a 32-item knowledge quiz, eventually titled the Digital Literacy Assessment Survey, was developed and tested for content validity. Second, the Digital Literacy Assessment Survey was administered as a pre-test in a second-grade classroom at Burris Laboratory School in Muncie, Indiana. Third, the "Eight Days . . ." lesson was administered to 22 students in the second-grade class. Fourth, the knowledge quiz was again administered as a post-test at the immediate completion of the "Eight Days . . ." lesson and again, eight weeks later. Finally, students engaged in, semi-structured interviews designed to elicit feedback about their perceptions of the lessons.

The classroom teacher met with the parents of her second-grade students to explain the purpose of the study and request that they allow their children to participate. She also shared that each student, regardless of whether they participated in the study, would learn about digital literacy through the curriculum. Then, on the second day of school, the teacher shared information with students about the project. If parents denied consent or a child chose not to participate, their data were not included in the study. The pre-test was administered in two sessions of 16 questions over 2 days before the "Eight Days . . ." intervention was taught. Testing was broken into two sessions to mitigate the possibility that the children would suffer from test fatigue. This process was repeated for the post-test, which occurred after the intervention was taught.

The "Eight Days . . ." lessons were administered during the first two weeks of the semester. Each lesson lasted 30 to 45 minutes and was administered during the regular school day. At the end of each session, a four-question exit ticket was given to assess students' understanding of each topic. For the remainder of the semester, the classroom teacher used results from exit tickets to inform her instruction with an eye toward reinforcing concepts with which students seemed to struggle. For five school days following the final lesson, there was no instruction in digital literacy or the use of technology. The post-tests were administered by a member of the EMDD team over two successive days.

During the next eight weeks—whenever technology instruction happened in the classroom—the teacher reviewed relevant digital literacy components prior to students' completing the related activities. Immediately after the 8-week period, students again completed the Digital Literacy Assessment Survey in two, 20-minute sessions on two successive days. Finally, semi-structured interviews were conducted with students to collect qualitative feedback about their perceptions of the "Eight Days . . ." intervention and their resulting digital literacy knowledge. The interviews took place during the instructional day with minimal interruption to the classroom.

The student user experience was defined by both their learning outcomes and their levels of enjoyment during the learning process. In general, results showed a significant improvement in the number of correct answers from the pre-test to the post-test. It is also worth noting that even eight weeks after the first post-test was administered, results from a second post-test showed that students retained the information. Additionally, semi-structured interviews allowed the project team to better understand which aspects of the lessons students enjoyed most, which were less appealing to them, and why.

Teacher User Experience Testing of Professional Learning

The Digital Literacy Pathways professional learning series was first marketed to teachers in Muncie Community Schools, Yorktown Community Schools, Delta Community Schools, and Burris Laboratory School in Indiana. Teachers in Indiana are required to complete 90 hours of professional development every five years in order to renew their teaching licenses. Digital Literacy Pathways was designed to meet a portion of these requirements. Each teacher enrolled in this series was asked to complete a number of assessments to evaluate efficacy and user experience. Prior to beginning the training, teachers completed a pre-assessment that asked them to rate their knowledge of and confidence in teaching digital literacy. For example, teachers were asked about whether they believe they have the skills needed to effectively use and teach technology, their opinions about the efficacy of using technology in the classroom, whether their school provides adequate technology training and resources, and how confident they feel about their knowledge of the eight components of digital literacy. Teachers completed the same assessment after completing all ten modules. Pre- and post-survey results were compared to evaluate whether the Digital Literacy Pathways professional learning series achieved one of its primary goals: to improve teachers' knowledge of and comfort levels with teaching technology in the K–5 classroom. Additionally, teachers were asked to complete a separate culminating survey focused on overall user experience. For example, teachers were asked whether the professional learning series was engaging, fun, interesting, informative, educational, credible, valuable, and worth the time they invested in completing it. Likewise, at the start of each module, teachers were asked to rate their confidence about teaching the topics covered in the modules. For example, in the module focused on online communication, teachers were given the following prompt: "Based on the description above, rate your degree of confidence teaching effective communication using technology to foster digital literacy by recording a number from 0 to 10."

The formative and summative research outlined here achieved a variety of usability and user experience research goals. First, it allowed the EMDD team to test concepts and designs early and often, ensuring that researchers did not pursue designs and development that would be difficult or expensive to change. This research also provided the team with an opportunity to monitor student learning—both for K–5 students and for teacher participants in the professional learning series. It also allows the design and development team to make continuous improvements to content and delivery methods, ensuring that all platforms associated with this transmedia learning experience meet the needs of their various audiences.

Conclusion

Development of the Professor Garfield website and Digital Literacy Pathways professional learning series is ongoing. Iterative and summative usability and user experience testing has been instrumental in the EMDD team's ability to ensure that associated websites, lesson plans, and learning activities provide sound teacher and learner experiences. Additionally, high participant approval comments such as "thorough" and/or "all-in-one resource" for digital literacy instruction speak to the strong need for such a resource among these respondents. The high approval ratings of concept, content, user experience, and usability provide promising evidence that the Professor Garfield offerings tap into a robust opportunity space. UI and UX testing has reduced the risk that the Professor Garfield project team would build the wrong product, thereby saving time, money, and other precious resources. It helped identify problems in early stages of development when they were easy and inexpensive to fix. It helped the team understand teachers' and students' success rates, both when it comes to their use of interactive experiences, as well as their success in learning.

References

Blackwell, C. K., Lauricella, A. R., & Wartella, E. (2014). Factors influencing digital technology use in early childhood education. *Computers & Education*, 77, 82–90.

Brooke, J. (1996). Sus: A "quick and dirty" usability. *Usability Evaluation in Industry*, 189.

Ertmer, P. A., Ottenbreit-Leftwich, A. T., Sadik, O., Sendurur, E., & Sendurur, P. (2012). Teacher beliefs and technology integration practices: A critical relationship. *Computers & Education*, 59(2), 423–435.

Hague, C., & Payton, S. (2011). Digital literacy across the curriculum. *Curriculum Leadership*, 9(10).

Inan, F. A., & Lowther, D. L. (2010). Factors affecting technology integration in K-12 classrooms: A path model. *Educational Technology Research and Development*, 58(2), 137–154.

Instefjord, E. J., & Munthe, E. (2017). Educating digitally competent teachers: A study of integration of professional digital competence in teacher education. *Teaching and Teacher Education*, 67, 37–45.

Samsung Newsroom. (2015, June 23). Survey finds majority of teachers do not feel prepared to use technology in classrooms. *Samsung Newsroom*. news.samsung.com/us/survey-finds-majority-of-teachers-do-not-feel-prepared-to-use-technology-in-classrooms/

18 Conclusion

Defining a Flexible Framework for Analysis or Design of Socially-Concerned Transmedia Stories

Kevin Moloney

In the prior chapters, scholars, authors, and producers described multiple overlapping approaches for the study and development of socially-concerned transmedia stories. From the conceptualization of native, emergent, and feral transmedia stories, to the use of design thinking, transmedia design, and other human-centered techniques, the first six chapters presented a foundation for storyworld analysis and development that is inclusive and empathetic. Those chapters set the stage for a deeper read of the two that follow—chapters seven and eight—in which the approach shifted to a first-person look into how two internationally successful transmedia content producers approach their subjects and become impassioned and driven by them. No matter how brilliant the design of a storyworld and its network of media might be, the story is always the most important consideration. In the three chapters that follow—Chapters 9 through 11—the very human story of bringing water to the parched mountain communities of Morocco unfolded through university student engagement, culture, history, tradition, art, poetry, and interaction. Chapters 12 through 15 focus on a few critical tools—immersive technologies such as augmented and virtual reality, and ethical and low-cost techniques for audience targeting—and present intriguing cases that exemplify the methods outlined to that point in the book. The two chapters prior to this conclusion, Chapters 16 and 17, bring in the critically important methods of usability and user experience to test functionality and engagement and describe a case of the usability of a design for transmedia learning. These chapters present a menu of design choices made by scholars and designers from which the reader may assemble or iterate an entirely new approach to studying, teaching, or producing transmedia stories.

Due to the complexity of the storyworld design task—particularly for factual, ethical, socially-concerned storytelling—no single recipe for analysis or production will answer all needs. Others (Gambarato, 2013, 2018; Jenkins, 2009a, 2009b; Jenkins et al., 2013; Lupton, 2017; Moloney, 2018; Phillips, 2012; Pratten, 2015; Scolari, 2013) also inform the analysis and production task; however, they focus almost entirely on native transmedia stories, and do so without considering the human-centered approaches presented here, nor presenting tools to strategically target the publics that can best use the information in them. At Ball State University's Center for Emerging Media Design & Development (EMDD), we provide graduate student project teams with a program-specific *Transmedia Project Design Template* (Moloney, 2021) that they will use first to analyze case study storyworlds. Using it again, they then develop their own storyworld design document as a guidebook for story development and production, and to avoid breaks in goals, continuity, or story network connections. This template brings together the content presented in this volume as a framework for analysis and design. For purposes of wide adaptability, it is presented in the following in broad strokes. The most recent iteration of EMDD's document is available at the link on the reference list (Moloney, 2021).

Analyzing and Designing Socially-Concerned Transmedia Projects

The following are recommendations for data categories when undertaking a qualitative or mixed-methods study of a socially-concerned transmedia project or guidelines for the planning and production of one for pedagogical or professional purposes: 1) contexts, 2) empathy research, 3) storyworld, 4) targeting, 5) aesthetics, 6) story network, 7) user contribution, and 8) results testing. This volume describes uses of design thinking (Chapters 3–5 and 15–18), transmedia design (Chapters 5–6), transmedia action research (Chapters 9–11), and usability and user experience methods (Chapters 17–18), all of which are equally useful tools for project analysis and design. This flexible framework can be adapted to deploy any of the methods offered in this volume.

1 Contexts

Primary to any storyworld development is the context from which that storyworld builds. As Chapter 2 described, no storyworld—least of all a factual one—exists in isolation of real-world story contexts. This level of analysis or design examines the *historical* or *socio-political history* of the project's subject. Any good author will research these subjects thoroughly before writing or production begins, but including these contexts in a design document will keep a project from drifting too far away from the subject at hand. Transmedia production is complex and requires a team to accomplish in a timely manner. Making these factors part of the guiding documentation will help them all stay in sync.

This category is also a good home for the results of a formative step in the design thinking process: the *problem space*. Design thinking and other empathy research techniques provide a human-centered structure for determining what problem should be solved with the project. This problem space should be narrowly defined to be accomplishable. As contributor Jennifer Palilonis often notes to incoming EMDD students:

People often say that they want to solve the problem of world hunger. That statement rarely gets any pushback because we all think of world hunger as a terrible issue that needs to be addressed. However, the truth is that world hunger is not a problem. Rather, it is the result of myriad contributing problems like climate change, lack of access to education, food shortages, and more. So, saying you want to solve the problem of world hunger—while an admirable and lofty goal—misses the mark because you haven't adequately defined a solvable problem. But if you focus on any one or more of the complex problems that contribute to world hunger, you just might move the needle toward a less hungry world.

(Personal communication, August 9, 2021)

2 Empathy Research

If undertaking the analysis of a socially-concerned transmedia storyworld, a researcher should examine the storyworld to consider whether producers engaged a human-centered approach to its design. Did the producers of the storyworld engage in conversation with both the subjects and the publics of a project? Or was the design top-down and prescriptive? Or was it somewhere in between? Did the producers decisively target effective audiences for their work? Or did they simply publish the work in hopes an audience might find it? This process might be invisible in the result, and whether a human-centered design process was used would likely require interviewing the story's producers.

If designing a project, the producer should at this stage plan the full process and toolset for empathy research—from defining the problem space discussed previously to processes for learning how stakeholders perceive their own problem and what storytelling solutions might contribute to solving it. This process might include interviews and surveys of experts, story subjects, and potential audience members to define all of the following categories. Plans and prototype stories might be co-created with either subjects, expert stakeholders, or audience members. Appropriate user contribution to the storyworld can be determined. As described in Chapter 15, these empathy research techniques can be put to work in targeting the most valuable publics for each story you might design. Excellent methods for these processes can be found in IDEO.org's (2015) *Field Guide to Human-Centered Design*.

3 Storyworld

As described in Chapter 2, factual transmedia storyworlds are not created; they are delimited. After empathy research helps narrowly define the problem at hand, it can also inform what subject areas a particular project will engage. Regardless of whether the project builds a native or emergent storyworld, or analyzes a feral one, the stories that inhabit a storyworld connect in infinite ways to an ever-wider network of stories, subjects, contexts, and interactions. It is, therefore, critical to draw borders around the subjects that will be directly included in the project. Tight definitions like this can be found in the *New York Times'* 1619 Project (Moloney, 2020), and the sprawling, disjointed effects of poor delimitation can be seen in the *National Geographic's* Future of Food project (Moloney, 2015). A journalist might call this stage defining the *scope of coverage*, or determining which subjects and stories are in and which are out of the project.

Starting-point stories should also be defined here. These stories form entry points around the mediascape through which the audience will hopefully enter and move through the wider network of stories both inside and outside of the project's borders. They could be like the overture of an opera that provides a taste of what is to come, like the exposition of a dramatic arc, like the call to adventure in a hero's journey, or even like the lede of a news story. How, where, and with what information a story starts can mean success or failure for a project.

Once the starting-point stories are determined, scholars can analyze or producers can create the stories that follow, building over time the complex storyworld to unfold in series across a narrative arc, hero's journey, inverted pyramid, or other storytelling structures across multiple stories the way we see in the *Star Wars* galaxy or Marvel Cinematic Universe.

4 Targeting (Media Channel)

To activate an audience targeting plan, a producer must define the media channels on which the stories will be told. A media channel is the place where a story will be encountered, like specific books, mobile apps, websites, magazines, theaters, galleries, game consoles, billboards, and other publication venues. Each is a connection point with a specific audience (Moloney, 2019). Which channels are used can be economically, ethically, and effectively determined through design thinking (Chapter 15). In case study analysis, scholars can observe the array of channels selected to determine what the audience outcome of a project might have been. Here again, interviewing a project's producers is the most direct way to determine this from the outside. Unfortunately, many projects overlook this set of decisions and select both media channel and media form by convenience rather than through research.

5 Aesthetics (Media Form)

A media form—like text, still photographs, video, virtual reality, games, and others—can each appear on a variety of media channels. Once producers determine through empathy research which channels will reach the desired audiences, they might then evaluate media forms that effectively communicate the content, appeal to those audiences, and work effectively on each channel (Moloney, 2019). For example, text is excellent at describing the invisible and can connect history and other contexts to the subject. Still photographs isolate moments in time for a reader to stare at in wonder or critical examination. These two would likely be a terrible choice for virtual reality, though. Video and film deliver a narrative arc better than most others. Audio engages the mind's eye and connects a story to the listener's personal world deeply. Games describe systems in ways all the others cannot and create a personal, active agency in the story being told. Each media form brings particular storytelling affordances, and to neglect them for convenience of production is risky at best.

Here storyworld cohesion can also dissolve if a producer fails at creating a unified design aesthetic across all stories. This is where the emotional tone of storytelling, the text and color palettes, the design of interfaces, and other aesthetics can be analyzed or described in a project design document. Both scholars and producers benefit from a close eye on what each media form accomplishes in storytelling.

6 Story Network

When I studied advertising in the 1980s, the mantra we recited was "reach and frequency"—reach the audience through the media they use and hit them with the message frequently and repeatedly. Transmedia storytelling creates a more complex execution of this mantra. We achieve reach by placing stories on multiple digital, analog, or brick-and-mortar media channels to pull diverse audiences into the storyworld. Rather than hitting them repeatedly with the same message on all those channels as 20th-century advertising did, we tell multiple different stories in multiple different media forms. As the audience moves from one story to the next, their attention to the subject lingers and engagement both lengthens and deepens. An effective transmedia producer will design how stories will connect from one to the other, allowing the audience to move in both linear and nonlinear modes through the content. In socially-concerned storytelling, a producer would likely avoid the mysterious techniques of game designers or entertainment producers. If a member of the audience engages with only one story node on the network, that story should be complete enough to have value. However, engagement with other stories should build expertise in the subject matter and deepen their real-world engagement. While a producer might model ways this has been effectively done elsewhere, a scholar might examine the effectiveness of a network design in accomplishing this goal.

7 User Contribution

As illustrated throughout this volume, transmedia storytelling embraces co-creation, storytelling as a conversation, and all the engaged interactions the 21st-century mediascape provides. Allowing space for user contribution helps develop a sense of ownership in the story, membership in the community the storytelling creates, and fuels adoption of the project's goals. When studying cases, scholars might evaluate both what spaces were provided by the project producers and what unplanned others might have emerged for user contribution, and what the outcome was. When designing a storyworld, producers are now expected by their publics to let them in and value the contributions they make—from likes and shares to the reporting and creation of stories related to the storyworld. Empathy research with members of a project's public can reveal surprising and engaging ways that users might contribute and actively "spread" (Jenkins et al., 2013) the story.

8 Results Testing

Through what capture mechanism will a producer determine the effectiveness of a transmedia story? These techniques often include the common, inexpensive, and simplistic analysis of engagement statistics such as online and mobile page or video views, unique visitors, time on a page, and others provided by basic web analytics. Though these statistics are a valuable starting point, they might not reveal actual success. These numbers don't reveal whether the project has reached key new publics or if it has simply "preached to the choir" by engaging publics that already support the story's mission. Time on a page might reveal deep reader or viewer engagement, or might reveal that the viewer loaded the page and then left to feed the cat. Analog and brick-and-mortar media are notoriously difficult to track. To determine success usually requires a deeper look and a more specific set of methods. Prior chapters offer examples of some tools in design thinking, transmedia design, transmedia action research, and—most particularly—usability and user experience testing as methods to know how effectively the media in a project reach, engage, and communicate to an audience. An effective producer will develop project-specific methods not only to test how compelling media are but also to understand the level of interest and engagement from the audience and how much they learned from it. Though methods for this are many and beyond the scope of this volume, they can be found in the disciplines of education, advertising, product design, and political activism in addition to human-centered design and usability testing. In my early days as an advertising student, the critical metric was not engagement, but conversion. How many people bought the product or service? Similar actions can be discovered through storytelling by designing ways for the audience to show they have bought in. Did they take an action from registering for a newsletter to joining an organization? Did they donate or write a letter to a government representative using the producer's easy online form? By first determining the goal of the project, a producer can define means to measure success that go beyond clicks, views, and social media likes and shares. For scholars studying these projects, effectiveness is more difficult to determine from the outside, but many methods exist across disciplines that are useful.

Again, the best tool is to interview the producer if possible and compare their claims to visible and independent results.

Conclusion

This volume is a diverse snapshot into the complex, iterative, and variable process of developing socially-concerned transmedia stories. The work of contributors here provides different valuable approaches to accomplishing the same goal: making the social world a better place through storytelling in journalism, documentary production, education, history, community organizing, and fact-driven social change movements. The world needs more and more effective, vetted, double-sourced, fact-based information and much less mis- and disinformation. Whether one identifies religion as fact or fiction, scholars, producers, and students of socially-concerned transmedia storytelling can learn much from any method that builds community, knowledge, and collective action through story. Like them or not, we can learn from Padre Marcelo Rossi and his Pentecostal competitors (Chapter 1), as well as others from successful contemporary political campaigns to disturbing conspiracy theories. Stories can build community, and communities can change the world.

References

Gambarato, R. R. (2013). Transmedia project design: Theoretical and analytical considerations. *Baltic Screen Media Review*, 1(1), 80–100. https://doi.org/10.1515/bsmr-2015-0006

Gambarato, R. R. (2018). A design approach to transmedia projects. In M. Freeman & R. R. Gambarato (Eds.), *The Routledge companion to transmedia studies*. Routledge.

IDEO. (2015). *The field guide to human-centered design*. IDEO.org. www.designkit.org/resources/1

Jenkins, H. (2009a, December 12). The revenge of the origami unicorn: Seven principles of transmedia storytelling (Well, two actually: Five more on Friday). *Confessions of an Aca-Fan*. http://henryjenkins.org/2009/12/the_revenge_of_the_origami_uni.html

Jenkins, H. (2009b, December 12). The revenge of the origami unicorn: The remaining four principles of transmedia storytelling [Weblog]. *Confessions of an Aca-Fan*. http://henryjenkins.org/2009/12/revenge_of_the_origami_unicorn.html

Jenkins, H., Ford, S., & Green, J. (2013). Designing for spreadability. In *Spreadable media: Creating value and meaning in a networked culture* (pp. 195–228). New York University Press.

Lupton, E. (2017). *Design is Storytelling*. Cooper Hewitt.

Moloney, K. (2015). *Future of story: Transmedia journalism and National Geographic's future of food project* [Doctoral dissertation, University of Colorado]. https://scholar.colorado.edu/downloads/2227mp94w

Moloney, K. (2018). Designing transmedia journalism projects. In R. R. Gambarato & G. C. Alzamora (Eds.), *Exploring transmedia journalism in the digital age* (pp. 83–103). IGI Global. www.igi-global.com/chapter/designing-transmedia-journalism-projects/198024

Moloney, K. (2019). Proposing a practical media taxonomy for complex media production. *International Journal of Communication, 13*(2019), 3545–3568.

Moloney, K. (2020). All the news that's fit to push: The New York Times Company and Transmedia Daily News. *International Journal of Communication, 14*(2020), 4683–4702.

Moloney, K. (2021). *Perfesser Kev's Transmedia project design template*. Center for Emerging Media Design & Development. https://transmediajournalism.files.wordpress.com/2021/08/transmedia_bible.pdf

Phillips, A. (2012). *A creator's guide to transmedia storytelling: How to captivate and engage audiences across multiple platforms*. McGraw Hill Professional.

Pratten, R. (2015). *Getting started in transmedia storytelling: A practical guide for beginners*. CreateSpace Independent Publishing Platform.

Scolari, C. A. (2013). *Narrativas transmedia: Cuando todos los medios cuentan*. Deusto.

Index

1619 Project *see New York Times*

action research 5, 93, 103, 107–122, 238, 242; participatory 107, 109; theory 5, 107–108
activism 4, 13, 109, 131, 189, 242; environmental 131
adaptation 17, 31, 109, 111, 113, 114, 120, 189
Adler, Kris 131
advertising 8, 13, 19, 57, 86, 178–179, 241–242
advocacy 6, 49, 223
aesthetics 7, 78–79, 83, 85, 238, 240–241
Albania 113–114
American Public Television 205, 207
Arendt, Hannah 80
art 6, 13, 18, 42–44, 74, 78–87, 95–96, 100, 110, 115, 126–132, 138–141, 145–148, 156, 201, 226, 229, 237; immersive installations 145
Art: The Response 145–147
audience: engagement 2, 7, 102, 195–197, 206, 211, 218, 222, 225; experience 213; targeting 6–7, 15, 43, 45, 178–189, 221, 237–240

Baldwin, James 213
Ball State University 4, 42, 181, 183, 211, 225
Batman 18
Before the Flood 115
Benjamin, Walter 77
Berger, John 141
Bigfoot 18
Bill and Melinda Gates Foundation 182
Black Lives Matter 1, 178
Blue Roots Project 15, 41–45, 216
Blue Sky Days 63

brainstorm 30, 42, 199, 216
Brui-Art: Le son du paysage 130–132
Bugs Bunny 16
Burke, Tarana 18
Business Model Canvas 30–31, 40
Butler University 203

California: Californianos 72; gold rush 67, 71; Republic 71
campaigns, social communication 6
Cemetery Wall, The 132
Center for Emerging Media Design & Development (EMDD) 42–43, 181–182, 185–190, 211, 215–217, 225–226, 228–229, 231–232, 234–236, 238
Centre Intermondes 151–155
character wheel 94–104
chronos 80, 87, 100
Chupacabra 18
Circle of Blue 5, 41–43, 215–216
Civil War (United States) 69
climate: change 6, 11, 27, 110–120, 126, 134, 138, 143–145, 187, 239; games 111–112; grief 115
Cloud Encounter 144
CloudFishers 127, 128
co-creation 32–33, 43, 97, 108–109, 113–114, 131, 181, 241
co-design 76–78, 94–95, 103
cognitive: load 171; responses 64, 171; training 161; walkthrough 220–221
Come Closer 143
Coming Home Virtually 6, 169, 174
communication: design 4, 85, 93, 101, 103; strategic 101, 225; strategies 5, 92, 96–97, 104
communication, socially concerned 1–2; stories 24, 26–27, 33; storytelling 35,

178–179, 189, 210, 213–214, 218, 223, 237, 241; storytelling genres 178; transmedia project 222, 238; transmedia stories 7–8, 35, 219, 238, 237, 243
communities, marginalized 113
community-based adaptation 111
community engagement 85, 94, 98, 107–115, 118, 125, 128, 195, 198, 206; immersive 115
concept testing 220, 229
conspiracy theories 1, 243
constraints 23, 25, 28–29, 31, 42, 45, 175, 199
content: design 76; logic 231; strategy 40, 210; validity 234
contexts 7, 12, 48, 80, 92–93, 100, 119, 133–134, 136, 169, 182, 189, 195, 238–241
control mapping 162
coronavirus *see* COVID-19
COVID-19 18, 77, 81, 169, 174; pandemic 18, 77, 169, 174–175
Curricular Fog Water Kits 137

D.A.R.E. America 48
Darrow, Clarence 205
Dar Si Hmad for Development 6, 125–127
Debs, Eugene V. 6, 17, 193–208
define (design thinking phase) 25, 185–186
demographics 57, 183–188
design: challenge 226; human-centered 1–2, 4, 24–25, 239, 242; methodology 5, 92; practice 84, 87, 91, 93, 104; process 24–27, 76, 85, 87, 94, 103, 182, 197, 239; research 2, 4, 87, 92–93; social innovation 76; visual 210, 213–214
design thinking 2, 4–7, 23–29, 33, 35, 37–39, 42, 44–45, 94, 104, 178, 181–189, 194–200, 204–208, 216, 225, 227, 237–242; phases 23–25, 44, 181–190
DESIS Network 76
Diary of a Young Girl 16
digital literacy 7, 102, 225–229, 231–233, 234–236; curriculum 7, 229; instruction 225, 227–228, 236; lesson 226, 229; pedagogy 226, 229
Disney 12, 16, 26
displacement, social 143

documentary 1, 5–6, 13, 17, 41, 57, 63–64, 72, 74, 134, 137, 170–171, 178, 181, 183, 186–187, 189, 194–200, 203–207, 217–218, 243
Doyle, Arthur Conan 18
drillability, principle of 11
Drinking Fog: Fog Collection in Southwest Morocco 127
Drug Enforcement Administration (DEA) 51
drugs: prohibition 52; trade 52; war on 49, 53–54, 56
Duprat, Camille 140, 150, 152, 157

empathize (design thinking phase) 25, 38, 166, 181–182, 185
empathy research 2, 7, 23–31, 35, 37, 39–40, 42–45, 180–182, 183, 188–189, 194, 196, 212, 217, 226, 229, 328–242; analogous 30, 43; interviews 29–30, 39; methods 212; strategies 37, 43
engineering, humanitarian 125–126, 133–137; education 133
environment: degradation 143; immersive 151; protection 166, 169
Environmental Education Centre of Eleftherio Kordelio 118
epos 80, 100
eSafety 227–228, 232
ethos 4, 9–11, 16, 18, 51, 64, 80, 86, 100, 138, 181
Eva: A-7063 169–170
Everyday Hero 78
experience: design 2, 23, 42, 210, 212, 225; economy 26; immersive 151, 165–166, 173, 194; journeys 216–217; research goals 235
extractability, principle of 11

Facebook 93, 95, 98–99, 178–179, 187, 194, 197, 199, 207, 216–217, 219
Field of Dreams 179
First Point Volleyball Foundation 217
Fisher, Walter 10, 91
Flint, Michigan 5, 37–41, 45, 174; water crisis 37–43
focus groups 227
fog: collection 125–129, 135, 138, 147; collection nets 127–128; collection systems 125; communities 133, 136–137; generators 125–126, 128, 135; harvesting 125–126, 128, 150;

initiatives 128; machines 131; net installation 134, 136; observatory 135; water 6, 126, 128, 132–138, 145–146, 149, 151, 159, 215, 219–220, 229, 235, 238
fragments 77, 81–87
Frank, Anne 16–17
FRONTLINE 178
Fuller, Buckminster 148
Future of Food *see National Geographic*

Gadsden Purchase 68
game 11, 13, 16, 32, 60, 84, 112–120, 165, 169, 172–173, 217–218, 221–222, 240–241; climate 118; mechanics 119; role-playing 169, 172; serious 116; video 172
Game of Thrones 16
Generation-Z 186
genos 80, 100
Global Lab 4, 5, 108, 134
Google Analytics 179, 222
graphic design 24, 188, 231
Greater Wellington Regional Council 116
Greece 19, 80, 118–119

Half The Sky 194, 197
harm reduction 15, 47–60; Action Center 50, 53–54
Harry Potter 9, 16
Highrise 13, 19
HIV (human immunodeficiency virus) 51, 53–54
Hogwarts School of Witchcraft and Wizardry 9
Holocaust 16–17, 169–170, 203
Homer 19
House Select Committee on Narcotic Abuse and Control 52
Houtryve, Tomas van 5, 63–66
How might we questions 182–183, 199, 226

ideation 25, 39, 42, 44, 99, 181, 185–186, 190, 195–196
identification 163
IDEO 23–28, 181, 239; ideo.org 25; OpenIDEO 25
ImagisLab 92, 104
immigration 68, 70
inclusion processes, social 76
Indiana donut 183–185, 187

innovation, social 4, 76–77, 81–85, 92–94, 97, 102
Inside Out 141–142
Institute for Geosciences 114
Interactive Qualifying Project 107, 112
interactivity 82, 161, 178, 214, 218, 231; design 210, 213, 215, 231; designers 212, 226; experience 214, 221; systems 231
interdisciplinaires 148
iteration 41, 45, 189, 238; prototyping 212; testing and development 212, 226, 229; usability 220, 229

Jenkins, Henry 8, 11–13, 18–19, 38, 108, 186, 210, 237, 242
Johns Hopkins University 52
journalism 1, 4, 5, 13, 14, 26, 41, 42, 56, 57, 161, 163, 164, 182, 189, 196, 217, 243; immersive 161; inverted pyramid 240

Keller, Helen 205
Kinder, Marsha 8, 11, 178
King, Martin Luther 52
Kor, Eva Mozes 170–171, 203

LadHyx Hydrodynamics Laboratory 140
Latin America 2–4, 65
learning: stealth 121–122; virtual 232
LEGO *Ninjago* 13
Lesson Learned From That Dragon Cancer 6, 169–172
Lines and Lineage 15, 63–67, 74
Lmouden, Raiss 131
logos 80, 100, 111
LonelyGirl15 13
Lucas, George 5, 11–12, 15–16, 18, 48, 56
Luceo 5, 48, 56

Marvel 8–9, 15, 178, 240; Cinematic Universe 8, 178, 240
Matrix 8–9, 13, 19
McGill University 143
media: channel 39, 99, 187, 240; environments 161, 165; form 3, 16, 186, 240–241; immersive 161–162, 166, 169; industries 3; literacy 226, 228; public 6, 170, 193–200; structure 96
mental model 165–166, 171, 173, 175
#MeToo 1, 18

Mexican-American War 67, 71
Michigan Department of Health and Human Services 56
micronarratives *see* narrative
Middle Earth 9, 11
millennial 43, 183, 186
Minow, Newton 193
Mist Collector 15, 145, 159
Misty Way 145, 150–152, 155
Morocco 6, 126–127, 131, 134–138, 144, 237; Amazigh 126, 131–138, 193; Anti-Atlas mountains 125–126, 134–135
Muncie Community Schools 235
mythos 9–10, 16
#MyWaterStory 41–45, 216

naloxone 47, 53, 58, 59
Narnia 9
narrative: arc 219, 222, 240–241; content 82, 97–98, 100; engagement 163–166; framework 77, 101; hegemonic 5, 76–77, 82–83; micronarratives 81, 83, 85, 87; progressive 77; traditional 84
Narrative Design for Social Impact: The Project Model Canvas 40
narrative paradigm 10, 91
narrative world 80, 82, 84–85, 87, 96, 98–99, 100, 164, 166; *see also* storyworld
narrowcasting, bundled 180
National Football League 67
National Geographic 14–15; Future of Food 14, 19, 240; Society 14
National Public Radio 193
neoliberalism 77
Nephelograph (also Néphélographe) 145, 155–157
New York Times 13–14, 178, 240; 1619 Project 14–15, 20, 178, 240; Company 14, 178; *The Daily* 14; *for Kids* 14; *Magazine* 14; *Race/Related* 14; *The Weekly* 14
New Zealand 116
Nixon, Richard M. 49
Norman, Don 23–24
Notre Dame, Cathedral of 10
Nuit Blanche (art event) 148, 156–157

Obama, Barack 67, 73
Odysseus 19
Odyssey 19
Okeanus 156
Ong, Walter J. 79–81

opioid crisis, American 5, 15, 47–48
Oz: Land of 9, 11, 16, 20; *Wizard of* 9

participation 2, 6, 26–27, 44, 84, 98, 101, 107, 109, 120–121, 144–145, 155, 215–219; recruitment 198
participatory learning and action 107, 109
pathos 111
pedagogy, progressive 107, 109, 122
performance, principle of 11
persona 7, 28, 185, 198, 216–217; audience 217
perspective-taking 164–173
photography 56, 63, 68, 74–75, 110, 135; photo-elicitation 114, 117; photo journal 34
Pico, Pío de Jesus 65–66
Plug Social TV 5, 15, 91–98, 101–104
podcast 14, 216–218
poetics 143, 159
Politecnico di Milano 4, 92–93, 104; Department of Design 92
Pope Francis 216
Porous Sail prototype 145, 149–150
problem: space 238–239; statement 25, 185–186, 225
Professor Garfield's 21st-Century Literacy Project 225
Proteus effect 164
prototyping 25, 42, 44, 86, 185, 187, 190, 196, 212, 221, 226–229; A/B testing 220; for empathy 31; solutions 226, 228; wireframing 231
public broadcasting 170, 193–197
public relations 8
public service 11, 48, 183

Rangel, Charlie 51
Raville, Lisa 53–54
reality: augmented 162, 170; virtual 161–163, 169–170, 174–175, 219, 237, 240–241
rebab 130–133
Red Cross Red/Crescent Climate Centre 112
reference world 10, 86
research, participatory 109–110, 122
results testing 7, 238, 242
Revolutionist: Eugene V. Debs, The 17, 193, 197, 203, 205
rhetoric 77–78, 81, 84
Roosevelt, Theodore 204–205

Roots 20
Rossi, Padre Marcelo 3–4, 7, 243

Sahara Desert 6, 127, 135
saturate and group 39, 199
Schmoke, Kurt 51–53
Schorno, Daniel 151, 156–157
scope of coverage 240
Sea-narios Game 117
secondary worlds 9, 20
Seeing a Void 149
Selma 20
seriality, principle of 11
simulations, immersive 162
situational model 163
slavery 14, 67, 69
Smithsonian Institution 14
social change 2, 4, 6, 10, 19, 76–78, 83, 87, 102–103, 107–109, 113, 121–122, 218, 243
social cognitive theory 6, 162, 164, 166, 173
social media 13–14, 18, 37, 41–45, 57, 60, 75, 81, 83, 93, 98, 136, 169, 179, 185–189, 194–195, 197–199, 203–204, 207, 212, 216–222, 242; campaign 37, 42, 199, 204, 216; networks 93, 185, 188
social television 93–94
spreadability, principle of 11, 186
stakeholders 5, 24, 27, 29–30, 32, 35, 39–40, 56–57, 76, 78, 82, 87, 94–97, 100, 103, 107–111, 113–121, 182, 186–187, 195–197, 228, 239
Stanford University 24, 67
Star Wars 8–9, 15–16, 178, 240
STEM (science, technology, engineering, and mathematics) 107–108, 117, 122, 126, 130, 133–138; material 138; training 135
storying 84, 121
storytelling: context 197, 238; creation 86, 99; cross-platform 194, 210–214; design 27, 37; experiences 26, 45, 98; immersive 6, 161–166, 169, 171, 174–175; journalism 243; map of 94, 100, 104; network 7, 238, 241; production 5, 87; purposes 161; qualities 86; social innovation 76, 94, 97; solutions 239; strategies 82, 101; structures 240; techniques 86, 101, 197; testing 217
storyworld 239; analysis 237; Canvas 100, 104; cohesion 241; creators 214; design 237–238; elements 128–130;

strategy 40; transmedia 5–6, 11, 17, 113–114, 118, 125, 133, 186, 195, 198, 205, 212, 217–222, 239
subjectivity, principle of 11
system usability scale (SUS) 232

targeting *see* audience, targeting
technologies, immersive 161, 163–165, 169–171, 174–175, 239
telos 80, 100
test (design thinking phase) 185, 188–189
Texas Revolution 69
Through the Looking Mist 145–150
Timmy Global Health 182
Tolkien, J.R.R. 11
topos 9–10, 16, 80, 100
transmedia: action storyworlds 113; activism 109; Building Model 99–104; campaign 17, 180, 212, 215, 216–218; committee 195, 198, 206–207; communication 4–6, 92–93, 104, 179, 188; communication strategy 179, 188; concept 95; content 6, 93–99, 237; creators 23, 211; credibility 214; curricula 94, 137; design 5, 84–87, 91–93, 97, 100–104, 178, 195, 213, 216, 219, 221, 237–238, 242; documentary 5–6, 13, 63–64; elements 197, 199, 204, 206; emergent 5, 8–9, 12–13, 15–19, 109, 237, 239; experience 29–30, 193, 197, 198, 215, 222–223; feral 5, 8–9, 12–13, 16–19, 186, 237, 239; franchises 178, 214; galaxy 126; ideas 195; learning 134, 228, 236–237; logic 125, 137; mindset 137; narrative 79, 211; native 5, 8–9, 12–15, 17, 19, 237–239; network 219; pedagogy 133, 136–137; platforms 212; practice 4, 81, 91–93, 96, 102–103, 105; project 8, 12–13, 86, 95–96, 99, 180, 194, 205, 207, 221–222, 238; seven principles of 11; storyworld (*see* storyworld)
transmedia action research 5, 107–122, 238, 242
transportation 163–164
Trump, Donald J. 71, 73
Twitter 3, 45, 93, 95, 179, 199, 216, 217, 219

UI/UX *see* usability
United Nations Commission on Narcotic Drugs 48

University of California Berkeley 70–71
usability 1, 2, 4, 7, 210–215, 219–223, 229, 231–232, 235–238, 242; design 2, 42, 210, 212; designers 210–211; evaluation 1, 210–211; feedback 226; formative testing 215, 219–220, 229, 235, 238; issues 219; methods 220, 238; needs 210; principles 7, 212, 215; research 4, 7, 211, 229, 235; researchers 232; summative testing 221–222; strategy 215; testing 4, 212, 215, 219–223, 229, 232, 235–236, 242; and user experience 1–2, 4, 7, 161, 194, 210–213, 215, 218–238, 242
usability and user experience *see* usability
user: contribution 7, 188, 238–239, 241–242; experience (*see* usability); extreme 33, 39, 188; interface design 210
user-centered: approach 2, 194, 196, 226, 228; design 7, 109, 113–114; process 23

Vallejo, Mariano 70–71
visualizations 119, 136

Wachowski, Lana 10–12, 18
Ward, Marcellus 51–52
water crisis: Flint, Michigan (*see* Flint, Michigan); global 216
Water Quality Indiana 6, 181–189
Westeros 16
WFYI: Nerds 195, 198–199, 205–206; Public Media 6, 17, 170, 194–208
Wilson, Woodrow 205
Wonderland 9; Alice's Adventures in 147
Worcester Polytechnic Institute 4, 107, 133
worldbuilding, principle of 5, 11, 76, 86–87, 99; techniques 76
World Water Day 44, 216

yeti 18
YouTube 57, 60, 93, 95, 98–99, 179, 205, 219

Zayed University 148
Zorro 18

Printed in the United States
by Baker & Taylor Publisher Services